William Fox-Pitt is the first British rider to become eventing's world number one, a distinction he achieved in 2002 and repeated in 2008. Born in 1969, he represented Britain throughout his teens, winning young rider team gold in the European Championships of 1988 and 1990, and completing Badminton at the age of 20. His first Burghley win five years later established him as a regular on the senior British team and guaranteed him a ticket to the Atlanta Olympics in 1996. Over the past decade, he has ridden consistently at the highest level, representing his country in five gold medal-winning teams in the European Championships, leading the British ranking list for eight years and claiming regular victories at four-star level, headed by Badminton in 2004. His success continued in 2008 when he won bronze with Team GB in Beijing. William lives in Dorset with his wife, racing journalist Alice Plunkett, and their children Oliver and Thomas.

Minty Clinch, who worked with William on this book, is a freelance journalist specialising in adventure travel. She has written several biographies, ghosted and otherwise, including Mark Todd's *So Far, So Good*.

D0230728

WHAT WILL BE

The Autobiography

William Fox-Pitt
With Minty Clinch

An Orion paperback

First published in Great Britain in 2007
by Orion
This paperback edition published in 2009
by Orion Books Ltd,
Orion House, 5 Upper St Martin's Lane,
London WC2H 9EA

An Hachette UK company

1 3 5 7 9 10 8 6 4 2

A CIP catalogue record for this book is available
from the British Library.

ISBN 978-0-7528-8169-0

Printed and bound in Great Britain by Clays Ltd, St Ives plc

The Orion Publishing Group's policy is to use papers that
are natural, renewable and recyclable products and
made from wood grown in sustainable forests. The logging
and manufacturing processes are expected to conform to
the environmental regulations of the country of origin.

Every effort has been made to fulfil requirements with regard to reproducing
copyright material. The author and publisher will be glad to rectify any
omissions at the earliest opportunity.

www.orionbooks.co.uk

To all the horses that
have given me so much

CONTENTS

ACKNOWLEDGEMENTS

Without the ponies and first few horses I learnt to ride on, my career would definitely have taken a different path, so first and foremost I am indebted to my parents – my mother spent days finding me the right mounts, determined that I should not lose confidence. All along, their support and encouragement has been tireless.

Thank you to my family, friends and owners for their endless loyalty and patience. To Andrew, my brother, for all he had to put up with during our childhood and for being so good about it now. To Fiona Larkin, a special person, whose patience and sense of fun is etched on my memory. I have relied heavily on many people for help and support. Thank you to the trainers I have had the good fortune to learn from, especially Lars Sederholm's incredible horsemanship and Sheila Cotter for getting my dressage riding started.

To my team of supporters who have been major players, particularly Jackie Potts and Alex Van Tuyll without whom none of this would have happened. To Alice for her love and driving force. She copes with my antisocial life, is a brilliant mother to our boys Oli and Thomas and is the best person at making me laugh at myself.

Thank you finally to Minty Clinch, who has been fantastic to work with and without whom nothing would have ever made it on to paper. And to my publisher Orion, especially Susan Lamb for taking this book on.

CHAPTER ONE

My Family and Other Animals

I certainly never expected or dreamed of a career as a top event rider. For as long as I can remember, I was surrounded by animals and I loved them all. We always had ponies and riding was something we did as a family. My younger brother Andrew was good and very brave, but I thought he was crazy. I was cautious and calculating and I enjoyed riding up to a point.

I soon learned how to handle that imbalance. From the age of reason, say five or six, I realised I had natural advantages that I could exploit. Obviously I was stronger and bigger, but more importantly I knew how to wind Andrew up. He had a hot temper and I was the opposite. If I could get him to blow a fuse, he would hopefully get the blame for the resulting chaos. It didn't always happen that way because I was older and supposedly more responsible.

Even though we were generally pretty horrible to each other up to the age of ten, Andrew and I were a team. My parents were both highly motivated and had incredibly busy lives. When they got married in 1966, my father, Oliver, was thirty-four and an ambitious financial analyst trying to make his mark in the City. After several ventures, with varying degrees of success, he set up his own company, Fox-Pitt Kelton, in 1971. The City has always been his life and the investment world is what he does best. It's his gamble; it gives him highs and lows. He loved it then and he loves it now, having just set up a new business, Master Capital, at the age of seventy-five.

Before she married at the age of twenty-five, my mother, Marietta Speed, was a top-class event rider who had represented Great Britain at the World Championships at Burghley in 1964, come fourth at Badminton in 1965, and second at Burghley that same year. I was born on 2 January 1969 but, with the life my mother led, full-time parenting was never a possibility. She was always on the road, and it was the same when Andrew came along eighteen months later.

In order to cater for their conflicting passions and responsibilities, my parents divided their time between London, where they had a house in Westminster, and east Kent, where my mother kept her horses at her family home, Knowlton Court. My grandfather, Jack Speed, died before I was born, but his widow, Monica, still lived there, running the house, the farm and overseeing the stables. To this she added being the perfect grandmother. She was a formidable character, much loved by everybody and totally in control of everything that went on at Knowlton, something my newly married parents must have found quite challenging. She completely doted on Andrew and me, and nothing was too much trouble. When we were small, she looked after us whenever our parents were away. She was gifted with incredible patience and warmth and she spoilt us to death.

From an early age I lived for the weekends. Andrew and I both hated London, because it represented school and restriction, whereas Knowlton was the ideal place for two small boys to run wild. I started riding aged two on Nigger, an elderly grey donkey retired from beach duties. There wasn't a lot of action, but his felt saddle sticks in my mind and at least he was kind, which is not always the case with donkeys. Silver Star, my first pony, came along next, but the only thing I remember vividly is her dying. Riding wasn't a passion or even a focus, I was lucky it was just there.

We were very fortunate, because our parents allowed us to find our own boundaries so we enjoyed an outdoor life with dogs, making camps and riding bikes. I loved camping, though I have to admit to enjoying my creature comforts now. By the time I was six, Andrew and I were on the loose on our ponies. There were rules, of course: we had to wear hats, we weren't allowed to trot on the roads and, above all, we were forbidden to jump unless there was an adult with us. Supervision was minimal between breakfast and lunch, though we obeyed the lunch bell promptly because we were usually starving. Today's parents are more neurotic about losing sight of their children, but sadly they have to be. As long as we could be out of doors, we were never bored. If we had to stay in, options were table tennis, snooker or cards, rather than watching television. I was not a great reader then and I am still not now.

Our first matched white ponies were Willy Wiff and Tiddlywinks – great names. Tiddly used to bolt so, although he was mine initially, he rapidly became Andrew's, and I had Willy, who was bone idle except when he bucked. Andrew would never worry about the bolting, fast was great and falling off even better, just so long as no one told him how to ride. For me, doing it properly was the more important thing and falling off was the end of the world. However, jumping off was fine, which is what I did every time I lost control. To this day I can't bear being out of control and I never want to ride an out and out puller.

Sometimes we used to do pairs showing classes, yelling at each other and looking a total mess, despite our best efforts to get our white ponies clean. How we envied children with immaculate bay or chestnut ponies! Having been advised that if you want boys to ride you must do everything for them, my mother normally had the ponies ready for us, but we did help with the show preparation. We would get well stuck in because if we succeeded, we'd have more chance of a rosette.

Minnie Monster was my first proper pony, the first one I remember trying before he was bought. Willy and Tiddly were local hand-me-downs that worked pretty well. Minnie was a handsome, 12hh, charismatic, grey gelding with a good reputation. He gave me my first taste of success at the West Street South Pony Club Gymkhana Games Championship in 1977. I was seven and the games consisted of races involving flags and sacks and bending poles, but no jumping, which was the best thing as far as I was concerned. As overall champion in Jubilee Year, I got a massive red, white and blue rosette. It felt great and I thought I had it made, but jumping was becoming an issue. There were logs all over the place at Knowlton, logs I'd looked at for years and thought, 'You'd have to be mad to jump that.' Andrew would gallop up and go over them and I'd gallop up alongside him and go round the edge. The more my mother urged me to give it a try, the more bloody-minded I became.

One day I decided I had to jump, but on my terms and in secret. Ignoring the family rules, I made Minnie stand in front of a minute log for ages while I psyched myself up. Then I took the longest possible run, kicked him into a flat-out gallop, held my breath and shut my eyes. He'd jumped it a couple of hundred times with Andrew so he flew it as if it wasn't there. The anticlimax was huge: what was the fuss about?

If he'd stopped, I certainly wouldn't be riding today. As it was, I got no praise from my mother, just a roasting for jumping on my own. There was no boasting to Andrew who had been jumping logs for two years. Not that he'd ever taunted me. He didn't need to because we both knew he was doing it and we both knew I wasn't. He was the doer, I was the thinker. He was the baddie, the wild child, cheekier and ruder than I ever dared to be, and he usually got away with it.

Once I could jump, I had to hunt. It was not my initiative – I was terrified – but my mother loved it, as did my father who went with her on Saturdays, so Andrew and I were expected to join in. I started locally with the West Street South Hunt over less demanding country which was perfect for me. Soon afterwards we were introduced to the Cottesmore, a Leicestershire hunt at the other end of the scale, where we were based during the Christmas holidays. To this day I retain a love for the Leicestershire countryside and feel butterflies rising in my stomach as I drive through some of the best hunting country in the world.

On the hunting field my instructions were 'follow me'. My mother never let doubt stand in her way as she led her small boys across some of Leicestershire's most celebrated country. We obeyed her as best we could, white as sheets as we scrambled and muddled through hedges, until inevitably she'd disappear over a fence we couldn't tackle. Panic would set in and I might veer left and Andrew right, each of us taking out a few furious riders. I remember Urky (Ursula) Newton, a formidable hunting character and someone many were petrified of, telling my mother to keep her brats under control or better still leave them at home. My mother would smile and apologise profusely, while taking not a blind bit of notice. Gradually we learned to keep up and I started to enjoy jumping.

On non-hunting days, we would sneak on to a local farmer's land and race round a circuit of hunt jumps. When it was too frosty, we'd turn the cowbarn, where the ponies lived, into a race track, setting out hay bales on the concrete and creating drop fences out of the steps. We spent hours in there riding flat out, often without saddles. We shared our two ponies with Adele and Rachel Jackson who lived in the village, and took it in turns to do time trials. Once our neighbour, Sue Cross, reported us for riding the pones to the point of exhaustion, but Granny was having none of it, saying they had a great life and if they didn't want to jump, they'd stop. End of story, except that whenever I run into Sue – as I did at Burghley in 2005 – she says, 'Every time I see you winning an event, I remember that day when you were flogging those ponies to death round that field.'

Between the ages of seven and fourteen, hunting changed from being the scariest thing I did to the thing I lived for. It taught me about survival and about sticking on no matter what. As I was on a pony initially, I had to fight for my line because the big hunts were competitive, with no hint of politeness, let alone kindness to kids. Eventually I thrived on the cut and thrust, but the more confident I got, the more Andrew lost interest. Before long I was able to hunt some of my mother's horses. Hunting is the best preparation for cross-country riding because it instils good horsemanship by developing the key elements of confidence and skill. However, although hunting was a passion and a goal, I was unaware how strongly it would influence my future as an event rider.

Sometimes we went to stay with our Fox-Pitt grandparents, Billy and Mary, who lived in Dorset. We were very fond of them but they were much more formal than Granny Speed, and Andrew and I spent most of the time there down by the stream trying to keep out of their way. My grandfather retired as a general after serving in the Welsh Guards. He loved animals, was a keen birdwatcher and was still hunting in his eighties, despite suffering from chronic bronchitis following lung damage during the First World War. Granny Fox-Pitt wasn't a very cosy character either and there were strict rules as to how we should behave. We would often go and stay with our ponies so we were able to pursue our passion for hunting and it kept us out of the house and out of trouble.

The downside of my idyllic rural childhood was that, in contrast, London was a prison. The Sunday night revolt against the journey back to town from Knowlton was a regular fixture, with Andrew and me often hiding until we were discovered and dragged protesting into the car. One night, we hid in some bushes with all four dogs, two Alsatians and two flat-coat retrievers, for what seemed like hours. We'd normally have been far too scared, but it was okay with the dogs and I remember thinking how lucky we were that they did not even whimper. We listened to the carry-on when our disappearance was noticed, but we only gave ourselves up when we were threatened with a police search. They knew we would not have dared to go far and I remember clearly this being the only occasion I saw Granny in a fury.

Not that she was all that amused by the chicken incident which took place at about the same time. She had a new batch of Marans pullets on point of lay, big grey and white chickens that she was extremely proud of. Andrew and I weren't sure if they could fly – they certainly didn't look as if they could – so we devised a test for them. I don't know how we carried a dozen birds upstairs to our bedroom without being detected, but Granny soon spotted the trail of feathers through the house. By the time she started banging on the door asking what we'd done with her chickens, we'd locked them in the wardrobe. We tried to get rid of the evidence as quickly as possible by throwing them out of the window. Because they had clipped wings, they fluttered to the ground rather than flew, but they all landed safely. That wasn't enough to stop us being in trouble as they didn't lay for a month.

In London, our house had no room to run around. There was always an issue with Andrew and I having too much energy, so my mother made us run around the block after school in the hope of stopping us from fighting and breaking up the house. Invariably the run turned into a race that I would win, which in turn led to an argument, so we were pretty much out of control even before we got inside.

My school in London was ultra-formal and strict and the only thing I liked was sport. As I was built like a giraffe, I was very ungainly, but I was quite quick and the medals handed out on sports days became a focus. There were not many gold ones but I won the odd bronze and although I was brought up to think that losing was fine, my parents always encouraged me to try not to.

Apart from our sporadic fighting, everything at home was always calm and relaxed – no shouting, but we were expected to behave. I was clobbered from time to time, but no doubt I deserved it and I learned to control my temper from a young age. It was as well I did because patience is the critical factor when dealing with animals and particularly in a career with horses.

I cannot escape without mentioning the guinea pigs; they were an obsession between the age of eight and twelve. I was introduced to them by Rachel and Adele in Leicestershire and breeding them became a hobby. From that I developed an interest in breeding anything – rabbits, dogs, hares, sheep and so on – which must have been worrying for my parents.

The guinea pig is the ideal breeding animal: it can reproduce nearly every month with a litter of perfectly formed mini adults that emerge ready to run around. I started with a pair of fluffy albinos and reached a startling total of eighty-six. I eventually decided that I'd have to sell some of them and I took my new role as a guinea pig dealer very seriously, not least because it would generate more pocket money and infuriate Andrew. As he wasn't a guinea pig fan, it was a double-headed benefit. My guinea pigs were kept in luxury in chicken coops and were looked after meticulously by Granny and Michelle whenever I was at school. Apparently they spent most mornings feeding them and mucking them out to make sure standards didn't slip in my absence. Michelle came to Knowlton in 1979 and has looked after everyone and run the place tirelessly ever since. If ever there is someone to track down or some information to be gleaned, Michelle is still the person to call on.

On Saturday afternoons after school, Granny and I would put the guinea pigs I wanted to sell in boxes and she would drive me round the pet shops in east Kent. Often I would decide the pet shop was unworthy – the cages too small or whatever – so we'd have to go on to the next one. Granny never once said, 'William, for God's sake leave them there,' though she must have thought it.

It was school that developed my enthusiasm for little animals. Every half term, some children were allowed to take a pair of science lab gerbils home and I couldn't wait for it to be my turn. Eventually it was, and guess what, they reproduced. When it was time to return them, I thought, 'Okay, school doesn't know there are any young so they won't miss them.' It's quite disturbing to think I was so devious at that age, but they were my secret. I left them in a nest in my sock draw without a word to anyone and took their parents back to school.

In the evening, I found myself in trouble. When my mother put away my laundry, she discovered the babies barely alive. She explained why they couldn't survive without their parents and decided we had to return them there and then. By that time, the school was locked, but not daunted, she climbed in through a window and I showed her where my classroom was so that we could reunite the family. The next morning I was excited at the prospect of seeing them, but what I discovered has scarred me for ever. Because of the separation, the parents had eaten their young, leaving the remains of a few limbs as evidence ... and it was all my fault.

I didn't just love animals, I was deeply sentimental about them. As we raised sheep on the farm, there were always a few orphan lambs about the place and I was wholly unrealistic about the need to eat the males. I didn't consider becoming a vegetarian because I didn't connect the two concepts, but there was no way I'd tuck into David or Timothy for Sunday lunch. Much to my horror, the Alsatians had other ideas, killing Timothy and taking a good few chunks out of David: it was my first exposure to death. After that, the farm manager told me that the lambs were only with us until they were strong enough to rejoin the flock. It was a white lie that worked.

Despite my commitments to the guinea pigs at the weekend, I would regularly accompany my parents to events. These trips were always fun and I remember keenly hoping they'd do well. My competition debut came after my breakthrough with the log. I agreed to take Minnie Monster to some hunter trials, though my approach was still cautious. Then, at the age of nine, it was time to tackle my first mini one-day event. As often happened, I went with Fiona Larkin, my mother's head groom. Fiona played a huge part in my early riding years, taking me to most competitions, organising me and teaching me what it was all about.

I remember it as if it were yesterday: the restless night, the nerves of competing, the joy of completing and the devastation that followed. Yes, I won my first event, but I was eliminated for jumping the wrong side of a fence. It was my fault so I wasn't hard done by and I certainly didn't let myself cry, but I was very angry and upset that I'd let everyone down. In a similar situation nearly thirty years later, my sentiments would be identical.

CHAPTER TWO

Pink is It

Imay never have liked school in London, but Wellesley House, my prep school near Broadstairs in Kent, was far, far worse. My parents wanted me to go to boarding school when I was eight, but they knew better than to insist outright, so they sold Wellesley House to me as being near my grandmother and promised I could come home every weekend. The alternative was going daily to Westminster prep round the corner from our house in Romney Street, but of course that was London, so they reckoned I'd agree to Wellesley. They were right.

I absolutely hated boarding school. I'd had a very happy life and I'd never been miserable before. Wellesley had a rule that you couldn't go home for the first few weeks of any term to give you time to settle in, but three weeks felt like a life sentence. Any communication had to be by post, which meant two days for letters to get home and two more days for the replies to get back, nearly a whole working week which, at eight years old, seemed like a lifetime.

I was an over-sensitive, home-loving child and I wasn't ready to be sent away. I'd have been all right if I could have used the phone, but that wasn't an option. On one occasion, I decided to sneak into my housemaster's office to call home on his phone. I knew that if I asked permission, he'd refuse, so I decided to take the risk. I looked at his timetable to see when he was teaching senior school and crept into his office. Just as I was on the point of dialling, he returned so I dived under his desk and hid unnoticed in the footwell for what seemed like hours, his feet inches from my hands. Miraculously no one was out looking for me – it must have been during a reading period – so I got away with it. I'm not sure I'd send a child to boarding school at eight, but some children cope well and communication is now so much easier and more acceptable to the school authorities.

At some point in my first term, I decided to go home. I knew I'd be sent straight back, but reason didn't come into it and I had a compulsion to talk to Granny. I wasn't running away to escape; I only did it because going home to talk about what I wanted to talk about would be quicker than writing a letter and far more practical. If I could have phoned, I wouldn't have done it. Planning it gave me a real buzz and I was quite proud of my attention to detail. I couldn't go in the dark because I hadn't been there long and I didn't know the way. Also it would have been too scary. Timing was the key: I needed a long period during the day when no one would notice I was missing.

In the end, I chose morning break. I knew it took half an hour by car to get back to Knowlton, but that didn't strike me as very far at that age and I knew which direction to take. So far, so good, but a small boy running down the road in uniform wasn't going to get away with it for long. Sure enough, the mother of another child drew up and asked me what I was doing. I said I was going home and she promised she'd take me there. Of course she stitched me up and drove me straight back to school.

Running away may not have worked for me, but I'm proud that I started a trend for it. My childhood was often like that. I wasn't socially competitive so I wasn't a leader, but I had ideas, I made plans and I gave instructions that others sometimes followed. Knowlton was the nearest point of refuge, not only for me but for my friends who'd come to stay for weekends or in the holidays. Granny was a no-nonsense character, and although she remained totally in charge at home until she was well into her eighties, she was essentially soft, always welcoming and very kind to Wellesley House boys.

My approach to my friends was less sensitive and I routinely put pressure on them to jump cross-country fences, even if they'd never ridden before. Naturally they didn't want to lose face by refusing the challenge, so I showed them how to do it on Tully, by far the best pony, then watched as they struggled with whatever other ponies we had at the time. After anything up to ten refusals, they'd get over the jump, often falling off as they landed. Then I'd move on to the next fence and repeat the process. I assume they enjoyed it, because they always came back for more.

After a while, I stopped moping around and things started to look up, but the weekly torture always started on Sunday night and Monday mornings were sheer hell. After two years, Andrew joined me, but that only made things worse. As his older brother, I'd fuss over him and boss him around when all he wanted was to be left to get on with school in his own way. Realising how much weekends meant to me, he'd often set out to sabotage them, disappearing at the moment of departure and lying low for hours.

We wouldn't be able to leave until we'd found him which might not be till 6 p.m. so wasting valuable weekend time. I used to try to find him and, if I did, we'd beat each other up. On one occasion, he bashed me on the back of the head with a stone. At this stage, we competed over everything. If I wanted to be at home, he automatically wanted to be somewhere else. It got so bad that Granny enlisted Tracey Simmons, who lived in a cottage on the farm, to be our playmate at weekends. She was a complete tomboy, game for everything, including learning to ride, but she was a civilising influence on us, if only because she was a third element in the equation.

We were typical brothers, fighting like cat and dog, but on the whole we got on well enough. We liked making camps and setting traps and we both enjoyed off-roading on the 50cc Suzuki bike I was given for my twelfth birthday. We weren't interested in how it worked, or at least I wasn't. Maintenance stopped at filling it up with petrol and mending a puncture.

On one occasion, we nearly killed Will Murray, a childhood friend who was staying with us. The challenge was to ride the bike over a ridge, touch an iron gate and come back. Andrew and I were sitting at the finish line doing the timing; each thinking it was great he was so slow, much slower than us. Eventually that turned into, 'Oh shit, where is he?' We wandered down the track imagining a breakdown, to find the motorbike entwined in the gate and Will lying on the other side of it. He had great gashes on his leg and arm, but he was *compos mentis* enough to ask why we hadn't shown him where the brake was. He has the scars to this day and he still believes we did it on purpose. It wasn't a problem at the time, but later it came back to haunt me when he married my dressage trainer, Lizzie Murray.

In the summer of 1979, my mother and father took Andrew and I on our first family holiday, leaving my new little sister, Laurella, behind. Our trip was to Wyoming in the USA. When it was announced we were going for a month, I was horrified, furious that it was to take me away for half the summer, but it turned out to be one of the best holidays of my life. My father worked very hard and if he did take time off, he wanted action, preferably skiing. He wasn't one for buckets and spades, beaches or luxury hotels, but dude ranching was right up his street.

We rode out western style every day and ate and camped with other families from America and Europe. We wore cowboy hats rather than crash hats and I loved the relaxed style and the laid-back approach. It was great boys' stuff, very light-hearted with lots of speed and no style. Andrew and I were given dobbins to start with, but were allowed to swap them for livelier ponies on day two.

Mine was a skewbald four-year-old, recently broken and still quite wild, so I took him on as a project, predictably spending lots of time searching for logs to jump him over. We covered a lot of ground on horseback, looking at the wildlife and tracking moose. I also enjoyed trying trout fishing, although I've never done it since. I was fascinated by prairie life and especially by the rodeo, which I thought was the coolest thing ever. We'd pester our parents to take us and we were mesmerised by the bulls and broncos.

When we got home, we put a headcollar and rope on the unfortunate Willy Wiff and a neckstrap round his loins. The harder you pulled, the more the neck strap tightened so the more he'd buck. He was probably in his twenties by then and our parents objected strongly, but Willy got his own back by kicking us once we fell off. The idea was that we would time each other to see how long we could stay on, but eventually we bucked him to a standstill. That was good news for Laurella, who inherited a very docile first pony a few years later.

When Willy quit, we decided to try our luck on some bullocks that were waiting to go to market. We knew what to do from the rodeo: we had to wedge them against the barn at one end of the crew yard and then jump down onto their backs for the buck off. Most of them escaped, so we concentrated on the few we managed to corral, but we never got them in the right position. As they were completely wild, that was probably lucky for us. Abandoning the rodeo attempts, we thought we should round up the ones that had escaped. Before we knew it, they were stampeding through the woods with us and the dogs on their heels, ending up a couple of miles away on another farm. They lost so much weight during their flight that they had to be fattened for another two months before they could be sold. I can still clearly remember the bollocking we got.

Although my mother concentrated her energies on my riding once Andrew stopped, I never felt under pressure. She was probably ambitious, but only in a supportive way. She has this ability to think outside the box and she always had the next stage in mind. Although I was distraught at being eliminated after winning my first event, she was encouraged by my performance and by my increasing confidence.

Not surprisingly I've never been small and, from the age of nine, she had me riding horses of all different shapes and sizes. There's no fault in that, but the Pony Club mothers thought she'd lost the plot when she sent me to my second event with Minnie Monster and Knowlton Corona. Minnie was 12hh, Fatty (Knowlton Corona) was a 17.1hh beast. My father had ridden him round Badminton three times. He had a reputation for taking a strong hold and he hated dressage, so there was no way he was going to stay in the arena for a nine-year-old boy. I remember trotting down the centre line and halting, then trotting straight out past the judge's car before I could turn him. The same thing happened several more times before I completed the test, but the judge took pity on me, and so did Fatty, and the cross-country was great. I thought I'd done a fantastic job, but the reality was that Fatty had taken me under his wing, as some old horses do, and aimed between the flags to carry me round the course.

To outsiders, it must have seemed crazy to put a slightly nervous child on such a massive horse, but I never thought it was odd at the time. If I'd been really worried, I could have refused, but in those days I usually did what my mother suggested. I would want to meet her expectations and going clear cross-country was at the top of that list. Having a run-out wasn't great, but a refusal was the worst crime because it meant you hadn't kicked hard enough.

At this stage, my mother began to look for ponies that would keep me interested. Bronze came next and was my first chestnut, a huge excitement on the grounds that he wasn't grey, but I didn't have much of an affinity with him in other respects. He was very feisty, fairly mad and too mental to hunt. Minnie was a kind pony, but he could run out, so my mother thought Bronze would get me going forwards. I wouldn't say he was a bad choice; just that he always went a notch quicker than I'd have liked. He also gave me my first bad fall in the pairs competition at the Goodnestone Hunter Trial. I was following my mother on one of her young racehorses through a sheep pen made out of hurdles and Bronze jumped in too close behind her, then veered right, clipped the hurdle and turned over. I was winded and taken off in an ambulance. There was certainly no hopping back on this time.

To counter the after-effects of the fall, and in the interests of diversity, I was found a second pony that was as bone idle as Bronze was buzzy. Tully was a priceless Connemara, at 14.2hh a real overgrown pony rather than a small horse. He was the laziest thing ever to come out of Ireland and he had the shortest stride, so he couldn't do dressage. Not that he had the remotest wish to, but on the upside he was safe, totally genuine and he taught me how to use my legs. Whereas Bronze went around like a motorbike going flat out, with his head bent into his chest, Tully stretched his nose way out in front as I tried to boot him forwards. However, I loved him from the start. He was a friend for years and became part of the family.

My mother also encouraged me to ride the young homebred horses. Some were nice, some weren't, but either way I enjoyed the challenge. It was a great advantage, teaching me to appreciate what different horses have to offer, rather than thinking there might be a better one round the corner. I was very excited to be given Solitaire, a fiery chestnut mare, when she was four and I was thirteen. We called her Runt because she was only 15.1hh and I rode her for seven years. She was the first horse I produced through to advanced, which was a bit of a joke, given my height.

In those days, winning was rare for me. I routinely got a pink rosette for fifth place and, if I was lucky, a special for best boy, so my victory in the Eridge Pony Club One-Day Event sticks in my mind. Runt flew round the cross-country for her first win, but the scoreboard said I'd been eliminated. Fiona was with me, so we went to ask the organiser, Jenny Nolan, what had happened. She said the fence judge at the bogey fence, a big log over a ditch, had heard someone say, 'Give her a whack,' as I was approaching. Seemingly this was outside assistance, so I'd been disqualified. As Fiona hadn't been there and I hadn't used my stick, I thought this was grossly unfair, especially as it meant the whole West Street South team was eliminated. Mrs Nolan refused to change it. I knew I hadn't cheated and both Fiona and I were mortified, especially as it handed victory to the Eridge team. It was a harsh lesson that the judge's decision is final.

That was my first contact with the Nolan family, though by no means my last as I've been a close friend, rival and team-mate of Jenny's daughter, Pippa (now Funnell), ever since. I hadn't met her at that point, but she was one of a number of talented juniors in Kent at that time, along with Alexandra Remus, who was being hailed as the next Lucinda Green, Tina Gifford (now Cook) and Polly Martin (later Phillipps). Pippa wasn't a threat to me as neither of us was winning anything, but the Eridge episode inevitably left a sour taste and I avoided her for ages on the grounds that she was her mother's daughter.

A year later, I came second to her at the south of England area trials, my first experience of Pippa the Winner. She was always very serious and professional, a year older than me and much more schooled and polished, but then so was everyone else. I was lanky, with very little style, and I always looked awkward. I lived for the cross-country; dressage was the price I paid for the fun. At the age of thirteen, I had shot up to 6ft 2in and, from then on, my height was one of the biggest issues I had to deal with in my riding.

Both my parents had competed regularly at Badminton, my mother much more professionally than my father, but neither was really into dressage. I'd never had any formal lessons, but luckily we had a Polish neighbour, Colonel Wilhelm Lewicki, who lived at the end of our drive. He was an amazing horseman with a cavalry background who'd escaped to England at the end of the Second World War. Wil was trained in the Polish cavalry school and was a member of the Polish Event team in the '50s and '60s. In those days, the Poles were world leaders in three-day eventing, but their talent was hard hit by the loss of many officers killed during World War II. Wil's arrival in Britain during the Second World War was an extraordinary stroke of luck – he was walking in Warsaw one evening when a German soldier rushed up to him and warned him that Warsaw was being ransacked that night and he should get out. The solider was an eventing friend he had met whilst competing at the World Championships in Rome. He left with some friends for Britain via Paris, where he joined the Polish regiment based in Cheshire. His next home was in Gloucestershire where he trained John Sheddon, the first Badminton winner, and then he moved to Dorset. Amongst his pupils was Tadkiz Kopanski, a prominent figure of the equestrian world and Chief Executive of the Pony Club for years. It was also in Dorset that my mother met him through my aunt, Sarah Fox-Pitt. He trained my mother at the height of her eventing career and competed himself, qualifying for Badminton three years in a row in his fifties. On each occasion, he led the dressage, but pulled out before the cross-country.

He famously broke both hips without falling off, while trying to prevent a horse from refusing, a credit to his power and determination.

These formidable qualities were now focused on me. Neither Bronze nor Tully put much effort into their flatwork, which was fine because I had zero interest in it either, but Wil Lewicki was an old man and he looked forward to my weekly lesson. Although I felt it was for his benefit rather than mine, I knew it was my duty to call every Saturday when I got home and book a lesson. He'd drive up from his house in low gears, progressively burning out his clutch, invariably reversing into a tree or a parked car, and limp into the indoor school.

He had an amazing empathy with horses and they all loved him. He was endlessly patient and he really knew how they moved and what made them tick. Up to that point, my only instruction had been at the Pony Club, where the best pupils, which didn't include me, trotted round on the bit and the rest didn't have a clue. Wil Lewicki did not tolerate that kind of sloppiness. He stood in front of me hour after hour, sharing his subtle understanding of the basics. He showed me what pressure with the legs should feel like, how to adjust the pace with my seat bones, how to tell which of the horse's legs was moving at any given time and how to establish a contact. He taught me about timing and precision, the need for endless patience and the futility of trying to force an issue.

For me, it was Chinese torture. I'd learned to ride positively, not to sit through lessons that often took place at a walk. He'd explain that if I asked Tully to halt with one leg in a certain position, it would act as a brake, and that it could lead to a good or bad result, a square or a crooked halt – practising that for an hour felt like all day. Even when we jumped, he worked on my technique, repeating a sixteen-inch fence endlessly in the search for perfection.

Of course it was invaluable, but it took me years to be able to put it into practice. He taught at a level so far above my head that I could see no conceivable gain, but I realise now how privileged I was to absorb things that I would never have learned from anyone else at such a young age. The more experienced I get, the more I fall back on his instruction, but at the time, I thought it was the most boring thing I'd ever done in my life.

CHAPTER THREE

Breaking New Boundaries

W hen my mother told us she was going to have another baby, Andrew and I were puzzled. 'How will it fit in the car?' I asked. Our sleeping space was a major priority. My parents had always wanted four children, two and two, with a gap in between, but we'd been unaware of that plan. I remember being proud when my headmaster Bill Sale came in to tell me that Laurella had been born, though it didn't mean much to me either way at the age of nine.

Due to complications, my mother spent several weeks in bed in the run-up to Alicia's birth in 1981. This meant that Fiona and I were left to tackle the summer shows on our own. That was fine because, like me, she has a cautious disposition. Just before her spell in bed, my mother had bought me my first horse, a grade B show jumper called New Bliss, and her instructions to Fiona for the Broadstairs Show were succinct: 'Tell William he can jump one class and then he's got to do the B & C.' Knowing that this was an adult class with jumps of 4ft 6in or so, Fiona must have thought my mother had gone mad.

As we walked the course, she'd say, 'Here's the first fence, right,' then she'd take me straight past it to the next one, but I don't remember being scared. New Bliss was a schoolmaster, so it was logical that I should do whatever he was capable of. All I remember was turning, pointing and kicking. As luck would have it, he jumped two clear rounds and we won, beating some good pros, in what must go down as one of my biggest riding flukes. He was the perfect horse, but he wasn't sound behind, so dressage was out of the question.

He was soon joined by Full House, the world's clumsiest show jumper, but totally honest across country. As I'd be eligible for junior competitions when I was fifteen, he was to be my first real event horse, but I never went to try him. His owner rode him round an event at the start of the season and I took over at Graveley Horse Trials the next weekend. Although I rode *hors concours* because I was too young to compete in adult classes, it was the biggest day of my life. I set out with great excitement, quickly curbed by a pretty awful dressage and a very average show jumping round. However, the day ended on a happy note with a clear cross-country.

The next milestone was the junior novice trial in Brougham in Cumbria, an eight-hour drive to what was only my second competition outside Kent. Both my mother and Fiona came, so I was conscious of its importance. Somehow, Full House and I managed to come second, beaten by Polly Lyon (now Williamson), the first of many times that would happen in the early days of my career. Polly had left school aged thirteen (after which she was educated at home) to become a full-time event rider, so being runner-up to her was no disgrace.

At this point my learning curve accelerated because my mother decided I should take Full House to the two-star National Junior Championships at Windsor in May. To do that you had to be selected, but first I had to qualify by competing in the junior intermediate class at the Portman Horse Trials. The biggest stumbling block was the dressage, which required sitting trot and a complicated canter movement, none of which I'd done before. I did it somehow, then knocked a couple of show jumps and went clear cross-country, narrowly surviving a near miss at the coffin to finish fifth.

That day was a highlight of my childhood career, but my euphoria at fifth place only lasted until I read my dressage sheet. 'Horse showing plenty of potential, rider sitting on the back of the saddle taking unfair tugs at horse's mouth. Poor horse,' wrote the judge, Major Derek

Allhusen. He was probably right and I was mortified, but my mother was characteristically loyal and played it down as nonsense. In any case, it was mission accomplished because I was selected, and was able to make my three-day event debut at Windsor when I was fifteen.

I was at Eton by then, conveniently close, but ironically a school that embraced every known sport except riding. For my first three years, no one knew about my other life, but the need to compete at Windsor during term time meant the secret was out. When my mother first asked for permission for me to go to Gill Watson for dressage lessons during term time, she received a letter from Jack Anderson, the Lower Master, saying, 'Riding is a holiday sport and we wish it to be kept as such.' He was quite a tyrant, so when he said something he meant it, but my mother rolled up her sleeves and persevered until he understood that it was important. Time off was a matter for delicate negotiation and I was always held to ransom along the lines of, 'We'll see how good your work is before we decide if you can go.' This proved effective because my mother was at home getting Full House fit and I knew how unimpressed she would be if I was grounded.

She believes that if a job's to be done, it's to be done properly, so she wasn't going to let me be mediocre at dressage if there was an alternative. Perhaps after Derek Allhusen's 'poor horse' comment, she realised I needed to do more than sit and kick, so she organised a taxi to take me for an hour's instruction with Gill Watson on one of her school horses every Thursday afternoon. Gill was the junior and young rider team trainer and I was so in awe of her that I barely breathed or spoke. Her lessons were torture, but I did like the focus and the pressure, and appreciated the need to deal with my riding issues. I wanted to improve. Gill became a major part of the next six years of my life. Her patience, professionalism and wonderful nature have been a highlight of nearly every British rider's formative years. We are so lucky to have a system in place that has provided her as the Under 18 and 21 team trainer for over two decades.

Despite Gill's help, I was completely out of my depth at Windsor, an event of Olympic proportions as far as I was concerned. I looked round and saw all these juniors with dressage saddles and long stirrups, while I had my knees over the front of the Stubben jumping saddle I used for all three phases. My mother installed Full House at a local livery yard the week before the event and my school allowed me out to ride him for an hour every afternoon.

When we walked the course, she lined up notches in every fence with hedges and trees in the background, and gave me precise instructions as to where to turn to align them effectively. Every other fence was a rider frightener, which terrified me, but I really didn't need to worry because Full House was 150 per cent brave, too brave. Across country, he would clobber his fences, fighting into them with his head in the air, but no way was he going to refuse.

My mother convinced me that I'd be fine as long as I followed the plan, so I lay in bed on the Friday night and went through it all in my head, never imagining I might come in to a fence on a bad stride. Mind you, that was because I had no concept of a stride, good or bad. My mother doesn't believe in looking for one, just in balancing your horse and taking the right line. That works, within reason, and I was a blank canvas, so I probably took each fence exactly the way she suggested. I had various hairy moments, but that was more to do with lack of control than from taking the wrong line. As a typical boy rider with no knowledge of tack or studs, I made sure my stirrup length was comfortable and left everything else to my mother.

Full House did a tolerable dressage for those days, though it would be dreadful now. He took me round my first steeplechase like a runaway train and went clear in the cross-country, albeit not in the most stylish fashion, as you might expect from a green horse in bottomless ground and a rider who couldn't see a stride. After the second day we were surprisingly in seventh place, but the show jumping was a major disappointment. I tackled it as if it was the cross-country and I was probably lucky only five came down. I'd have been happy to finish twentieth had I been there all the way through, but dropping down from seventh was bitterly disappointing, especially as I had to go back to school and tell my mates it had gone belly up. The selectors rubbed salt in the wound by advising a martingale and a stronger bit, but it would be a while before my mother would concede.

My father had been at Eton so he was happy when I did well enough in Common Entrance to follow in his footsteps. Meeting my contemporaries at the New Boys' Party, I was initially struck by what a mixed bunch they were. I'd been at prep school with Jacob Grierson, but the rest were strangers. Most of them appeared to be fairly studious so I didn't feel they'd be natural soul mates. I was in Michael Meredith's house. He turned out to be a great housemaster, always fair and supportive, and he played a vital part in my smooth passage through school. I was one of thirteen new boys in his house, most of them extremely bright, but my two best mates, Charlie Winter and Charlie Clay, were as unmotivated academically as I was. We were probably the odd ones out, surviving rather than thriving, but we had a lot of fun together. My problems at Wellesley had all been about lack of communication, but at Eton I had my own room and phone. I was happy there from the start.

I remember the Dame, our house matron, telling me that we had a lie-in until 8 a.m. on Sundays. At this stage, I'd never managed to stay in bed past 7 a.m. so I couldn't imagine how I'd fill the time. Reading certainly didn't come into the equation. Seeing my look of dismay, she said, 'Don't worry dear, you'll learn to lie in.' And I did. Within three weeks, I was finding it as hard to get up as everyone else did. I had been used to a uniform of cord trousers and Aertex shirts, so it was bizarre to put on stiff collars and tail-coats every day, but I saw it as part of the deal and it's surprising how quickly everyone gets used to it.

The best thing about Eton was that you were treated as an individual and were encouraged in any sphere you fancied, but you were never forced into anything in particular. The risk was that you'd end up doing nothing and no one would notice, but I was intrigued by the choice of subjects and hobbies. Because of my height, I was encouraged to take up rowing, singularly the most uncomfortable sport I've ever tried. I caught more crabs than you can possibly imagine and I managed to fall into the river several times. On the one occasion I coxed the boat, I steered it into a barge and that was the end of that.

Chasing a ball around never did anything for me, so I wasn't into cricket, though I enjoyed rugby up to a point. As a family, we can do athletics. My father had a hurdling blue from Oxford and he encouraged all of us to run to county standard. He's a real enthusiast and an equipment freak so, much to my embarrassment, I was using spikes and starting blocks when my contemporaries were in plimsolls. He put up hurdles and the high jump in the garden at home and made sure we all practised regularly. He encouraged us every inch of the way and turned up at athletics meetings to cheer from the sidelines; he was usually the only supporter there.

I didn't choose to go to Eton, but I'm very glad I did. It worked well for me because I was independent and fairly self-motivated, but there was a certain barbarity in the way it was run. Everyone was put under pressure, the best example being the way each term's exam results (known as trials) were read out in front of the whole year. I will never forget Willoughby and Burrell being singled out as General Total Failures (GTFs) – two GTFs and you were out of the school. All lists and, therefore, all roll calls in each house, were in order of performance in trials, so in theory the dimmer or lazier you were, the less likely you were to be rescued in the case, say, of a fire.

Academically I was average, but I got nine O levels and three A levels. My mother always wished she'd been an actress, but I was far too self-conscious for the stage. I couldn't sing a note, but I really enjoyed art. When I first went to Eton, I remember going to chapel, as we had to every day, and watching some boy read the lesson. For the next three years, I dreaded the day that boy would be me and I was only able to relax in chapel when the deed was finally done.

I'd come to terms with school by this time and I'd learned how to make the system work for me so I didn't feel I needed to push the boundaries. I hated smoking and drugs were not my thing. We were allowed to drink a couple of pints of beer in the Tap, the Eton pub, on Saturday nights. Sometimes we might be tempted to push the limit, but I would always be the one to suffer or get caught, so I soon realised it wasn't worth it. I made a small number of very good friends, none of them at all horsey. My mates thought I used school as a bit of a dormitory, but I was beginning to love competing and my mother worked continuously at home to make sure I could.

A couple of weeks after Windsor, I got a letter from Colonel Hubert Allfrey, the chairman of the selectors, saying that although he wasn't putting me in the squad for the European Championships, he wanted to long-list me so that I could benefit from the training. 'William obviously finds it difficult to control his nerves,' he wrote, 'so the more exposure he gets, the better.' It's hard to imagine he could have spotted any great talent at that stage, but he could see my enthusiasm and commitment and the huge backing I had from my parents. As it turned out, Full House was lame for the rest of the year, but I felt I was on my way.

CHAPTER FOUR

Bargain Basement Superstar

M y heart sank when I first saw Steadfast. The back partition of the lorry opened and there was a heavy, ordinary-looking animal. He extricated himself from his tight stall and stumbled down the ramp, exhausted by the effort required to finish second in a novice class at Witton Castle. I hadn't expected another horse, but my mother was on the case, buoyed up by the certainty that riding was the best way to keep a teenager on the straight and narrow. She thought that Full House was too feisty and tricky and wanted a calm horse that I could ride forwards, rather than fight to control.

Steady came from Judy Bradwell, a 17.1hh charger by the thoroughbred stallion, Ascertain, but the other half was part Clydesdale or Shire. I fancied myself on a classy thoroughbred racehorse and I was hoping for something amazing, so this dark bay elephant with a huge white face was a massive disappointment. Full House was no oil painting, but Steadfast, with his huge feet, legs, body and head, was something else again.

He felt fine when I tried him, but then I hadn't a clue what I was looking for. He wasn't going anywhere when I galloped him, but he jumped the novice cross-country practice fence willingly enough. I took him back to the lorry, told my mother he wasn't very exciting and assumed that that was that. Wrong, of course. The next day, she called me at school to say she'd bought him, subject to vet. When I heard he'd failed – lame on the circle, lame on the flexion test, bad front feet X-rays and breathing problems – I couldn't believe my luck. Wrong again. The next day, she called to say she'd got him for half the original price. She smelled a bargain. I saw a lame heavyweight, but it was one of the best decisions she ever made because he turned out to be the most incredible horse. At the time, he was eight, with a couple of events under his belt, and his owner had sent him to Judy to sell. She told my mother, 'He'll get William going and give him confidence, but when he wants to go on, you'll have to sell him because, basically, he's a novice horse. Meanwhile, he'll fill the gap.'

This piece of horse-trading illustrates the parental way with money. No one ever discussed it, but I was brought up not to spend it. My father was ambitious on his own account. He was driven, not perhaps to the point of obsession, but not far off, and he was a role model to all of us, going to work at the crack of dawn and returning when we were in bed, spending his weekends strimming or chopping down trees. During my early childhood, my parents ran Knowlton Horse Trials, a novice event at first, but with intermediate and advanced classes as well by the time it finished in 1982. My father worked tirelessly to design, build and upgrade the fences, in the belief that no job was worth doing unless you did it to the best of your ability.

Neither of my parents ever bought an expensive horse or drove a smart car. They never went on posh holidays or stayed in hotels, preferring to overnight with friends. When we went skiing, we'd drive out, well stocked up with tins of corned beef and baked beans, stay in a self-catering apartment and have dinner in a restaurant perhaps once during the week. On the mountain, we'd take a little picnic, a sandwich and a bottle of water, which we'd eat in the snow, rather than pay over the odds in mountain restaurants.

At home, we did jobs for pocket money, sweeping leaves off the drive, cutting down branches, mucking out and, of course, selling guinea pigs. Everything was negotiable, but we didn't get anything for nothing. If we showed an aptitude for anything, our parents backed it with all their energy and supported us endlessly. We were then expected to practise and participate to our full ability. Even at pre-prep school, we practised the sack race in the garden in the run-up to sports day.

I rode Steady round one novice event in the spring of 1985, then quickly forgetting his potential limitations, qualified him for Windsor in the intermediate at Bicton, where he came eighth. He also finished third in the intermediate at Chilham Castle, my first grown-up points, as I was now old enough to compete in adult classes. As Full House had already been selected for Windsor at Belton, I had two strings to my bow. The only problem was that the three-day event clashed with my O levels. I'd done four the previous year, so I had five this time round. Now that I was getting more involved in eventing and competing against riders who were in it full time, I slightly resented my education, but deep down it gave me a bit of a loophole, which I frequently used to console myself when things went wrong.

In order to avoid getting my hopes up only to have them dashed, I'd run through the worst-case scenario in my head before I started. Even so, I was more optimistic when I went to Windsor than I had been the previous year, if only because it was more familiar second time round. All being well, Full House would take the cross-country in his stride and, as I had more control, he flew round, getting better all the time. Steady wasn't really ready and was still green at ditches and water, so we scraped round, with him responding bravely to my ignorant commitment. Both horses went clear within the time, finishing seventh and eighth after cross-country. Steady knocked one show jump down to end up ninth, which was as good as I could have hoped for, while Full House, as usual a bit of a physical wreck after towing me cross-country, demolished six and dropped right down the order.

After two bad Windsors, show jumping was rapidly becoming a real issue for me. When the listed juniors were invited to do a dressage and show jumping competition in Birmingham, it was decided I should go, even though it clashed with the 110m hurdles in the Junior

County Championships in Reading. Competing for Berkshire in the race was important particularly for my relations with the school, but the logistics were complicated and I arrived at the Birmingham showground with my mind spinning. The first person I bumped into said to me, 'Don't panic. Take one of these little blue pills my mother gave me and you'll be fine.' She was immeasurably more sophisticated than I was, so I accepted it. While I was wondering why it had no immediate effect, the organisers changed the running order so I had to hurry off to Reading without jumping. I suppose the pill was valium, because it hit me at the athletics match, leaving me wandering round the track like a zombie. I tried to wake myself up, but I came way last in the race. Neither the school nor my parents had a clue what had happened, but the experience made me realise that there would be no short cuts in the battle to control my nerves.

After my second Windsor, my mother sent me off for training for the first time, driven perhaps by my increasing recalcitrance at home. By now, we would often argue over horses, not because I knew best, but because I was starting to want to do things my own way. I started querying some of her theories rather than accepting what she said as gospel. I had to learn to take criticism, but I found it difficult to take from my mother. I must have been pretty stroppy, because she sent me to Waterstock for three days with Steady and Runt.

Lars and Diana Sederholm ran Waterstock like a military campaign, with precise timetables in operation throughout the day. The Sederholms were great family friends. As they had three daughters about my age, I was allowed to stay in the house, but I was very much there as a student. Working with eventing gods like Yogi Breisner and Richard Walker was scary, but I knew it was a great opportunity and I was very conscious I had to make a success of it, especially as both my parents had trained there in the 1960s.

I found it pretty difficult keeping to the Sederholm timetable because I was looking after the horses myself. I liked to do them well, but although I'd learned how to groom and clean tack at Pony Club, I had very little experience of actually doing it, so everything took me a long time. On the riding front, I spent hours in sitting trot on Runt with no reins and very short stirrups, the beginning of a long, agonising road to getting it right. On the last day, when I went to saddle Steady for my lesson with Lars, I found him lying down asleep. I didn't want to disturb him, so I went and told Lars I'd be late. He looked at me as if I'd fallen out of a tree and said, 'Get back there and get on that horse right now. Your lesson finishes at 2.30 p.m. and if you miss it, that's your lot.' I was mortified at the thought of disturbing Steady when he didn't want to be woken up. Lars tells the story as an illustration of how soft and hopeless I was, but as a child, I never got a horse out of bed to ride it and I still wouldn't now.

The Waterstock days were a one-off, but despite the experience I gained there and from the junior system, I was still heavily involved in the West Street Pony Club. The Pony Club is an invaluable all-round grounding for any child with an interest in ponies. The structure is there from five years old and there is a lot of fun to be had from rallies and mini-camp right up to the Pony Club Championships, which has an illustrious roll of honour. It was through the Pony Club that I met Sheila Cotter, a local dressage trainer. Sheila and I immediately hit it off and from then on she came down to Knowlton regularly. She was the first person to build on Wil Lewicki's instruction. She was strict, but she always treated horses sympathetically, giving them time to warm up and sensing when they were getting tired. While I was competing in juniors and young riders, she established my position. She taught me many other dimensions to dressage, a great contribution because my height was a natural weakness I had to overcome. Lars touched on my position, but Sheila beat it in until it finally stayed. I wouldn't like to think how many hours it took, but every one of them has paid off. Now my height often works to my advantage as long as I'm in balance. My upper body is great leverage, but I am always aware of the problems I can cause if I'm in the wrong place.

After Windsor, I was long-listed for the junior squad and I represented Britain as an individual for the first time at Rotherfield Park in the autumn of 1985. I received my first ever Union Jack badge, a source of enormous pride. More importantly, I was eligible for twice-yearly training sessions with Gill Watson, who I had been sent to by taxi from school a couple of years before. Riders were invited to take a couple of horses for a few days of intensive training. I learned a lot on the courses, but they were also good fun as we stayed in digs and went out in the evening as much as possible.

I have many memories of water and muckheap fights and, on one occasion, of coming up against a gang of locals in Aston Rowant. They set about picking a fight, but they were a lot older and we didn't fancy our chances, so we legged it. Most members of the squad were girls, but there were always a few hopeless boys with mothers who did everything. It didn't take us long to realise that a girl who thinks you're a hopeless boy will rush to help, especially if your incompetence threatens to hold her up, a valuable early lesson in the on-going battle of the sexes.

By 1986, Full House was out of the picture. Once again he'd been lame after Windsor and needed the rest of the season off. I appreciated what he did for me, but I found it hard to handle the disappointment that came with it. He taught me a lot about patience. I had to learn to be tolerant of his often uncooperative temperament and physically I learned that the best cure for injuries was time. My mother's breeding programme at Knowton involved two founder brood mares, Go Try, her 14hh Connemara show jumper, and Rise and Shine, the first horse she rode at Badminton. Of the two, Go Try was the successful female gene in a dynasty of Fox-Pitt horses; my sisters are still riding her descendants today. Runt was one of hers, as was Loch Fyne, an elegant grey we nicknamed Thomas. He promised a great deal when I started riding him in 1986 as back-up for Steady.

After a quiet year in 1986, with Steadfast off the road with a check ligament injury, 1987 was to be the big one. It was my A-level year and my Eton housemaster Michael Meredith was concerned, not surprisingly, as my mother had planned my last appearance in the Junior National Championships at Windsor and my first three-star three-day event at Bramham to coincide with the exams. Thomas, then aged seven, was my back-up for Windsor, but when we walked the cross-country, we felt he was too inexperienced to tackle it, so we withdrew him. However, Steady was fantastic, finishing in fifth place on his dressage score, a personal best.

My mount for Bramham was Le Djinn, an incredibly versatile horse and my mother's last successful event horse. He'd won the Grand Prix d'Auteuil and several other races in her colours in France, and then carried her to victory ahead of forty rivals in the Melton Hunt race, a famous four-mile steeplechase over natural country. She'd also completed Bramham on him in 1976, a decade before she passed him on to me to ride in Pony Club events. At one of them, I was leaving the arena on a loose rein after an average test when he bucked me off and disappeared. That was the kind of horse he was, his sadistic streak tempered by a terrific sense of humour.

By way of preparation for Bramham, and with both of us aged eighteen, I rode him in my first advanced at Bicton. The fences were a big shock to me but, as usual, I had complete confidence in the plan, rightly so because Le Djinn went clear. He was a cantankerous old bastard, a temperamental, super-talented chestnut who was very grumpy in the stable. Get in his way and he'd give you a swipe or a kick – and he wasn't kidding. When I first rode him, I was too terrified to do his girth up, leaving it to Fiona or my mother, who took no nonsense. His job was to educate me to the next level, not a task he particularly relished, though he did love cross-country. During the dressage test, he'd buck and swish his tail so fiercely that it hit the back of my hat, especially if I was wearing tails that tickled his back, and he'd often knock a show jump or two because he didn't care.

At Bramham, with the tails of my coat pinned tightly to the saddle cloth, he performed to type, earning a dressage mark in the eighties, not quite last but not far off it. After going clear in the cross-country and knocking three show jumps, we finished just outside the top twenty, but Le Djinn had done his job. It was a massive experience to have had at eighteen and a privilege to compete at this level against

Lucinda Green, Ginny Leng (now Elliot), Mark Todd and Ian Stark. Lucinda, who competed against my parents, has been very supportive throughout my career, but I was in awe of the others, especially Ginny. At the time, she was eventing's leading lady, the ultimate perfectionist, but I wouldn't get to know her for a few more years.

Back at Eton, Michael Meredith was tearing out his hair and bribing me to work even more overtly than usual, while at home I'm sure my father was starting to give up on my education. I took my French oral before Windsor and my biology practical before Bramham, but the bulk of the exams were scheduled for the following week. During the competition, I was supposed to spend every spare minute revising. Imagine trying to read French literature in the lorry for three hours between the vet's inspection on Sunday morning and the show jumping phase in the afternoon. Concentration had no chance.

After the excitements of Bramham, settling down to A levels was a big ask. I had no time to worry so I didn't, though I probably should have done. Inevitably they weren't going to go well and they didn't, but as I never got wound up about exams, that wasn't a problem. When they finished, I left Eton without a backward glance and with many good memories. There were some informal leavers' parties, but nothing ceremonial; it was just a sense of job done, over and out. Like all eighteen-year-olds, I'd become a big fish in a small pond, and I was looking forward to moving on.

University was always non-negotiable. I hadn't applied, but my parents knew how to turn the screw. Either they'd support my horses through my university days or I could opt out and earn the money to pay for them myself. It wasn't much of a choice, but it was totally fair. In the meantime, I had a gap year to look forward to. Secretly I hoped that one gap year would turn into two and that I might not go to university at all but, of course, my parents' decision was a good one. Why should I be allowed to throw all my eggs in one basket when I didn't know if I'd be any good at eventing anyway?

I sometimes feel guilty they put so much into my education for so little return. I know I benefited a lot from it, but I didn't achieve what my father hoped for. He was more academic than any of us, working hard at school and at Oxford, whereas my plan was to ride through my university days. To achieve this, I wanted to be fairly close to home, though not in Kent. Eventually I got into London University's Goldsmith College more by luck than anything else. My mother made me ring them from every service station on the way up to the Pony Club Dressage Championships at Weston Park. I wasn't too concerned if I got through or not but, by the time we arrived, I had an interview, not because of my A-level results, but because my eventing represented an outside interest which they appreciated. Their gamble paid off, because I later rode for London University and was a member of a pretty successful team.

It was July and I remember walking Steady back from dressage at Iping horse trials when my mother told me my grandmother had died. She'd been confined to the house for three years, still taking a keen interest in everything we were all up to but partially paralysed by a stroke and affected more recently by Alzheimer's disease. By this time, she'd stopped fighting and started deteriorating, so I was expecting it, but I remember that day of mixed emotions very clearly. I knew it would be a relief to my parents who'd been so worried, never wanting her to go into a home, but troubled by a catalogue of nurses. Some were kind and caring, others completely crooked. For Andrew and me, the loss of the person who'd played such a major role in bringing us up was the saddest thing that had ever happened.

My parents organised a lovely funeral and she was buried in the Knowlton churchyard next to her husband, Jack. She missed the news of my moderate A-level grades, but she would have been delighted at my selection for the European Junior Championships at Pratoni del Vivaro in Italy. At Rotherfield two years earlier, I'd been selected as an individual – as it was a home fixture, Britain was allowed eight individuals in addition to a team of four – but at Pratoni, we were only allowed six riders in all. Steady was not a potential gold medallist, but I hoped I'd earned my place in the team after coming fifth at Windsor and following up with some good results.

The riders, including Tina Gifford and me, flew out to Rome, while our mothers drove Steady and Tina's horse, Song and Dance Man, out to Pratoni, a mad trip we were lucky to miss out on. They spent three days on the road, stabling the horses each night and sleeping in the horsebox themselves. Steady trod on a nail along the way, so he didn't trot up very well at the first horse inspection. 'Pottery,' the vets said, but to me he was always pottery so I was distraught when the selectors decided to leave him off the team. I believed that any chance of a medal had evaporated, but morale plummeted still further when my mother asked Colonel Bill Lithgow, a team selector, for an explanation. He told her Steady wouldn't be sound by Sunday so I now had to contend with the prospect of a lame horse as well.

It was a harsh moment, but there was no scope for negotiation. On the plus side, the blow revved me up and Steady went brilliantly, coming third in the dressage, going clear in the cross-country within the time and clear show jumping. I finished second behind Polly Lyon and won the silver medal. It was one of the most memorable moments of my career and a fitting end to my days as a junior. It was also a huge personal triumph and a very proud moment, for me, Steady and my parents, who'd made it all possible.

CHAPTER FIVE

Cold Calling

As gap-year activities go, canvassing for George Bush Sr was unusual, but I was keen to spend some time away from horses and my father was right behind me. He'd been sent to the United States for three years during the Second World War and later studied economics and business at Stamford University, so he had friends in America, among them Bush's brother, Buck, who got me the job.

In January 1988, I went to stay with distant cousins in Boston and worked for the Bush campaign in the run-up to the New Hampshire and South Carolina primaries. I had no experience of politics and no great enthusiasm for it, but my first solo foreign travel was comfortingly low risk. From the start, I loved the work and I was pretty successful at cold calling. I often got the predictable reaction, 'Who the hell are you and what do you care who I'm voting for,' but no one ever put the phone down on me. I suppose the English accent helped when I rang to ask if party representatives could call round to put their case.

At other times, I was a dogsbody, setting up functions and booking meeting halls, but it was good experience, not least because it was so very different from anything I'd done before. I couldn't stay beyond the end of February because the new eventing season, my first in young riders (aged nineteen to twenty-one), was about to begin. Le Djinn had retired, so I was pinning my hopes for the Young Rider Championship at Bramham on Steady. He had come fifth in his first advanced class at Weston Park after Pratoni, so he was proving he could make the step up to the next level. Scanner was my other chance, a stunning bay we'd exchanged for New Bliss after we'd established that he was chronically unsound behind. I dreamed Scanner would be a superstar and take me to Badminton. Maybe he would have done, but he was very temperamental, nappy and a slow developer, so it took me most of my teens to get him up to advanced. He too was rarely sound but, at this point, he'd finally achieved the advanced qualification he needed for Bramham.

Young riders have to go further and faster than juniors but, in those days, they also carried weights, which was to my advantage. When Mark Todd (Toddy), New Zealand's Olympic gold medallist from Los Angeles and Seoul, later said, 'The day they get rid of weights, you and I have had it in this sport,' I could see what he meant, because it's difficult to create a level playing field unless every horse carries the same amount. Then again, a small girl with three stone of lead puts more strain on a horse than a heavier rider with none, so that's not fair either. Subsequently, weights were abolished on safety grounds: the Horse Trials Association was terrified a rider would be killed, triggering an outcry about a horse being exhausted by carrying dead weight he wasn't accustomed to.

As I prepared for my first British Young Rider Championships at Bramham, I was careful to control my diet, so that I'd be as close as possible to the minimum weight of 11st 11lb. As I'd always been skinny, I wasn't used to going short of food, so it may have been unwise to accept a glass of champagne at the welcome cocktail party in Bramham House. I was happily talking to Nigel Taylor, then at the top of the game, when I thought, 'Bloody hell, he looks a bit odd.' The next moment I had a vision of him falling violently away from me, but the reality was that it was me who was crashing backwards. Having hit the floor and passed out, I came round to hear Nigel saying, 'No problem, he's only drunk.' I staggered to my feet and said, 'I'm not drunk, not drunk,' and walked out of the hall to lie down for a bit. The next moment, I fell headfirst down the stone staircase, top to bottom. When I landed, someone put me to bed and, half an hour later, I was fine, not a bruise anywhere, but people still wind me up about it.

I didn't even have a hangover, though there's nothing I hate more. I've never had a good relationship with alcohol because I'm a lightweight and I can only drink half as much as anyone else for the same effect. The next day, Scanner did a very good dressage just behind Polly Lyon, with Steady tenth, but I gave Scanner an appalling ride cross-country, which I ascribe to lack of nourishment rather than booze. There was a decent corner that I didn't feel he was ready for, so I went for the longer, safer option and still let him run out. Steady was his usual consistent self, finishing in the top ten, but I was mortified to have done such a bad job on Scanner when I had a real chance of winning or, at worst, coming second in a very competitive event. In the days when parents encouraged their children to consider a career in eventing, young rider classes attracted forty entries, whereas twenty would be a strong field two decades later.

Even more disappointingly, Scanner was never really sound for the remainder of my gap year, so Steady was on his own. At last I was eventing full time, often living by myself at Knowlton and absolutely loving it. The senior British eventing team had been successful with silvers at the Los Angeles and Seoul Olympics, so the mood was buoyant, with big sponsorship deals in the offing. My target for 1988 was the European Young Rider Championships at Zonhoven in Belgium. Again we were a squad of six, but this time I made it into the team along with Polly, Pippa and Susanna Macaire. Polly and I had been together in Pratoni, but Pippa and Susanna were the old guard, so they called the shots. When they wanted to get up, we all got up; when they went back to the hotel, we all went, so it was a bit two and two, but pretty stress free overall.

The chairman of selectors, Christopher Schofield, cheerfully announced he was sending me out as the pathfinder for the team. As the only boy, I took the responsibility very seriously, though he probably had me tabbed as cannon fodder or felt that my weak dressage reduced my chance of an individual medal. My mother was indignant, as those who go early tend to get worse dressage marks but, of course, that was the deal so off I went round the twisty sandy course.

I'd walked it with Gill Watson, always the voice of caution and someone whose main priority was the team result, and then with my mother, who'd given contradictory instructions along the lines of, 'Go like hell here, cut this corner and don't make too big a loop there.' I heard both voices in my head, but Steady wasn't the fastest of horses, so there was no art in hitting the best speed. On deep, loose sand, he would only make the time if he went flat out. The course was daunting for both of us, with a lot of water jumps, which he never liked. Steady needed positive riding, because if I had any doubts, he'd pick up on them. He was cautious and lazy and he didn't have a very big jump, so he didn't like to meet fences on the wrong stride.

I was the only young rider to have a mother as a manager, mostly because she was the only one with enough experience to give sensible advice. Although we sometimes disagreed about horses, we worked effectively together. She has a direct manner that people who don't know her can find intimidating, but we'd always got along very well. 'How can you expect the horse to be calm, if you aren't?' she said. 'You can't rely on others to help you control your nerves, you have to do it yourself.' I've always rated this piece of advice very highly. I suppose she must have been nervous when she competed, but she was a gutsy rider, very steely in a crisis, and she didn't believe in sports psychology, just in getting on with it.

In my first international young rider team competition, it was inevitable I'd have plenty of commands ringing in my ears as I urged Steady on. Where Gill felt I should get round safely with ten time faults, my mother thought ten time faults would scupper the team's chances of a gold medal. She wanted me to go for it and I was eager to take on the challenge. I certainly felt the pressure, but I also enjoyed it, all the more when Steady and I completed the cross-country within the time.

'No worries then,' said Gill, no doubt unaware of my mother's alternative approach. 'The time's obviously quite easy.' After a poor dressage, I moved up to fifth after the cross-country, finishing with the fastest time of the day. With a clear show jumping round, I finished fourth, so near and yet so far. We won team gold, with Polly taking individual gold on Highland Road and Pippa finishing in eighth on Sir Barnaby. Before I started, I'd have accepted ending on my dressage score, but I was bitterly disappointed at missing out an individual medal. Zonhoven is a dreary place, but it was a great competition and a job well done. Team gold was a cause for celebration, but we were focused on catching ferries and getting the horses home as soon as possible, so we left immediately after the medal ceremony.

CHAPTER SIX

You'd Have to be Crazy

I can't imagine what possessed us to enter Steady for Badminton, but he was qualified from Bramham and Zonhoven, plus he was the only horse I had at that level so he had to go. Lots of young athletes have personal goals, but not me, and Badminton definitely wasn't on my radar at that time. I used to walk round it thinking, 'Mad people do this,' and suddenly I was out there with the loonies. I wondered if Steady and I were really up to it. I knew I'd be pushing him, a souped-up Land Rover rather than a Ferrari, to do a four-and-a-half-minute steeplechase and a thirteen-minute cross-country. Now I know I was right to be concerned. He was never a Badminton horse in a million years.

The selectors were keen that the winning team from Zonhoven should take the opportunity to compete, so they made sure our entries were accepted. Polly, Pippa, Susanna and Daniel Hughes also took up the challenge, creating a lot of peer pressure. From the moment I got to Badminton, I felt like a tennis pro might playing at Wimbledon for the first time, totally gobsmacked and in awe of everything; just driving into the stable yard created terror and uncontrollable excitement in equal measure. Nowadays, the excitement is less, but I'm still just as terrified.

I'm also very superstitious and notoriously good at losing things when I'm nervous. I couldn't find my crash helmet on my first Badminton cross-country day, but how could I possibly compete without it? As no one could track it down, I did the steeplechase in Mary King's groom's hat, then switched to a new helmet my father bought for the cross-country. Normally I would have looked on that as the kiss of death, but on this occasion I forced myself to be pragmatic about it. What else could I do?

Our dressage was pretty average because Steady had suddenly become a head shaker. Head shaking or twitching the nose can be caused by an allergy and Steady did it for the first time on the Thursday, in advance of his test on the Friday. It caught us by surprise and I had no idea what to do. The result wasn't awful, but certainly not as good as he could do.

To everyone's amazement, he flew round the steeplechase, all four and a half minutes of it, inside the optimum time and headed happily off to phase C. As I came down the undulating avenue towards Badminton House and the start of phase D, the crowds appeared in waves as I breasted the hills, then vanished as I disappeared into the dips. I felt sick, overcome by nerves, encouraged only by the odd little voice calling, 'Good luck.'

The compulsory ten-minute halt in the box before the cross-country was an out-of-body experience. I react to nerves by getting lethargic, even to the point of falling asleep. Lars, Fiona and my parents looked at me doubtfully, wondering if I was up to the job. When they legged me up, I remember thinking, 'There they go,' rather than, 'Here we go,' as if it was happening to someone else. I didn't know if Steady would go round at all, but as soon as I was on him, the doubt vanished. As we headed for the first fence, I left my worries and nerves behind me. I'd walked the course with my mother, so I had a definite plan, no ifs, buts or maybes. Even today, I hate setting out thinking, 'I'll see how he's going and decide which route to take when I get there.' I have a plan and a fallback plan and that's it.

On this occasion, I was there for experience rather than to win, so I picked the long routes at the ski jump, the lake and the Tom Smith's Walls. At the Vicarage Vee, the long route was so horrible it wasn't an option, so I took it straight, although I was petrified, not least because it was a fence I'd dreaded jumping. The coffin was also pretty unfriendly, but Lars told me Steady would be fine, provided I went in strongly and kicked. Only a few riders went straight all day and my plan was to go in the long route, then take the direct route over a rail out. Steady was no athlete, so he was always going to find this manoeuvre testing. He jumped the ditch with insufficient momentum, landed unathletically on the bank and put in an annoying stop at the rails. I was mortified because I knew I'd let him down, but it was very exciting to get round. Ginny Leng (Elliot) won with Master Craftsman. I had a couple of show jumps down, but finished in the top half, proudly earning my completion plaque. How exciting it was to have done Badminton.

The 1989 European Young Rider Championships were held in Achselschwang in Bavaria. Pippa and I were back in the team, along with Tina Gifford and Daniel Hughes, the replacements for Polly and Susanna, who'd been fast-tracked to the seniors following good performances at Badminton. With Tim Randle and Belinda Cubitt competing as individuals, we were a great group, three boys and three girls who got along well. There was a lot of rivalry, banter and flirting. Daniel and Tina were an item and I fancied Pippa, but I don't think it was mutual. We never got it together, but I wonder if we might have done if there'd been a few more opportunities. I still hadn't forgiven her mother for the area Pony Club incident, but I no longer held it against Pippa and we've been close friends ever since. Luckily it stopped at that: the mind boggles at the competition there'd have been between us if we'd been a couple.

This championship gave me my first experience of sportsmanship – or lack of it. Running the first kilometre or two after the steeplechase was something I did to give my horse a bit of a break without any weight on his back. I'd done it at every three-day event, including Badminton, and I did it at Achselschwang. Gill was worried I'd trip and lose Steady, but his well-being was of more concern to me, especially as I knew that if he escaped, he'd put his head down to eat rather than run away.

As the British team led after the cross-country, the Germans tried to turn the tables by claiming that there was a rule saying that you had to go through every marker flag on phases A, B, C and D mounted, rather than just at the start and the finish of each phase. We were sitting in the lorry relaxing and reliving the day when the blow fell. I'd been eliminated and the whole team with me, as Daniel had failed to complete, following a nasty fall on the flat.

Our *chef d'équipe*, Giles Rowsell, protested, but the Germans put their money on the table and insisted on an investigation. No one on our side seemed too optimistic and I went to bed thinking, 'What bastards.' I didn't sleep a wink, but the incident did show me the lengths to which some nations will go to get their rivals eliminated. I am competitive and ambitious, but I'd never want to win on a technicality. They must have been trying it on because I can't believe they thought I was cheating, but turning such an irrelevant detail to your own advantage is no way to win.

The ground jury still hadn't decided the next morning, but I was given permission to do the trot up. Eventually the Germans lost their money and I was allowed to jump, much to everyone's relief. Less positively, our team lost the gold medal because Tina had a stop at the first show jump. Pippa was second and I was third behind the Swedish gold medallist, Stefan Lidbeck. The home team kept their heads down at the medal ceremony, but it was a shame fate didn't play into our hands, as we'd have dearly loved a victory. On a personal note, I was happy to have won team gold and individual bronze in front of Granny Fox-Pitt. She'd been suffering from Parkinson's disease for years, so she was rarely able to come and support me.

Back at home, my honeymoon was at an end. Two years had passed since Goldsmith's had accepted me, so it was time for me to keep my end of the bargain and head off to university. I lived in Pimlico with various housemates, including Charlie Winter, known as Chill, who was a great friend from school. He had a part-time job while he was doing the rehab he needed after an accident so he could pass his medical to get into the army. I'd chosen Goldsmith's for its location in Deptford in south-east London, just over an hour's drive from home, and I only spent one weekend in town over four years.

I read French, not from any passionate interest in Molière and Racine, but because I thought it would be the easiest way to get a pass with minimum work. Both my parents are fluent and they made sure some of it rubbed off on us by insisting we always spoke French in the car as youngsters. It's a very good idea and I shall certainly do the same with my children, though it did mean that we spent a lot of journeys in total silence.

They also insisted on French exchanges over a period of three or four years up to the age of thirteen. These were always met with fierce resistance from Andrew and I, but there was no escaping them, perhaps because our parents wanted a couple of weeks' peace during the long summer holidays. The families were chosen for their availability rather than for their suitability. On one occasion, I spent most of my days with a local farmer milking his goats as no one in the family ever got up before lunch. On my last exchange, aged thirteen, I worked in a show jumping yard for Madame Bonnafoux. I may have learned some good stable boy French, but I've never been so exhausted in my life. Veronique, the head girl, and I had to do twenty-six horses, so I mucked out twelve and rode six every day. We had a two-hour lunch break and, invariably, Veronique had to crash on my door to wake me for afternoon stables. By the end of the day at 7 p.m., I had no energy for anything beyond supper and bed. Standards were very different and it was normal for the horses to stand in their stables all day, but it was good experience and, surprisingly, I enjoyed it.

Thanks to the exchanges, I could speak a bit of French with a reasonable accent by the time I got to Goldsmith's. The course required literature and linguistics as well as language and it was a major struggle after my double gap year. To my relief, the timetable was comfortingly relaxed. I never had to be there till noon on Monday and I was gone for the weekend by noon on Thursday; if Friday lectures crept in, I borrowed someone else's notes. I doubt I'd have got a degree if I hadn't had an amazing teacher called Sandra Blane. She was six foot tall with masses of curly red hair and she had a gift for putting a point across. If she was speaking, everyone listened. She was a keen dressage rider, so we shared an interest in horses, but she wasn't very tolerant of the amount of time I spent riding. 'Do you realise you're in danger of failing,' she told me firmly as my finals crept up. 'Carry on like this and you'll be lucky to get a third.' She was a powerful woman and she taught French literature with real passion, so I can thank her for the mediocre 2.2 degree I eventually achieved.

London was unusually social by my standards. When Chill and I had friends over, we'd start shopping at 8 p.m. so the food was rarely ready before 11 p.m. But at least it was edible, because we could both cook. My grandmother introduced me to the basics at an early age and both Chill and I had talked our way onto the Eton cookery course, mostly because it guaranteed a decent meal once a week. Demand was high and places limited, but I convinced Michael Meredith that I should do it, despite his initial doubts. 'When in your life, Fox-Pitt, are you ever going to have to cook?' he demanded, but he allowed himself to be persuaded. I've since proved him wrong, because I have often needed to cook and it is something I enjoy doing.

I'm sorry now that I didn't have more time for university life. My only contribution was riding for the university team in dressage and show jumping. The deal was you borrowed horses from local riding stables, warmed up for ten minutes before the dressage test and did the permitted maximum of two practice fences before the show jumping. Our trio did pretty well, reaching the National Championships at Marchington in Staffordshire. After we won that, I was selected to represent Britain in the World Student Games in Rotterdam in 1990.

As a team we came nowhere, but I drew an amazing little horse and took the individual show jumping title, inappropriately I felt, as it was always my weakest discipline. I don't remember much about the competition apart from drinking endless schnapps, perhaps because I was far too taken with my team-mate, Lucy Wordsworth, a student from St Andrews I'd met at the qualifiers. Rotterdam was our first opportunity and we took it. Luckily she was about to graduate and she moved down to London to work in an art gallery shortly after the Dutch trip. She was my first more serious girlfriend, attractive, dark, good fun and very self-sufficient. Her mother, a powerful lady, terrified me, which stood Lucy in good stead when she came to stay at my home.

As 1990 was my last chance at the young riders individual title, my mother and I decided to keep Steady for the Europeans at Rotherfield rather than take him to Badminton. We entered the three-star at Saumur instead, where he finished in eleventh place. By now, I had a genuine second string in Faerie Sovereign (Bobby), by the great eventing sire Ben Faerie. He'd done some hunting and eventing with Natasha Ward, but she was giving up and her mother, Veronica, who owned him, asked me to try him. The contact had come through Belinda Cubitt, squad mate and friend from Aschelschwang, and I was excited to have my first paying owner.

He was a funny, chunky, little horse, with a big head and a very short neck and back. He had no mouth and pulled like a train, but he was compact, powerful, very brave and a brilliant jumper. We immediately struck up a good partnership and we were selected for the Young Rider National Championships at Bramham. He performed better than I could have hoped, finishing third and giving me the luxury of two horses to choose from for the European Championships. As they drew close, I decided that Steady was my best bet for Rotherfield and that Bobby should take me to my first Burghley.

With Bramham as his only three-star three-day event and just three advanced classes under his belt, Bobby was minimally prepared for his four-star debut. He'd also had an interrupted preparation, standing in his stable for three weeks after knocking his knee at Dauntsey in July. My mother was always positive, but she knew Bobby was all brawn and lacked experience, very different from Steady. On the way to Burghley, she surprised me by telling me not to worry, to take the long routes and pull up if need be. She seemed even more anxious than I was, but we were both overreacting because Bobby did a reasonable dressage for him and went clear cross-country. He was a minute over the time, mostly because I chose the long route at the water. As I couldn't hold or turn him, weaving through the fences took forever. Overall, it was a very good introduction to Burghley and was the culmination of a highly enjoyable season on the road with Veronica and Nikko.

During the run-up to the European Championships, I received my first offer of sponsorship, thanks to Victoria Osborne, a friend I'd met through juniors and young riders. She was working for Smirnoff and somehow she persuaded them to give me £5,000 and free vodka for a year in return for having my lorry painted bright red with white writing. I was dead chuffed to have a sponsor, especially such a cool one as Smirnoff. With a paying owner and a paying sponsor, I was at last bringing in some money, a fraction of what was required, but at least it was a start.

Our old lorry, newly painted in the Smirnoff colours, arrived at Rotherfield in the nick of time. With Pippa now in seniors, Polly, Daniel and I were joined in the team by Lynne Bevan and Horton Point. Steady did a really good test, second to Polly on her new horse, Folly's Last, and I sensed an opportunity on the cross-country when I learned that everyone was getting time faults. Steady bombed round until the owl hole fence, a tiny step up to a bounce to the hole in the hedge. I was so confident that I failed to balance him on the turn into it, so he tripped on the step and stopped. He made nothing of it the next time and finished within the time, but twenty penalties for the refusal cost us victory the next day. He finished fourth, the end of an amazing consistent run in young riders, but I was furious with myself for letting him down because he really deserved that gold medal.

CHAPTER SEVEN

Vive la France

In 1991, I moved out of young riders into the real world of adult competition. I was ready for it, but poor Steady had to shoulder the responsibility, because he was still my only competitive horse at the highest level. I entered him for his second Badminton, knowing that he owed me nothing. Aged fourteen, he'd already taken me much further than I, or anyone else, could possibly have expected. For that, I'm indebted to a horse with a huge heart and a mother with a meticulous approach to horse management.

Steady didn't have the best conformation and he was always very hard to keep sound. His front legs were back at the knee, which predisposed him to check ligament problems. He also had chronic navicular disease, so he was always trained on the softest ground and usually led down hills to minimise concussion in his front legs. This might seem a neurotic approach, but it worked for him and, where Steady was concerned, nothing was too much trouble. His wind problems made it even more complicated to get him fit, but again I followed my mother's routines, doing the boring roadwork myself whenever I could to make sure he used himself correctly. We drove regularly to Dover, where my mother dropped us off at the bottom of the cliffs; I would walk Steady up and then she collected us at the top. When we came to a suitable hill on the way back from a competition, we'd take advantage of every opportunity to repeat this routine.

Our planning and effort paid off at Badminton, with a much improved dressage, a clear cross-country and nineteenth place, a performance that put me on the long list for the European Championships at Punchestown. Shortly afterwards, I went to my first senior team training, along with Ian Stark, Karen Straker (now Dixon), Lorna Clarke and Richard Walker. None of my mates were there. After her spectacular successes as a teenager, Polly Lyon was short of a top horse and Tina Gifford was still in young riders. I felt a bit out on a limb, roped in simply for the experience and to benefit from Ferdi Eilberg's dressage training and Steve Hadley's show jumping expertise, which I certainly did.

When the team was announced, it became clear that the selectors felt the same way. Shortly before they left for Punchestown, Lorna's horse went lame, but they preferred to take a punt on it coming sound rather than to expose a rookie like me. Although I was desperate to go, I knew deep down that the challenge of a senior championship would be a step too far for Steady and me. As it turned out, many of the horses finished exhausted in unexpectedly hot conditions, so someone up there must have been looking after me. When I heard there was a steep hill at the end of the steeplechase and that the cross-country was difficult, I knew there was no way Steady could have coped. Lorna had to pull out before the competition started, but the team cleaned up, with Ian and Richard winning individual gold and silver and Karen taking bronze, despite a refusal on the cross-country.

The distraction of a new girlfriend made my disappointment easier to bear. I first met Wiggy Channer at Philip Clapham's twenty-first birthday party in July, an eventing gathering at the Clapham family home at Mattingley in Hampshire. I was chatting idly with friends after dinner when Wiggy sat down beside me. I turned towards her and thought, 'Wow.' She was beautiful, with deep blue eyes and plenty of personality. When it was time to leave, Wiggy said, 'If you're ever up in Bicester, give me call.' I was pretty sure I wouldn't be in Bicester, where she lived with her parents, but was equally sure I'd be giving her a call. I never needed to, as Belinda Cubitt, one of Wiggy's neighbours and a mutual friend, invited us to a party, and that was that.

That first summer was a dreamy, blissful idyll. As Wiggy had finished her first year of a veterinary degree at Cambridge, we were able to spend pretty much the whole time together. We rapidly became infatuated and she made the most of her only horse being off the road to stay with me at Knowlton. It was a much more intense relationship than I'd ever had before, but it seemed normal and relaxed, at least to me. Looking back, it must have been very difficult for everyone else at home. My parents agreed, perhaps reluctantly, when I asked if she could stay at Knowlton. Basically I'd gone from nought to a hundred in a very short time, from casual romance to the love of my life, and they didn't know how to put on the handbrake without alienating me.

Not content with just being there, Wiggy began to take charge. She realised her own riding was not progressing, but she's not a great bystander and she felt we should all benefit from her veterinary expertise. In later years, her suggestions about feeding and supplements were very useful but, in 1991, she'd barely begun her course.

Gradually, infatuation was replaced by a form of reality. I'd never dealt with anyone remotely like her so our relationship was a learning curve for me. Being with her made me see how lucky I was to enjoy my life so much. Despite being highly intelligent and good at her subject, she hated university and was disappointed that her riding was apparently going nowhere. She didn't particularly want to be a vet, but she was spurred on by resentment of her maternal grandfather, an old-fashioned practitioner from the James Herriot era, who didn't think it was a proper career for a woman. Luckily he was still alive to enjoy her graduation in 1995!

Our problems accumulated when she got trodden on by a horse and broke her foot, an accident that put her on crutches. In October, our focus was a big family party to celebrate my parents' silver wedding and, belatedly, my twenty-first and Andrew's eighteenth birthdays, so she helped out with that. My father was always a keen party giver and an enthusiastic planner, my mother less so because she had to do most of the work.

As Steady had missed out on Punchestown, the Boekelo three-day event in Holland became the highlight of our autumn campaign and Wiggy, still on crutches, insisted she should come. My mother suggested she should be back at university, but there was no deflecting Wiggy once she'd made up her mind. She was pretty miserable throughout our week there, either sliding around in the mud or holed up in our bug-infested lodge in the forest. My approach has always been laid-back, giving the impression that I need to be kicked into gear, though, in reality, I'm extremely self-motivated. However, Wiggy has an opinion on most things and that included how I should ride my horses.

Maybe she didn't do such a bad job, because good old Steady closed out his three-day career with me in tenth place. His next mission was to introduce Laurella to eventing, a campaign that peaked with a tenth in the Junior European Championships. He then spent an honourable retirement hunting with my mother and brother.

By now, finding a genuine successor was my top priority, but replacing Steadfast wasn't as easy as it sounds. I had several alternatives, but none of them were right for the places I wanted to go. Faerie Sovereign coped amazingly well, but his conformation was a disadvantage. That spring, I was offered the ride on Uncle Sam, a big thoroughbred owned by Annette Harries, a local Pony Club mother whose daughter had given up. He was fantastically talented, a machine of a kind I'd never ridden before, but he was largely insane. Annette insisted on keeping him at home, doing all the schooling herself and selecting which events he should go to. She got her pleasure from producing him, but not having him stabled at home made it difficult for me to establish an effective partnership with him. Nevertheless, we came tenth at Bramham, my first good senior result at one of my favourite events, but sadly soundness problems put him out of eventing shortly afterwards.

A year earlier, Tor Lane-Fox, a distant cousin, had told me that Sarah Kellard, a rider based at Bramham, had a nice grey gelding for sale. Tor reckoned he would be pretty cheap because he was far too big for Sarah and he bolted. In the hope Steely Dan was a man's horse,

I bought him for £2,000, with the promise of a further £2,000 if he made it to intermediate. He was handsome but thickset, with an indifferent gallop and a switch in his head that could go at any time, leaving me with the permanent impression that I was about to cannon into a tree or a barbed-wire fence. Despite his quirks, he gave me my first three-day win at Tweseldown in 1990. As his victory upgraded him, I paid Sarah her £2,000, only to find Steely Dan dead in the field as the result of a haemorrhage shortly afterwards.

I had a much better prospect in Thomastown, a chance ride I picked up after randomly parking my box next to his owner, Lesley Wallace, at a one-day event. As we got chatting, she told me how upset she was because she had four children and she'd lost her nerve. By chance, I'd seen her show jumping, so I wasn't lying when I said, 'He looks like a really good jumper. You'll be fine.' And she was. Later, she decided to give me the ride, although she was another owner who liked to keep her horse at home because he was very much part of her family.

In 1991, he was an eight-year-old, very green on the flat, but with an excellent jump, rather like Steady's, but with more spring. He was an impressive grey, half Irish Draught and so on the heavy side, but brave. He was quite tense and his flatwork came on very slowly, but he won at Windsor in 1991, my first victory in a two-star three-day event. That autumn, he broke down badly at Blenheim on the steeplechase. I am sure his extravagant jump was a contributing factor, causing excessive jarring and concussion on landing. We thought we might lose him but, after two years of careful rehabilitation, he made a comeback against all the odds.

My first year in senior competition was a rollercoaster, with some good wins in addition to the inevitable fifths. My confidence was building steadily and I felt I was on track to become a professional event rider. On the downside, I learned that horses, particularly good ones, can go wrong, often when it matters. I'd been so lucky with Steady, but I needed to learn what it takes to keep a string of event horses on the road.

For the first time, I had real backing in the form of sponsorship from Hackett, a men's clothing company that started with second-hand period garments and then moved into retro suits and contemporary leisure wear. The preliminary approach came out of the blue at Gatcombe in 1991 at the final trial for all European Championship contenders before Punchestown. I knew Justin Llewelyn as a commentator and as Mr Taittinger, so I was intrigued when he asked me if Smirnoff planned to continue their sponsorship beyond the agreed year. When I said they didn't, he introduced me to Jeremy Hackett, who'd set up the company in the mid-1980s with his business partner, Ashley Lloyd Jennings. After sponsoring Rodney Powell for some years, they were looking for a younger, cheaper, up-and-coming event rider. Given the female bias in the sport, that didn't give them much choice, especially as Justin recommended me unreservedly. No doubt they'd have preferred a shorter model, because they had to tailor most of the clothes I wore to fit my inconvenient frame, but in other respects, the deal worked brilliantly. For a non-clothes person like me, stocking my wardrobe with Hackett kit worth £2,000 every year was a physical impossibility, but my friends and relations benefited whenever birthdays and Christmas came along.

From the outset, Hackett were dream sponsors, asking for very little in return for their investment. My lorry was resprayed once more, the bright Smirnoff red replaced by Hackett's tasteful dark green, and my grooms and horses wore clothes and saddle cloths branded with their logo at all events. I had to wear whatever formal clothes they stipulated. Photo-shoots and autograph signing were quite painful initially, but gradually they become more tolerable as I learned to handle the embarrassment. I spent one particularly uncomfortable day in the Sloane Street shop, dressed in my riding gear, ready to challenge the shoppers on a racehorse simulator. Jeremy regularly asked me to take course walks for his clients at major events which I enjoyed and, on one occasion, Chaka was put on parade in Jermyn Street to mark the opening of their new shop, but their overall approach was very understated.

From my point of view, having my own income at the age of twenty-one was a minor miracle. Most young riders make their mark by taking risks, investing in their talent by undercutting their elders, so my contract opened up avenues that weren't available to my contemporaries. I knew I was lucky to have an edge and I didn't plan on letting it go.

After Boekelo, Wiggy returned to Cambridge, but I was to spend my next academic year in France. The deal was for students to organise their own placements, preferably in a university, but I negotiated an apprenticeship at L'Ecole Nationale d'Equitation in Saumur, the home of the celebrated Cadre Noir. I lived with the De Beauregards, a very kind family headed by Le Colonel, the *écuyer en chef* at the Cadre Noir and a highly respected rider in his own right. Sometimes I was responsible for looking after their son, but more often than not, it was their horses I cared for in their absence.

For my first two months, I was a bit of a dogsbody, helping out in return for instruction. The Ecole Nationale is a respected and demanding school with magnificent facilities, including five indoor and numerous outdoor arenas, a cross-country course, gallops and miles of hacking. State funding provides for 350 horses and a range of activities, among them vaulting and carriage driving, inspired by the college's military origins. As with most state-run enterprises, there was an impersonal element; the horses were fed and watered automatically and the staff kept strict office hours, 8 a.m. to 4 p.m. Very little went on at weekends, but the quality was never in doubt and I learned things there I've never forgotten.

During the week, I rode the two college five-year-olds I'd been allocated. I was fortunate to be taught by John Paul Bardinet and Tristan Chambry, two of the main instructors on the French three-day event team at the time. Their training was much more intensive than what I'd been used to. There was no pottering along, more a relentless insistence on making the horse connect and work. None of my fellow riders spoke a word of English, so I developed good equestrian French and it was a fantastic opportunity to be able to study their methods.

At the end of the year, I returned to Britain to embark on a mission to Romania with Lucinda and David Green and Mary Thomson (now King). Lucinda roped me in, partly because I had an HGV licence so I could share the driving, and I was looking forward to the experience. The plan was to take three lorries full of food and washing machines, all to be donated to the Romanian orphans. The Greens, who were particularly devoted to the cause, had done the run several times, so they knew the set-up was soul-destroyingly corrupt. On the one hand, things that were handed out to the orphans were repossessed and distributed to the administrators as soon as the charity workers left. On the other, the machines were abandoned as soon as they went wrong, even if the fault was as simple as a blocked filter.

All this left a bitter taste, but it was an unforgettable adventure. We made the most of our situation, living in the lorries, preparing meals from food we'd bought along the way and sharing a lot of laughs, despite the circumstances. Mary is particularly good company, a great party person, and she always managed to lighten the gloom when the situation threatened to get the rest of us down.

After Christmas, I returned to Saumur with three of my own horses, Faerie Sovereign, Wopiti and Briarlands Pippin, a very exciting newcomer owned by Susanna Macaire, my fellow team member from juniors and young riders. Pippin was essentially a man's ride, too big and strong for a girl, so she offered him to me. He was a massively talented horse with a huge stride and was potentially very competitive, so much so that I dreamed I had an outside chance of being selected for the Barcelona Olympics in 1992 if everything went well at Badminton. With this in mind, I really got stuck into my preparation. My French colleagues couldn't understand my approach to my horses. Why didn't I give them French feed? Why did I take them for walks to pick at the grass on Sundays? Why on earth did I put loads of rugs on them, then leave the tops of their stable doors open? Were all the English riders that weird?

In the run-up to the new season, Jean Teuleure, Marie Christine Duroy and Didier Courreges, France's leading riders, were in residence.

I was privileged to train with them and watch them on a regular basis. I was amazed at how polished they were on the flat, so precise compared to the English or anyone else. Their horses seemed more talented and better trained, in a different class, and their attention to detail was outstanding. By January, when my horses were just breaking into a trot and getting fit, theirs were doing dressage every day and show jumping on alternate days. I found it difficult to believe they could be beaten. Jean, Marie Christine and Didier were always very friendly and helped me endlessly with my dressage and jumping. Even now, they still do so at the major championships, and it is great to have that connection.

CHAPTER EIGHT

My Day in Hell

As far as Goldsmith's was concerned I was still in France, but in reality I was competing in Britain full time on Faerie Sovereign (Bobby) and Briarlands Pippin, both rewardingly competitive after their intensive training in Saumur. I was hoping none of my tutors would notice my premature reappearance but, of course, they did: they just turned a blind eye, knowing I was a lost cause. The two horses peaked at Brigstock, each winning an advanced class and, as Badminton approached, I felt things were going well.

I know now just how dangerous that feeling is and, sure enough, Pippin soon developed a bad corn. Although it's an insignificant ailment in the wider context, it's tricky to cure in a hurry when your sights are set on a major event. As Pippin was already pretty fit, I took him to a water treadmill to keep his muscles toned and avoided riding him in the final run-up to the competition. My aim was to get him there if I possibly could; I did, and in doing so I learned a lesson I will never forget.

Both horses went quite well in the dressage; Pippin might have gone better had a bit of inevitable tension not crept in, but cross-country day started with a morning of torrential rain. Going first of all on Bobby, I flew round the steeplechase, only for him to pull up lame. Adrenaline heightens optimism and, as I set out on phase C, I hoped he might have suffered a minor knock that would right itself. Instead he got worse and I had to call an ambulance when I reached the 4km marker. The poor horse stood shivering in the rain for ninety minutes before it came to rescue us. By that time, we were both frozen through and I still had Pippin to come.

He was lacking jumping practice after his short lay-off, but he felt good on the first part of the course. The year before, he'd had a stop at the lake with Susanna and I'd decided that if I were to take him off his line for the long alternative, he might well do it again, whereas if I rode him straight with plenty of impulsion, he'd make the direct route easily. He was eating up the ground, so I had no reason to change my mind on my approach. What I didn't know was that he'd lost a shoe. As a result, one front leg slipped on take-off for the big rails into the lake. Skidding off balance, he hit it with his shoulder and flipped upside down into the water.

At the time I was unaware how incredibly lucky I was to be thrown clear. For a moment, we lay there side by side, but when I got up, he didn't. He was able to thrash his head, but he couldn't move his body. At that stage I dared to hope he was winded, so I held his head out of the water while I waited for him to recover. As time went by and he still couldn't move, the nightmares came crowding in. Help arrived promptly, a team of men dragged him onto dry land under the horrified gaze of thousands of spectators. I'm not sure why it took so many top vets so long to realise that he'd broken the base of his neck, but the delay before they put him down made the tragedy all the more agonising. Susanna rushed over and we sat there on the bank with her horse, soaking wet, covered in blankets and totally distraught because there was nothing we could do to help him. When it was over, Bobby went back to the Wards for his check ligament to heal and I set off for home with an empty lorry.

As the cold reality hit me, I was consoled by the thought that the newspapers would be unlikely to use his picture because he'd been killed. How naïve I was. The assumption got me through the night, but when I was hiding in bed the next morning, hoping it was all a nightmare, my mother banged on the door and told me my picture was all over the papers and that I'd better get up to field the phone calls. So I awoke to a barrage of hideous headlines such as 'Barbarian rider kills horse in fatal fall'. Both Mark Todd and the American, Karen Lende (now O'Connor), lost horses on the same day, but the lake fence made the most dramatic images, so it was me who paid the price.

On the Monday, the haunting pictures appeared in sequence on page three in the *Sun*, the take-off, the fall, me holding Pippin's head, accompanied by an article inferring that all event riders are cruel and inhumane and none more so than me. Later in the week, there were further incidents that would rub salt into my wounds and make me feel guiltier than ever. There was an instance when I was hacking out at home and a car pulled up and the driver opened his window to ask if I was ever going to compete again. There was another the next weekend, after I did a novice class at our local event at Chilham Castle. The *Evening News* knew how to make its point: 'William Fox-Pitt, who killed his horse at the lake at Badminton, was out competing on a young horse less than a week later.' And so it went on and on.

Susanna was very supportive, so matter-of-fact and accepting, never once saying 'if only' or suggesting it was, or even could have been, my fault. Looking back, I still blame myself, knowing I should have withdrawn Pippin when his preparation was interrupted. The next few weeks were the lowest and most miserable I've ever known. He was the first, and to date the only, horse I've lost, touch wood. I was young, but I accept that I was too blinkered by the opportunity to ride my first really good horse after Steady. Nowadays I realise how crucial a thorough preparation is. If a fitness programme is badly interrupted, I take the view that there's always another day. Bad and sad moments are part and parcel of eventing, but losing Pippin has given me a realistic perspective. When things go wrong, I now remember just how much worse they could be.

People can be incredibly kind in such situations. I remember how many consoling letters I received, even from people I didn't know. Lucinda Green, who had experienced a similar tragedy when Wideawake won Badminton, only to die of a heart attack when she was doing the lap of honour, was among the most encouraging. I received another memorable letter from Monica, the wife of Peter Durrant, now the chief executive of British Eventing. 'Just hang in there,' she wrote, 'and your day will come.' I'd only met her a couple of times and I wondered how she could possibly know that. Nevertheless, her words gave me hope.

Wiggy was great. She always thrived in a crisis, but unfortunately she had to go back to Cambridge on the Monday after Badminton. She'd visited me during each of my stints at Saumur and our romance was going swimmingly. Down in the dumps, I returned to university wondering if I could ever take such risks with a horse's life again. If I couldn't, I'd have to look for another career; a bleak prospect when I'd felt so certain only a few weeks before. Inevitably I worried about my future with Hackett, who'd put their money on the line, only to find their logo associated with a dying horse in the national press. They were incredible about it, devastated for both themselves and me, but quick to accept it and move on. Ashley did say, 'We hoped for exposure, but not quite that kind,' but they stood by me loyally, never threatening to withdraw or asking for an explanation. Ironically, by coming at a time when everything was new and fragile, the disaster cemented our relationship and made us a tighter-knit team.

Losing Pippin also introduced me to the harsh unpredictability that is inherent in eventing. High hopes are often dashed, but there are pleasant surprises when you least expect them. It's exciting to take a youngster round his first cross-country, wondering if he might become your next star. Unmanageable, uneducated novices can turn into top horses, always a very satisfying reward for hard work. At this stage, I still saw all my geese as swans, never looking at them critically as I would now, never recognising that dodgy legs or bad feet can easily crumble under pressure.

With her critical eye for conformation, Wiggy taught me a lot on that score. She always liked to tick off the boxes, no problems with back ends, straight front legs etc, and she was often right, although she never really appreciated that horses can break all the conformation rules and still win at the highest level. In the long term, we balanced each other out effectively, with me open to all comers and her taking a generally pessimistic view. Maybe her meticulous approach cost me an occasional ride, but overall it was not a bad mix.

Fortunately it didn't cost me Chaka, the first top horse of my career. His owner, Sir Michael Turner, had considered offering him to me for Burghley in 1991, but couldn't because I already had two entries, Uncle Sam II and Cleopatra, a grey mare owned by my young riders team-mate, Daniel Hughes. I can't imagine how she'd qualified and neither she nor Sam started, but I shall never know how different things might have been if Chaka had come to me a year earlier. Michael, a High Court judge, bought Chaka from Vere Phillipps for his son, David, to hunt and event at novice level, then sent him to Merlin Meakin, who specialised in competing young horses. Judy Herbert, Chaka's first serious event rider, produced him brilliantly, making the most of his talent on the flat, but his boisterous temperament meant she had to wagon him round the cross-country as best she could.

By Spectrach out of an Irish Draught mare, he was a man's ride, a great big thug of a horse, immensely talented, but extremely quirky. Michael, who was and is a very ambitious owner, could see trouble ahead. Judy had taken Chaka to four-star level, but he'd not gone well for her at Burghley in 1990 or at Badminton in 1991, so a change of jockey was in order. In the end, Australian rider, Greg Watson, took him to Burghley in 1991. Clearly they got on well because they finished third, but by 1992, Judy was back in the saddle. After Chaka spoilt his chance at Badminton with a stop, he went back to Greg for Burghley, but the Australian was on the Olympic long list in Barcelona that July so Michael asked me to fill the gap in the open intermediate at Stowe and the advanced at Dauntsey. Naturally I jumped at the chance.

Chaka was 16.3hh, a magnificent, dark, bay horse, then aged twelve, with a hard-nosed disposition, never soft or seeking affection. He wasn't aggressive, just very aloof, looking at people on the ground, whether riders or grooms, as his minions, there to serve him as best they could. Not surprisingly, he always struggled with the concept of a minion getting on his back and being his boss at times, making him an extremely reluctant partner when you were on top.

The only time I was allowed to sit on him before Stowe was under Michael's critical gaze and I felt like a rabbit trapped in the headlights, but that was nothing compared to the competition itself. As Michael was a steward, he was able pull rank to follow me round in his Land Rover and I felt his eyes boring into my back at every fence. Happily all went well and I was rewarded with a clear round, followed by a win in the advanced class at Dauntsey the next weekend. Chaka showed me what a brilliant one-day horse he was, in the lead after dressage and a real operator cross-country, with his effortless stride making the time very easy to get.

Now I knew what it felt like to ride a real horse. Of course it was magic to win an advanced on a spare ride, especially after my despair in the spring, but it was like being given one mouthful of ice cream, then denied the rest. In September, Greg claimed his rightful place on Chaka at Burghley, only to have a stop at the third fence. As a result, he had a run-in with Michael and it was my good fortune that Greg was apparently sufficiently rude to Michael for him to offer me Chaka for Badminton 1993. If every cloud has a silver lining, then there's no doubt that this one was mine.

CHAPTER NINE

Flying the Coop

In my final year of university, I was spending all my spare time at Knowlton, but I was increasingly torn between my parents and Wiggy. She was still at Cambridge, not due to complete her veterinary degree until 1995, but she was becoming less and less welcome at home during the holidays, to the point at which my parents no longer wanted her to stay in the house. As a result, I argued with them over ridiculously trivial things and the divide kept getting bigger. By the end of 1992, Wiggy and I had been together for eighteen months and we were becoming increasingly inseparable. Inevitably this wasn't easy for my family, who could see me withdrawing into my own world.

The other pressure was Chaka, based far away from home up in Northamptonshire. The logistics were already complicated enough, with me at university in London and Wiggy dividing her time between Cambridge, Knowlton and her parents in Oxfordshire. To us, it made sense to move out of the house and rent a cottage, but my parents wouldn't allow us to live together. After a very sheltered, carefree childhood and a good relationship with them, I'd had no need for a teenage rebellion. Now, aged twenty-three, I found myself making up for lost time. I became argumentative and irritable and, as Christmas approached, the situation became increasingly uncomfortable.

Leaving home, something I hadn't previously thought about, rapidly became a consideration and, by January 1993, it was time to go. I'd spoken to Wiggy's mother, Mary, and she'd generously offered me a base, a small yard and a flat at the Old Rectory where she and Philip lived. I drove off in Wiggy's lorry on 16 January, just after my twenty-fourth birthday. Between us, we had three horses: Loch Alan, the homebred grey my mother had given me for my twenty-first birthday, Dessie, owned by Wiggy, and one that belonged to Stephen, the working pupil who came with us. I had no kit, but I was allowed to take some essentials. As I drove away, it dawned on me what a risk I was taking, but it was time to see if I could cope without the comfort and security I'd always taken for granted. I was not only leaving the support of my parents, but a whole set-up that had helped me so much. There was Michelle, who had organised logistics for all my trips away, and Sue Palmer, so much more than the farm secretary, who dealt with the horse accounts and absorbed all my paperwork into her mountain of chores. I'm not sure what my parents thought, but I'm sure they believed that a taste of reality would do me the world of good.

Initially our enterprise was very fragile, with Wiggy and I studying at our separate universities during the week and living together only at weekends. Our first enormous stroke of luck came when we persuaded Jackie Potts to work for us. We went to an agency to find part-time help and she was the first person who came along. The initial deal was that she'd fill in for a few months before returning to America, but she's still with me fifteen years later, the most conscientious and reliable head girl that anyone could have and my backbone behind the scenes.

I was now nearer Chaka, then at livery in a hunting yard in Northamptonshire run by two women, Jenny and Pip. He'd been moved there by Michael Turner. We called Jenny and Pip 'The Rottweilers' because they were employed as Chaka's bodyguards and they took their duties seriously. They had no intention of losing control of Chaka and, as far as they were concerned, the less I rode him the better. As a result, relations were inevitably stormy.

The more I rode him, the more I liked him and I knew how lucky I was to have him, but working within someone else's system can never produce the best results. From the outset, the challenge was to prise the horse away from Jenny and Pip and install him at Bicester, but initially that was impossible, because our stables were too small for him and I was still at university. My first step in the Chaka war was to build two larger boxes at the Old Rectory, but the real battle was fought at Badminton. Wiggy and I based ourselves with a great friend, Alex McMeakin, while Jenny and Pip took Chaka in their lorry and I took Wiggy's lorry for Jackie to stay in. It was a nightmare week, one that was further complicated by the fact that I was in the middle of my finals.

It's normally the rider's job to trot the horse up at the veterinary inspection on Wednesday afternoon, but how was I to do it when I had an exam in London that same morning? By now my tutors had accepted my priorities, probably to the point of expecting me to do a runner but, having come so far, I didn't want to throw it all away. In the end, I sat the exam, my hand dripping with sweat as my mind wandered towards Badminton, then drove west at breakneck speed to make the inspection.

There were disputes over Chaka's diet and management throughout the competition, but he survived and his dressage was good, though not the best he was capable of. We had a fabulous cross-country round, clear within the time, and it helped lay a few of the 1992 Badminton ghosts to rest. In the show jumping, I missed my stride and he hit a fence, putting us down to seventh behind Ginny, who won on Welton Houdini. Her victory goes down in my mind as one of the greatest, because Houdini wasn't the most talented of horses, yet Ginny and her team produced him to such a level that he was able to beat a high-class field very convincingly.

My result was good enough to get me long-listed for the European Championships in Achselschwang in the autumn. This time, I knew I had a real chance of going, probably as an individual rather than in the team, but first I had to sort out some Chaka issues with Michael. Even before I finished my finals, I was summoned to his club in Berkeley Square to put forward my case for moving Chaka to my yard. I went with great trepidation, but with my sleeves rolled up, determined to fight my corner. I felt I was in a strong position after Badminton, but I knew it would take a lot to convince Michael. After all, Chaka had performed well, so Jenny and Pip had been doing a reasonably good job. Why give the horse to a twenty-four-year-old lad who'd recently left home to live with his girlfriend? As we're both open, direct people, we had a fierce debate. My case was that if he wanted Chaka, his pride and joy, to go to Achselschwang, he had to be in my system so that we could get to know each other. Michael accepted it finally, but he made me fight hard.

A little while later, Chaka arrived with more overnight bags than a Hollywood actor. I was ridiculously proud to have a top horse in my new yard, far prouder than I was of the 2.2 degree I received from Goldsmith's at about the same time. Every time Chaka sneezed everyone jumped, but he was used to that. He was very opinionated and contrary, but if you could channel his bloody-mindedness, he'd do anything for you. Then again, if he was bored or unhappy, he wouldn't cooperate. When the going got tough, he'd think, 'I've got a better idea,' and look for a way out. In a three-day event, the stop or the attempted stop, came after seven or eight minutes, but in a one-day event, he never reached that barrier. As a result, he was something of a Gatcombe specialist, coming first and second in the British Open Championship with me and third with Judy Herbert. In that respect, there is a strong similarity between him and Moon Man, a horse I ride today.

Big fences were small fry to him, and even though we had mutual respect, his commitment was by no means one hundred per cent. Chaka was a bit of barterer, always keeping a little back for himself. Out hacking, he could be very nappy and reluctant, particularly about walking downhill. Sometimes he used to pace so I'd get off, at which point he'd walk on normally. Then I'd get back on and he'd refuse to move. Round one to Chaka.

I had bad memories of Achselschwang from the Young Rider European Championships three years earlier, when the hosts had tried to get me eliminated for running beside Steady on phase C, but Chaka felt very good in his preparation and he went well in the final trial. Even so, I was surprised to find myself actually in the team with Ginny, Charlotte Hollingsworth (later Bathe) and Nick Burton. Tina Gifford and Helen Bell were the individuals and we made a divided group, with Ginny expecting individual gold and Nick and I, as the terrified new boys, saying 'yes sir, no sir' whenever anyone looked in our direction.

With Chris Bartle as our trainer, we all did quite good dressage, but he was worried that the long, hilly cross-country would take its toll. It rained all week and I too became increasingly anxious about how testing the cross-country would be. My concern was justified when Chaka ran out of steam two-thirds of the way round. He went out like a light, and my heart sank as I walked him back to the stables. Charlotte, our pathfinder, went clear but the rest of the team had disintegrated as well, with Nick retiring after an earlier fall, and then Ginny, who was in the lead after the dressage, having an unbelievable stop on the steeplechase. It was a battlefield and we were gutted, though delighted for Tina, who'd stormed round through drenching rain on Song and Dance Man to move way up the order.

On the Sunday, I couldn't get away quickly enough because the excuses, explanations and post-mortems were driving me insane. I should have stayed for the show jumping to support my team-mates and, especially Tina, who won the individual silver medal. Instead I focused on Blenheim the following week, as that was now the only positive on my immediate radar. I've always tried not to dwell on my disappointments, believing that you should move on as quickly as possible, but I thoroughly deserved the dressing down Mike Tucker gave me at Blenheim. Although I felt genuinely bad about letting my team-mates down in the competition, he made me realise that I'd failed them even more by leaving prematurely.

Tests on Chaka revealed he had a laryngeal virus, so he wasn't operating on all cylinders, not a good scenario because he was the type of horse who needed all his ducks in a row to be on form. Nowadays all my horses are tested, but we were inexperienced in those days. Many people didn't believe the veterinary reports, thinking we were covering up for our incompetence. Wiggy, Jackie and I found some consolation in the vet's findings, but we felt we'd failed in our first big challenge. Things didn't improve when I rode Thomastown, now back after his two-year injury break, at Blenheim. Over-brave as he was, he took a stride out at the double of corners and dived head first into the middle of the fence, flipping over and landing upside down, luckily not on me. I got back on, something you're no longer allowed to do, and he then gave me a fantastic ride, learning rather belatedly from his mistake.

By now, I was gradually accumulating a string of decent horses. The first was Loch Alan, a homebred from the Go Try line, a real personality and one of my all-time favourites. He did his first three-day event at Waregem in Belgium in the autumn of 1993, along with Faerie Diadem, a full sister to Bobby, the horse that gave me my first Burghley ride. I was also competing on a gutsy mare, Betty Boop, owned by Caroline Schwier and it was she who introduced me to Paul Ridgeon, the first owner who wanted to buy me a horse. He asked me to find a decent prospect to run in his colours. This was an exciting breakthrough for me and the bonus came when Wiggy persuaded him to buy a youngster for her as well.

We went shopping to Vere Phillipps's, a respected dealer I'd known for a long time through hunting in Leicestershire. I found a promising five-year-old called The Artist and Wiggy got Inchmickery, a middleweight, chestnut four-year-old. When John Thelwell retired from event riding, Paul sent us his other two horses as well. One we sold on, but we persuaded him to keep Willy B Free for Wiggy. He was the most perfect horse for her, giving her a couple of rides at Burghley, and she still has him today. Paul supported us generously, but he was also competitive and, with hindsight, I think the expectations that accompanied his impartiality created an element of rivalry between Wiggy and me.

At home, my mother was now fully involved in my sisters' eventing. Laurella was still riding Steady, a brilliant schoolmaster at the age of seventeen. She loved him dearly and got a real tune out of him but, after taking a second horse, the homebred Derivative, to the top in juniors, she decided she wasn't sufficiently in love with the game to continue. Alicia didn't have the same advantages at junior level, but later on she took over Loch Alan and The Artist. She got her young riders flag on The Artist and she still competes today whenever she can fit it in with her work. Andrew, the bravest rider of us all, took up polo in his late teens and played on the army team for many years.

CHAPTER TEN

Laying the Ghosts

The fall-out from the Chaka affair haunted me through the winter, along with the demons that come with unexpected failure. Initially I never felt Achselschwang was my fault, but the selectors weren't having any of that. If I was to redeem myself, it would have to be in the saddle, not in the laboratory. As the furore over leaving the competition prematurely died down, my doubts crowded in. I believed I was capable of getting a horse fit, but I'd never had sole responsibility before because my mother had masterminded the horses' training programmes while I was at university. Chaka had felt on good form, but his blood count had been low after Achselschwang. Would he have coped if he'd been fitter? It was not a question I could answer.

As always, Michael was passionately involved and intensely loyal. Although he was as devastated as I was, he's never been one to point the finger. Then again, he had no need to. He knew how hard I'd fought to take on Chaka and how disappointed I was that I'd let him down. He too was keen to look into any possible explanation but, by the time Badminton 1994 came around, we were daring to hope we'd just been unlucky. Nevertheless, I set about getting Chaka fitter than ever, ignoring the risk involved in increasing a horse's workload.

That winter, we were operating in chaos, our slim resources divided between our existing yard and one we'd rented a mile up the road. It was owned by Tony and Carol Merrick, a colourful couple who became very involved, but the logistics were a nightmare, with a non-stop tack shuttle between the two, and we knew we had to find an alternative once Badminton was over. As the land was flat and wet, I boxed Chaka to Barry Hills's fantastic woodchip gallops at Lambourn, a four-hour round trip, but essential to keep him trim, especially as I had no school at home. Even before Badminton we were looking for somewhere else to rent, but it took until the summer to find Stratton Audley Stud, ironically only a mile away. I also started taking Chaka to Lars Sederholm at Waterstock for show jumping lessons, along with Loch Alan and Thomastown. After my initial training with Lars on Steady when I was sixteen, he became a formative influence, cropping up with pearls of wisdom at various vital points during my career.

Chaka was a very good jumper, but he didn't often jump a clear round. If you increased the pressure to make him more careful, he'd stop. That was always his deal: he was crafty and he expected to get his own way so if he didn't, he looked for an exit. Having watched him compete with Judy Herbert, Lars was able to get inside his head and improve him but, more importantly, he gave me the first consistent show jumping training in my career. Believe me, I needed it. Although I'd had instruction from Gill Watson and Steve Hadley during my young rider days, I wasn't a naturally disciplined rider, relying on instincts developed on the hunting field, rather than establishing solid foundations. I had shallow roots and very little knowledge of what show jumping was about, but Lars got involved at a time when I needed to raise my game and I took his lessons very seriously, often feeling more apprehensive before them than at an event.

He was a demanding trainer, pushing both horse and rider to extremes and paying immense attention to detail. On some occasions, he'd concentrate on flatwork to the point when I wondered if we were ever going to leave the ground. For me, it was Wil Lewicki revisited, but by now I was old enough to appreciate the importance of getting it right. Lars often asked questions he knew were slightly beyond the stage I was at, taking a risk which could set me back, but when it worked, I grew as a rider. He was expert at assessing a combination, then pushing them out of their comfort zone to produce an outstanding improvement. He's a brilliant teacher and a consummate horseman in every sense of the word, but he'd be the first to admit that he's no diplomat, so you needed to be confident in your ability and receptive to his methods if you were to benefit from his philosophy. Over several years, he had a major influence on my riding and his words still ring in my ears, whether I'm riding at home or at an event.

Michael was accustomed to watching Chaka win back-to-back one-day events, but I insisted on a light pre-Badminton spring campaign. He accepted it on the grounds that his pride and joy would be fresher for the big one, but I knew I needed to deliver. For the first time, I rode a really good dressage test on Chaka, finishing third behind Mark Todd and Marina Loheit, so I started phase A knowing that we had a good chance. Horton Point, a spare ride for Mark, had never been the fastest horse and I knew Marina was unlikely to go for it, so the competition was wide open. Setting off on phase A was an emotional moment, because I was desperate not to let the chance of a potential Badminton win slip through my fingers. Chaka felt great as he flew the steeplechase and was full of running as he trotted into the ten-minute box before the cross-country. The first half of the course was a cruise, but he totally downed tools on me at the Vicarage Vee, running out to the left, crunching into the rail and falling into the ditch that is notoriously full of pig sewage. It was as much as I could do to get him back across the ditch to attempt the alternative. I knew my line was fair, that it would have been much easier for him to jump than to stop and I felt he'd shut down on me.

My dream dissolved in an instant, like a tape that runs smoothly until it turns into gobbledygook. Unable to believe it had really happened, my stomach sank into my boots, but I knew I had to make him go on because letting him off the hook would set up the run-out as a game plan for the future. The rest of the course seemed to last for ever, but we slogged along to the angled hedges at the second Luckington Lane crossing. By then, I'd lost my focus and failed to keep him straight so he jumped the wrong side of the flag at the second element. He had to jump the four-foot hedge again, almost impossible from a standstill in the road, but he did it, probably because it no longer mattered.

It's a long haul round Badminton when you'd rather be anywhere else, but going through the finish meant facing the music. The disappointment on everyone's faces was massive. I believe that most horses have reasons for not performing, but Chaka seemed not to be in love with the game, stopping with Judy Herbert, Greg Watson and now me. I'd thought we had a great partnership, but it had suddenly evaporated. Maybe I was not up to it, maybe Chaka wasn't a Ferrari. Certainly he'd felt like one up to the Vicarage Vee, but the fence was bang on the seven-minute marker, a stage on a course when some horses hit a barrier and he'd laboured from then on. I wondered if I should have eased up a bit and gone for the longer route. Then again, he might have found an excuse to stop somewhere else.

The upshot of my extended post-mortem was a total change of approach. Chaka would have to do more work. He did hill work, three or four times up a one-mile slope, and he did long, slow, relentless gallops, a key part of my mother's training routine. Slow gallops are tough on horses physically, but I preferred risking a lame horse to mollycoddling a useless one. Every time Chaka slowed at seven minutes, I'd keep him going. I didn't enjoy it, but I did it. I piled on the work and threw away the safety net: he would now have to run competitively at every event. I was no longer his soft option.

He rose to the challenge. He won convincingly at Cornbury, proving he hadn't lost his nerve, and followed up with a second, behind Karen Dixon and Too Smart, in the British Open Championships at Gatcombe, a course he loved. He was runner-up again at the Scottish Open Championships at Thirlestane, this time to the current world champion Blyth Tait on Delta. True to my promise, I ran him without hesitation, oblivious of hard ground and hilly terrain. Losing out narrowly twice in a row was disappointing but, ten days before Burghley, I felt Chaka had regained his respect for me. He might still grind to a halt, but he knew I was not going to make it easy for him. If I was going to win a big one, I had the right horse and the time was now. I'd proved I could compete with the big guns, Karen Dixon, Mark Todd, Ian Stark and Mary King. Now I had to go out and beat them.

I had two entries for Burghley, Chaka and Thomastown, who'd given me a good ride in the three-star at Punchestown in the spring. Since then, his owners, Mick and Lesley Wallace, had pleaded poverty and four children as an excuse not to pay their bills. I should have said, 'No money, no Burghley,' but I wanted to ride him. I was still new to competition at four-star level and a ride on Thomastown was ideal to pave the way for Chaka.

Sheila Cotter, by now nearly eighty, came to Burghley to help me with the dressage. She was my surrogate granny, totally on my side and was instrumental in improving my flat work, but it was always a challenge to get her parked safely, with no lost handbag or dogs. She also needed channelling to the right arena, so she'd be teaching me, rather than any one else. On this occasion, Chaka did a very good test, leading the dressage with forty-two penalties, a few marks ahead of Mary on King Kong, Mark on Bertie Blunt and Karen on Too Smart, with Blyth and Delta close behind.

Thomastown's dressage was mediocre and he was unlikely to do the cross-country time after his double tendon injury, but he was an excellent pathfinder, a bold horse who galloped round with huge enthusiasm. I hardly needed to use my legs, let alone spurs or a stick, as he flew through the quick routes. To my huge relief, he finished sound and well and I returned to the lorry for my customary nap to kill time before I had to get on Chaka. It's a bizarre feeling to nod off with your heart pounding and adrenaline pumping round your body, but it can be the deepest sleep, blissful while it lasts, though coming round is grim as reality returns.

On this occasion, I woke up hear Mark Phillips tipping Mary or Toddy to win during a radio interview. This made me more determined than I had ever been and the message got through to Chaka, who felt fresh and sharp. I might have missed an opportunity at Badminton, but it was not going to happen again at Burghley. He was a reluctant water jumper, but he went through the Trout Hatchery like a rocket. He met every fence on the right stride, as only sometimes happens, and I can't remember a single anxious moment. It was as though I was on a different horse from Badminton, with Chaka producing a fast, easy, clear round to hold on to our lead.

If Toddy hadn't been eliminated for missing a flag on phase C, he'd have been breathing down my neck but, as it was, I went into the show jumping with a fence in hand. It is an awful way to drop out of a competition and Toddy must have felt distraught, particularly as the officials let him ride round the cross-country before deciding to eliminate him. In his television interview, he was incredibly composed – God knows how. Chaka used his fence in hand, knocking one down despite Lars's training, but our round was good enough. I will never forget the pleasure and relief of winning my first four-star. It came at just the right time and was an antidote to bitter disappointments, the vindication of my training methods and the proof that pressure pays off. Even more importantly, it established me as a winner in my own mind: I'd started out as Mr Consistently Average, but now I'd delivered when it counted. If it never happened again, the pressure was off. A lot of good riders never win a four-star, so getting one in the bag aged twenty-five was magic, especially as I'd never won a three-star. I come from an exceptionally talented eventing generation, but I was the first to win a four-star; only Pippa and Leslie have achieved it since.

Michael was thrilled in much the same way as I was. He had a brilliant horse, but Chaka had missed the boat so many times that he knew he might never win at the highest level. I hoped my mother would see my triumph as some reward for her unstinting support. And Chaka? What did he think? He had a high opinion of himself, he was never low and he was well used to displeasing his rider, so failure never depressed him, but he didn't mind pleasing you if it didn't cost him too much. Horses know when they have done well and I was happy for Chaka. Quirky he might be, but he deserved his four-star win.

A monkey could have given out the awards for all I remember of the prize-giving ceremony, but my share of the winner's cheque was far above anything I'd received before. We celebrated with champagne at the horsebox, as always a rather isolating experience as one person's victory is everyone else's defeat. At least I'd won fair and square, leading from start to finish, rather than benefiting from someone else's misfortunes. Victory from the front is satisfying, but stressful: it can be easier to come from behind, when expectations are less, but then you have to rely on others making mistakes.

After my parents had left, my father driving a tipsy Sheila back to Kent in her car, Wiggy, Jackie, Daniel Hughes and I had dinner at the George in Stamford. We wanted to savour the moment rather than rush off, so we ordered more and more champagne. By the end, none of us was capable of driving anywhere, so we spent another night in the horsebox. Despite all the booze, I remember fighting sleep in the hope that such a wonderful day would never end. In the morning, we collected the horses from the empty Burghley stables and headed home.

Even in the midst of the celebrations, the Thomastown crisis had come to a head. Lesley Wallace and I had discussed his future, so I knew he might be going home to Basingstoke. When she and Mick kept their distance at Burghley, rather than getting involved as they usually did, I realised something was afoot. I asked the stable manager not to release Thomastown's passport. As it turned out, my suspicions were well founded, but when the Wallaces were told they couldn't have the document, they decided to take the horse during the prize-giving. Again I was lucky, because Rachel, my working pupil, saw them leading him out of the stable to load into their trailer. She was only eighteen, but she was a tough, feisty type, so she unclipped the rope, grabbed the horse by the head-collar and got the stable manager involved. He called the police, who put the whole thing on hold until I got back. After a massive row, we padlocked Thomastown into his box, they left and we resumed our celebrations.

When we got him home, we locked him in a stable in our original Old Rectory yard at the Channers, where his owners had never been, and issued legal proceedings. Eventually they settled out of court, paid what they owed and took him away. Sadly, I never rode him again. I had enjoyed riding him and he had done a lot for me. He was a slightly neurotic horse, not particularly friendly, but he was a genuine four-star ride. I was sad to see him go but then again, it was a miracle he ever got to Burghley with his medical history, so perhaps he left at the right time.

By now, we were in our new headquarters at Stratton Audley, a property previously known as the Marius Milton Stud. It is a beautiful, 1930s rectangle, with a clock tower and glass canopies over the stables. We had twenty stables and twenty-five acres of grassland, a solid basis for expansion, though with only nine boxes occupied, space wasn't at a premium at this stage. We installed the cheapest horse walker we could find and developed the existing arena in the lovely old walled garden. With my Hackett sponsorship, I could afford the rent, though we needed Mary Channer as our guarantor. We were sad to leave the Merricks, as they'd followed our adventures avidly, doing everything to help, and even being hands-on when we were away. Nevertheless, we knew we had outgrown the set-up, with nowhere to school the horses and insufficient turn out. Even if we couldn't fill the stables, and we never imagined we would, we were incredibly lucky to find such a good base so close to the Old Rectory, where we were still able to live in the bungalow. We'd become accustomed to having our saddles and bridles in the cellar or in the back of the car: now we had a dedicated tack room, plus staff accommodation, done up comfortably by Mary.

I'd got to know Ginny Elliot well at Achselschwang, so when she told me she had the perfect horse for me, a 17hh bright bay thoroughbred called Mostly Mischief, I was inclined to believe her. He'd completed the two-star at Lion d'Angers as a six-year-old, but now she was giving up and she wondered if I could find a syndicate to buy him. I liked him rather than loved him when I tried him, but

I'd learned that horses don't always give the right impression when you first sit on them. In fact, he felt quite average, but I was all too conscious of Ginny standing behind me telling me how amazing he was going to be. 'He'd go so much better for someone with longer legs,' she enthused, allowing me to believe that if anyone could maximise all of this potential, then it would be me.

I wrote a few letters to potential owners asking if they'd be interested. To my delight, I got a phone call from Monica Hunt, a keen member of the Horse Trials Support Group who'd never had an event horse before. Her only caveat was that she wanted to own him outright, rather than being part of a syndicate. I told her that wouldn't be a problem, hoping my voice didn't betray my excitement. When I got him home, he was stiff and again didn't give me a great feel, but I believed he'd loosen up with training. That was stupid because if he'd been going to loosen up, he'd have loosened up for Ginny. He was sound, with a great physique and a huge heart, but to say that he was unathletic would be an understatement.

Even so, it was a big thrill to buy an exciting horse from Ginny, so I set Blenheim 1996 as his target and went to work as best I could. He came with his own devoted groom, Alison Quinlan, who settled into Stratton Audley as Jackie's second-in-command. Alison loved all her horses and formed a particularly close bond with Cosmopolitan, so much so that she eventually accompanied him to the Atlanta Olympics. She was a brilliant organiser and a real people person, but sadly her bad back prevented her working for me long term and she had to leave in 1998.

Wiggy and Jackie shared the motto – 'no pain, no gain' – and a ferocious work ethic. If anything came easily, Jackie felt guilty and she has always been a pretty fierce taskmaster, with high standards and very little sympathy for those who fall short of them. That makes for a rapid staff turnover, but guarantees that those who stay are useful. She's been employed from a young age and she believes that you aren't doing a proper job unless you work until you drop. Sometimes this actually happened, as on the occasion she found one of her girls lying on the tarmac hyperventilating with half her clothes off in freezing weather. Jackie thought she'd have to call an ambulance, but the girl claimed she'd collapsed from exhaustion after walking the horses up and down the lane. As we didn't have a horse walker in those days, we always walked them in hand because I don't like them staying in their stables for the rest of the day after morning exercise. I never heard Jackie's response, but the girl didn't appear again.

Wiggy and I balanced each other out, with her applying science to every aspect of stable management and me taking my habitual laissez-faire approach. Wiggy taught me to minimise the risk, to pay attention to detail and to take precautious in any areas you could. All that was good up to a point, but a desire to get everything right can easily turn into paranoia. As far as I was concerned, horses were horses: if having covered every angle I was lucky, they'd stay sound, if I wasn't, they'd go lame.

Our finances were complex, with me covering the rent and the Channers paying Jackie's wages as Wiggy's contribution towards our business. As I was gradually getting more horses who were paying their way and Wiggy wasn't, that seemed fair. For example, Paul paid livery for The Artist, but not Inchmickery: he'd bought him for Wiggy, but drew the line at supporting him. We never had enough help on the yard which inevitably led to conflict, resulting in our first big domestic in August, 1994, when I wanted to take Jackie to Thirlestane to look after Chaka and Thomastown. No way, said Wiggy, because there wouldn't be anyone responsible left behind. As Jackie was key for Burghley, I needed her to come to Scotland, so I locked antlers with Wiggy for the first time.

I wasn't brought up to argue so I probably wasn't very good at it, but Wiggy belonged to the debating society at Cambridge and she knew how to put over a point. What's more, she put it extremely forcefully and at great length. On this occasion, she said that if Jackie came with me, she would have to stay behind to look after the horses. Eventually I said, 'OK, fine, you stay, I'm off.' That wasn't what she'd expected.

When I returned, we made a conscious effort to discuss the row and put it behind us, but it was the beginning of a pattern and it left a residue of bitterness that never entirely went away. The novelty was beginning to wear off by this time and, although the good times were still good, the bad times were getting more frequent. As I managed horses through experience and she through science, we were bound to have a lot of disagreements – and neither of us was going to back down.

CHAPTER ELEVEN

A Proactive Approach

Winning Burghley didn't change my life, but it shot me up the eventing ladder, and potentially opened up opportunities of attracting better horses. The selectors had always known Chaka was exceptional, but despite his victory, his inconsistencies meant they'd never put him on a team again. I'd been competing at the top level for a while, but success gave me renewed self-belief. Confidence is critical in any sport, but in eventing it is even more important than talent.

My main concern during our first winter at Stratton Audley was how I was going to find a replacement for Chaka, who was coming to the end of his career. Faerie Diadem (Dee) was making progress, but she didn't have the scope to go all the way. Loch Alan was my only hope and he was still a way off showing me he was a four-star horse. When I accepted an invitation to drinks from Dee's owner, Veronica Ward, I had no sense of premonition. The initial omens were unpromising, because Wiggy refused to come with me. She occasionally baulked at going out, meaning that we would have to cry off at the last minute, and this time her upcoming finals were a good reason. However, Veronica was a special owner and I felt strongly that I should go, so I set off without her.

While chatting with friends I found myself earwigging the conversation next to me, a discussion about a horse called Cosmopolitan. His owner, Frank Andrew, who ran the Milton Keynes Eventing Centre, was trying to sell him because his jockey was going back to Australia. I had no way of buying him, but as soon as I got back, I wrote to Frank saying I'd heard he was on the market and I'd always liked him, so if he couldn't find a buyer, how about me having the ride on him. To my astonishment, he called to invite me to try him. I was a bit confused because he hadn't had time to sell him, but I went immediately, excited and surprised that my proactive approach was working so well.

I was less excited when I saw Cosmo in the flesh. He was a plain bay, 16.2hh, though he looked bigger because he was so chunky, with a choppy trot and crooked front legs, but when I rode him I realised he could really jump and there was something about him. At the end of the trial, things became more transparent. Frank asked me what I thought and I replied that I liked him and there was a lot to work with. Good non-committal stuff, but then he looked at me shrewdly and asked who I had in mind to buy him for me. It was a question with only one answer: no one. As I was only interested in getting the ride on him, I left convincing myself that he was only a common little cob and I'd be better off without him.

The next day I got another phone call. Cosmo could come to Stratton Audley, but Frank wasn't going to pay any livery. I couldn't afford to deal on that basis; if Frank wanted to send his horse, he would have to contribute financially. The next day he accepted my terms and I went to collect Cosmo in a fever of anticipation. Was this the next big one? Would he be a winner? When I arrived back with this chunky cob, with his short neck and huge fat stomach, everyone laughed and he was affectionately nicknamed Hippo. We worked hard to get him fit and he certainly came alive over a fence, but I was worried to discover he had an unpredictable stop.

During that winter the stopping got worse and it came to a head at a small indoor competition when I could hardly get him over the practice fence. Very disappointed, I phoned Frank and explained that our target of Bramham in June was looking impossible and that the likelihood of even making a two-star competition was small. Luckily time was on our side, so I took him right back to basics. One thing I discovered was that he hated to jump from trot, so all jumping was done from canter and gradually his confidence increased. The less he stopped the more he enjoyed himself.

Another of Cosmo's problems was a lack of natural balance, which meant he would regularly fall over when he was worked on the lunge. Gradually he came together and by the time the new season started I was more optimistic. After all he was still only eight and, in many respects, he was precocious. The competitions went smoothly, as if there had never been a setback and, having jumped a couple of advanced tracks, we decided he was ready for his first three-star.

At fifteen, Chaka was feeling fantastic. He was a horse with an unusually good memory for a bad experience and he didn't like Badminton. He had gone well in 1993, but he was never relaxed there; only if he could leave his bad memories behind would he be in with a shout. In 1994, he was third after the dressage, only for it all to go wrong on the cross-country.

At Badminton in 1995, we had a seriously funny moment with Sheila, though it wasn't much of a joke from her point of view. At the age of seventy-nine, she was dashing from one side of the arena to the other to get the best possible view during my warm-up. Finding that her handbag was weighing her down, she asked the nearest spectator to hold it for her, adding 'please be careful because there's a lot of money in it'. At the end of the warm-up, she turned to reclaim the bag, only to find that the guy had done a runner – what a bastard. However, it demonstrated her complete focus while training me and fortunately there was some recompense when Chaka performed the test of his life, to go into the lead with forty penalties.

On the Saturday, Chaka nailed the cross-country, flying round without hesitation well within the time and making it seem like child's play. Had the Chaka I knew and mistrusted changed his spots? In my euphoria, I didn't know or care. That evening Wiggy and I realised that Chaka wasn't a hundred per cent behind. He looked a bit stiff, but with some physiotherapy from Amanda Sutton and a warm-up in the morning, we were confident he'd be fine for the trot up. The next day, he was full of beans and fine to ride, but it soon became obvious that he was seizing up very quickly if he had to stand around. As we hadn't consulted the vet, we didn't know what was wrong, but we did know that rumours, once started, would spread like wildfire, so we kept quiet. In any case, we still thought he'd pass. When we walked and trotted him, he looked okay and we thought that he'd perk up a bit with the crowds watching him. Maybe I didn't know him as well as I imagined; he was totally unimpressed by the inspection, and didn't get lit up in the least by the crowd.

While the judges were praising our performance, I was praying they'd get on with it. We stood for perhaps twenty seconds, but it was too long. Chaka walked away awkwardly and trotted up unbelievably lame. The crowd gasped, a moment I'll never forget, and I knew it was all over. The judges spun him straight away, leaving us devastated. Michael was a huge support, but Jackie was distraught. The vet diagnosed significant bruising in the stifle, a minor injury presumably incurred during the cross-country, though I never felt him hit a fence. His pain was typically at its worst that Sunday morning, then passed as quickly as it had come, leaving him fully fit by Monday. If we'd called the vet on the Saturday evening, he might have manipulated it or changed the shoeing to take the pressure off the stifle. How could we have been so stupid? Chaka was a stiff horse with many miles on his legs. I knew he wouldn't be back the next year, so my Badminton dream was over for the foreseeable future.

On the surface, this was just another episode in Chaka's familiar rollercoaster career, but it turned into one of my lowest moments and I found it uncharacteristically difficult to bounce back. At least Cosmo was going better and better, far outstripping my expectations, especially when he took the lead in the dressage in the advanced at Bicton. He was one-eighth Clydesdale, a sensitive, buzzy individual with a stilted gallop, but he had the guts to fight and an engine that never tired.

At Bramham, he lay second in the dressage behind a Frenchman, with the others well strung out behind, among them Loch Alan, an impressive mover, but a bit wooden in his approach to flatwork. I rode him early on round Mike Tucker's cross-country course, sailing through the new bogey fence, two circular pig huts on the turn. After the next three failed, no one attempted it until I came round with Cosmo. I'd had no feedback and no hint it was riding badly, so I fired him through and finished with half a minute to spare, embarrassingly fast, but twelve marks clear of the field. Had I known that no one had jumped the pig huts there is no way I would have taken the risk, but sometimes too much information can have a negative effect. Unlike Chaka, Cosmo was incredibly sound and careful, so I was cautiously optimistic. Happily he made no mistakes, so he won comfortably, with Loch Alan also doing a double clear to finish twelfth.

Bramham put Jackie and me back on track, but Wiggy was very tense as she sat her Cambridge finals. She struggled under the pressure, but finally she got her degree. Philip Channer came to Bramham to support me, but he was even more invaluable at fielding her phone calls and deciding whether I was able to speak to her from the ten-minute box or the practice arena before the show jumping. We were both in our own worlds: she trying to survive her finals, me trying to compete, so it was hard for either of us to appreciate the pressure the other was under. After the show jumping, I went straight to Cambridge to offer moral support, but I was too late to be of much use.

Chaka was in great heart, ready to have a go at improving on his runner-up position in the British Open Championships before challenging for his second Burghley, which would almost certainly be his last. At Gatcombe, I made a hopeless start to the campaign, getting six penalties for going the wrong way twice in the dressage. I remember sitting in the lorry feeling I'd let him down and that I'd lost any chance of winning. Michael was incredibly supportive, telling me not to worry and that it wasn't over yet, though I can't imagine how he found the generosity to say that when he must have wanted to throttle me. As it turned out, he was right. Chaka moved into second place after the show jumping behind the favourites, Mary King and King William. You don't often get a lead back from Mary, but this time she set off

Granny Speed (above left). She completely doted on Andrew and me (above right).

My parents, Marietta and Oliver, who married in 1966.

My mother (above) who competed at the highest level, including Badminton, Burghley and World Championships. I was keen to follow in her footsteps – here (below), I am riding my first proper pony, Minnie Monster.

The Fox-Pitt family. (Above from left to right) my mother, Alicia, Laurella, Andrew, my father and me in 1981; and again minus Andrew but with Alice in Athens, 2004 (below).

Riding of a different kind on a family holiday to Wyoming, 1979.

Alice and my first meeting! Pony Club Championships 1987, Steadfast (white face behind) and I look on as Alice's team collect first prize.

My long time dressage trainer, Sheila Cotter, at her 80th birthday in 1997.

Going native at Pabbay in 2006.

Our wedding, 29 November 2003.

One of the high points of a magical night – David Gilmour of Pink Floyd (one of my owners) playing at our wedding.

Nine-month-old Oli and me at the Badminton trot up in 2006.
(Kit Houghton)

Alice, me and Oli, with Thomas, a bump, only a month away in October 2006.

Toddler Thomas takes control of the yard.

like a rocket, took a bad fall and handed the championship to me.

When I was asked about Chaka's future at the prize-giving, I had no hesitation in saying Burghley was our target, but Michael had other ideas. 'I think we should retire him,' he said firmly. Chaka was everything to me, my best ride, my Burghley horse, and retirement had never been mentioned, so I was totally surprised and disbelieving, yet it seemed the right thing to do and I agreed without hesitation. He was certainly becoming more pottery at home, looking older and stiffer in the joints. Nowadays there is so much you can do to help older horses continue competing, but it was not an option back then and Chaka had already done plenty in his career. A few weeks after Gatcombe he went home to Michael and I never saw him again, remembering him with respect as the horse he was at the end of his career. He was a generous and enjoyable hunter, giving Michael and his son David two good seasons before his back caught up with him and he was put down aged seventeen.

The yard seemed empty without him and we missed him terribly, no one more than Jackie, but Cosmo was giving his all to be his successor. After he flew round the advanced course at Gatcombe, Bridget Parker, the chairman of selectors, added us to the long list for the European Championships at Pratoni, an unprecedented promotion for an eight-year-old with no four-star experience. When he earned selection by finishing second at Thirlestane, I expected to compete as an individual but, with no Ginny or Ian to call on, the regular team had fallen apart, so they scraped the barrel by adding me to the trio of Mary, Tina and Charlotte (Bathe). They'd all been in the team at the Hague in 1994, the last time the Brits won a gold medal at the World Championships. The journey was a nightmare as Cosmo was on a diet, while his travelling companion, a horse Lucy Jennings rode as an individual, was anorexic. Cosmo was outraged, crashing against the partition in protest as he tried to get at his companion's food. There were times when Rome seemed a very long way away.

I was haunted by memories of Chaka pulling up in Aschelschwang, but I put negativity behind me and Cosmo did as good a test as he could, lying tenth. As the team needed a steady clear, I was instructed by Ginny, our team trainer, to take the long routes at the two fences she didn't think he was ready for, a slight bone of contention, even though I was aware I needed to cater for his lack of experience. Sure enough, he put in a brilliant clear, but with six time faults, putting him in sixth. Most importantly the team took the gold medal position and we held onto it after the show jumping, with Mary King winning the individual bronze. Afterwards she told us she was five and a half months pregnant. Although she'd fallen off King William a few weeks earlier at Gatcombe, she had so much faith in him that she never thought anything could go wrong. Mary is a great example of someone who hasn't let success affect her. She had no riding background and very little financial support from her parents so she got to the top by sacrifice, hard graft and single-minded determination. There's no one more competitive, but she's a gracious loser, as friendly in defeat as she is in victory.

After the assorted problems with Chaka, Thomastown and Pippin, I was becoming increasingly aware that I'd need a string of talented horses to keep up in the sport. Like racing, eventing takes its toll and horses suffer from endless setbacks, so you need a decent string to provide cover when some are off the road. Until now, most of my horses had found me, but the time had come to get out into the marketplace and find good owners, just as I had done with Frank Andrew. Apart from Cosmo, I was riding Loch Alan and Dee, sixth and fifth at Blenheim and Boekelo respectively, decent but not earth-shattering results. Lismore Lord Charles, my second string at Boekelo, had come to me out of the blue, following a phone call from his owners, Nibby and Alan Bemrose. He was a lovely, big, quality horse, but one that was very difficult to manage, especially in the show jumping. No matter: at that stage, I still looked on anything I was offered as a great opportunity.

A year earlier, I'd had a call from Judy Skinner. I knew who she was because she had horses with Pippa and her daughters had competed against me as juniors, but we'd never met. When we did

I felt very apprehensive, but we were reassuringly similar in our approach.

There are many types of owner. The trickiest are the sentimental ones who say, 'This is my darling child and I want you to ride him until his dying day.' Fine if he's a star, but a waste of time otherwise. Others are dispiritingly commercial, saying, 'Get him going and then we'll sell him.'

Judy, on the other hand, was passionate about her horses, but encouragingly realistic. Her line was, 'I've got this horse, I think he's lovely, but if he is not up to it we will move him on and get a better one.' On this occasion, the horse in question was The Lord Chancellor, a five-year-old warmblood who'd developed a stop, which she thought I could sort by taking him hunting. He was too good to be a hunter, but careful, deliberate and no way brave enough to be a top eventer. He'd started his hunting programme with me in January 1995 and Judy must have been pleased with his progress because she bought me a second horse, an Irish five-year-old called Pie in the Sky from Vere Phillipps. He was a better bet, quite talented but, with hindsight, he wasn't a superstar.

On a personal front, things had improved between Wiggy and me. She had now graduated and was much more relaxed, and although she was determined not to work as a vet, she was still concerned that riding didn't challenge her intellectually. At the end of the 1995 season, we had a fantastic holiday in South Africa on the back of an invitation for me to compete in Cape Town. I was loaned horses to ride in each of the two competitions and offered a couple of days' teaching to make it more rewarding financially. Daimler, an amazing bush horse, was my mount for the South African National Championships, an event that took place in torrential rain.

I was the token foreigner, unaccustomed to riding though rapids crashing over slippery boulders, but Daimler was well up for it and we finished second. In the novice class I got soaking wet again, this time because my horse fell upside down in the pond. After waiting all day to see a ducking, the crowd were ecstatic. The teaching was equally crazy. South Africans have two paces, fast and faster. If I said, 'Slow down, steady, be careful' once, I said it a hundred times, but no one listened as they charged around on their ex-racehorses. It was an experience I will never forget, but at least everyone was determined to have fun, secure in the certainty that the faster you go, the less likely you are to stop.

Wiggy's holiday was equally fraught, partly because her snake phobia was a source of great amusement to everyone we met and partly because she won't fly in planes with less than 150 seats. That meant hiring a car to go from Johannesburg – where I did another competition in a blinding downpour – to Sun City – a fantasy gambling development in the desert. Our journey was beset with sense of humour failures as we got lost in the townships, but I cheered up when we arrived because the place was full of Miss World contestants. Needless to say, Wiggy was less impressed. We never saw a snake, but with so much to worry about, she'd never been happier to get home.

Now that she'd graduated, the time had come to propose. I believed that we had a great relationship and I couldn't imagine being without her. We had a good time together, sometimes serious and short on laughs, but she was bright and challenging and life was certainly never dull.

I planned to propose during our ski holiday in Chamonix with the Channers and I picked a great spot with a view of Mont Blanc on a blue-sky day. I turned to look for Wiggy and damn me if she didn't ski straight past. I'd positioned myself perfectly for my proposal, but my chance had gone, so I put it on the back burner until Valentine's Day. How embarrassing is that? I booked a restaurant in Elizabeth Street, one of many little tables for two squashed together in a row under bright lights. Each was occupied by a romantic couple and it was the slowest evening Wiggy and I ever had together, full of excruciatingly pregnant pauses and not surprisingly a proposal opportunity never arose. We went to a bar afterwards, but it still didn't seem right, so we decided to go home. We'd crashed across the road, nearly getting run over, and gathered ourselves on the other side when I blurted it out, not dropping to one knee and certainly not offering a ring. I'd never have dared to choose one myself and, anyway, why go to the expense when she might say no. She didn't, so there we were on cloud nine, in Belgravia at one in the morning, with our future finally sealed.

CHAPTER TWELVE

A Tarnished
Olympic Dream

Having missed out on the Barcelona Olympics, I was all the keener to make it to Atlanta in 1996, but my prospects didn't look good when Cosmo coughed as he pulled up on his last gallop before Badminton. I hoped it was a one off, but it wasn't: he coughed for weeks, scuppering my Atlanta ambitions and casting me into deep gloom. The Lambourn gallops were not lucky for me that spring, because Loch Alan pulled up lame on them two weeks before Badminton; it was another blow, though it probably did me a favour, as Badminton might have been a question too far.

Fortunately my rivals also fell on hard times so, contrary to normal procedures, Mary and I were allowed to ride our potential Olympic horses *hors concours* at Bramham to prove their fitness. Having won the year before, Cosmo had nothing else to prove and I found jumping round as a schooling exercise worryingly cold-blooded. We reduced the risk by missing out the steeplechase, but I was still in a dilemma because there was no point going fast, yet going slowly with no adrenaline running would be even harder. I was also aware that any mistake would be fatal. Cosmo delivered, with a good dressage and clear cross-country, and Lismore Lord Charles provided an unexpected boost by finishing sixth in the real competition. Mission accomplished.

By the time I was selected, Atlanta was only a month away. Like every other athlete, going to the Olympics had become a dream, but when I joined the team there was an atmosphere of pessimism. Atlanta would be too hot and humid for the horses, the competition was in the wrong season and the quarantine regulations would seriously damage our chances. Worse was to follow when I took Cosmo to the 'Atlanta Room' in Newmarket, a treadmill set up in a controlled environment by the research vet, David Marlin, to assess which horses would go best in the heat. I knew Cosmo's heavy build put him at a disadvantage, but my panic reached a new high when he was diagnosed with a heart murmur. It hadn't been detected before because it could only be heard from the right side and, after another raft of white knuckle tests, the vets decided the risk was minimal.

I did feel a surge of excitement and euphoria mixed with disbelief, when I went to Earls Court with the other riders to get our uniforms. With the team and the individual competitions separated for the first time, there were seven of us, plus a travelling reserve. The main contenders for the team were Mary, Ian and Karen (Dixon), with Gary Parsonage, Leslie Law, Charlotte Bathe and me to fill the other places and Chris Hunnable as the travelling reserve. Despite the vet's reassurance, I was worried to be taking a non-throughbred horse with a heart problem to the Olympics, but everyone had their own concerns. Atlanta, chosen because it was the headquarters of Coca-Cola, had nothing to offer, either to us or to the competitors in other endurance events, but we accepted we were going and we planned to get through it as best we could.

Our sense of doom increased when we stepped off the plane into temperatures of thirty degrees centigrade and more with ninety-five per cent humidity, the most unpleasant climate I've ever been in. My first feeling was, 'this is a joke'. How were we going to wear our dressage gear or gallop four miles across country when we could barely walk across the tarmac? The horses did their compulsory two weeks' quarantine in Pine Top, a beautiful place but with moderate conditions, living in wooden boxes with tin roofs – individual ovens that gave them no respite from the heat. The sand school was uneven and there was nowhere suitable to gallop. We shared the facility with the Germans. I felt the British administrators had not done the most successful recce, as we realised when we visited the Kiwis and the Americans: their horses were basking in cool, airy stables and their practice facilities were ideal.

We stayed in a hotel, commuting daily to Pine Top. We were all used to riding lots of horses and running our own businesses, but now we found ourselves in the middle of nowhere with lots of time to kill. Countdown training lore has it that the best approach to a major competition is to have your horse at his peak ten days before it starts, then to keep him ticking over until the big day. As tempting as it was to want to add the finishing touches in such a pressurised situation, we knew we had to back off. Instead we watched the Germans, non-believers in the countdown theory, as they lamed their horses one by one.

To avoid mutiny and to keep us amused, trips and evening outings were organised. We also got up early for team runs, something that comes easily to me because it's the only training I do, though some of the other riders were less than enthusiastic. At home I regularly put in two miles a day, usually between the bungalow and the yard, a modest programme, but I never had any problem convincing myself that more running would equal more weight which would jeapodise my chances in the saddle. For Gary and I, the Atlanta runs were a source of intense competition and the highlight of our day.

Gary was my mate in a slightly fragmented team, headed by the most senior members, Ian and Karen. Ginny came as our trainer, a tough call for her because she'd have preferred to compete, and training Ian and Karen, her former team-mates, put her in an unenviable position. Charlotte and I hadn't seen eye to eye since her mate, Rodney Powell, had fallen out with me over my getting the Hackett sponsorship and, despite the passing of a year, I didn't relish the prospect of spending three weeks with her. When we arrived, we sorted out our differences, putting the whole imaginary feud behind us, and we've been good friends ever since.

Things improved when the horses were installed in the Georgia Horse Park, built for the Olympics fifty minutes outside Atlanta. It was a shame we didn't go there earlier because the facilities were top class, but the powers that be decided to keep us away from our rivals, so that we wouldn't be influenced by their training programmes. We thought we had a rough idea as to whether we'd be competing in the team or as individuals, but we were kept guessing right up to the last minute. When asked, I said I'd prefer to be in the team, reckoning that Cosmo was a solid team horse and that I had a better chance of a medal with Karen and Ian than going it alone. We had daily trot ups, initially without incident, but gradually the hard ground took its toll. When Leslie's horse, New Flavour, went lame, he was replaced by Chris Hunnable and Mr Bootsie. Leslie took the terrible disappointment on the chin, but it is a cruel Olympic rule that strips you of all accreditation as soon as an athlete is substituted. Leslie had to watch from the sidelines with no access to any of us.

We moved into the Olympic village for four or five nights in the build-up to the opening ceremony, an event we were allowed to watch but not participate in because our competition started the next day. In the village, we were introduced collectively as the equestrian team, plus one basketball player. That was me, a false assumption caused by my height, but at least it provided us with a lot of laughs. As soon as the preliminaries were over, we were shipped out to the White Columns motel near the event site to avoid any risk of getting stuck in traffic.

The selectors' decisions as to who should be in the team and who should go as individuals were finally revealed at an impromptu meeting in the stables. With my place in the team secured, I assumed I'd be going first on the grounds that, as Cosmo had the least thoroughbred blood, he'd benefit most from starting in the cool of the morning. That was fine until Ian said he wanted the number one spot. The dressage was run much as normal, though there were misting fans to cool us down in the warm-up area. Cosmo was tense, but did a reasonable test, with a mark of forty-one. Ian went very well on Stanwick Ghost and the team was there or thereabouts behind the

Americans at the end the dressage, but I still felt it was an out-of-body experience. I expected to win a medal, yet there didn't seem to be any way of doing much about it.

On cross-country day, the first horses went off at 7 a.m., which felt like the middle of night. I remember Ian starting phase A on Stanwick Ghost in pitch blackness and doing the steeplechase in a muted dawn light. When he fell coming out of the water, a simple trip that could happen to anyone, the British camp went into panic mode. With our best rider gone, morale was at rock bottom, but our only possible means of recouping the situation was to attack. Instead, we were told that the priority was for the team to complete, no matter how badly, so we should draw in our horns and be ultra careful. As our mindset went into reverse, I began to worry about a bounce of mud huts, mostly because horses had to take off before they saw where they would land. Cosmo fought on the approach, as he often did, so we arrived on the wrong stride and he stopped. If I'd been more positive, he'd have been fine, but he was fractious because I was cautious, resulting in his only cross-country mistake with me.

With the chance of a medal receding with every stride, Cosmo slithered on over the newly laid, heavily watered turf. As he turned into the Olympic rings, with just five strides to go to the massive combination, he slipped and fell. We weren't in the penalty zone, but as I'd presented him at the fence, I couldn't circle without incurring twenty penalties. My only chance was to hop back on as he got up, kick him on and hope for the best. He coped brilliantly, but it was a shame the precarious conditions were not flagged up, because more substantial studs would have been an easy solution. Gary was seriously alarmed by the time he started, but he delivered his safe clear round. So too did Karen Dixon on Too Smart, but each added about twenty-five time penalties, far too many to make up for Ian's and my mistakes. No one would ride so meekly to instructions today but, back then, team riders rode to team orders. The upshot was as bad as it gets, a humiliating fifth, one point in front of the Japanese, with the Australians taking gold.

Our individuals were equally disappointing, with Mary, who'd been miles in the lead, dropping out of contention after a stop, one of just a very few in King William's career, and Charlotte retiring after her horse sustained a horrible injury. Later we had our own prize-giving for the also-rans, a dismal occasion for which we wore Olympic shorts, T-shirts and panama hats. The fifth-place rosettes were pink, so it was déjà vu, the Pony Club revisited. We couldn't get out of America quickly enough, but first we had to attend a formal dinner for owners and supporters.

We were part of the overall British disaster, a comfort in a way that we weren't the only ones to fall foul of the negative Atlanta vibe. Only Steve Redgrave and Matthew Pinsent managed to overcome it, rowing triumphantly to gold, while the rest of us tried to come to terms with the ugly reality of having underperformed. By the time Steve and Matt were on the podium, we were back at home, relieved to be away from the bombs and the ferocious security that still failed to prevent a fatal explosion. We were fit, experienced and well trained, but we had not been psychologically prepared. We failed because we never went for it. Maybe it was a blessing in disguise, because the dismal overall results persuaded the UK Sports Council to put money into victory rather than participation. Overnight, they abandoned the British belief that we were lucky to be taking part and set about creating winners.

Although the Olympic Games are significant and iconic, at least as far as eventers are concerned, Badminton or Burghley are way above them in terms of difficulty, in the same way as a tennis pro would put Wimbledon above Olympic gold. That said, for me Olympic medals are still a major personal goal. When my mother had offered me a choice of four four-year-olds for my twenty-first birthday, I'd picked Loch Alan and I still think he was the best one. I loved his cheekiness, the way he'd undo his stable door and go walkabout, setting off down the lane or doing the rounds of the other horses. You couldn't catch him until he returned to the action when he got bored and gave himself up. On the down side, he was a bit too small and wasn't quite brave enough, probably because he was too intelligent to go willingly into the danger zone. It was hard to get motivated after the Atlanta debacle, but one of the great things about eventing is that for most of us there are other horses to focus on. I came home in the middle of August and spent the rest of the month getting Loch Alan ready for Burghley.

Our performance was disappointing, with a good fourth after dressage ruined by a ridiculous fall at the Dairy Mound, the smallest fence on the course. He hated ditches, spotting them from a hundred metres out and slowing down the nearer he got. He'd often take off too early, quite a hair-raising feeling, but we managed to jump them well that day. I knew I had to generate impulsion to get us to the other side, but his suspicious nature certainly reinforced one of my earliest lessons: when in doubt, kick. After completing Burghley, I knew I'd never ride him round another four-star and my parents generously bought him back for Alicia. Although I thought he'd appreciate stepping down a level or so, he wasn't ideal for her either, but she did her best with him, living cheerfully with his foibles.

CHAPTER THIRTEEN

Tying the Knot

Eventing people tend to get married as soon as the season ends to allow time for a decent honeymoon while the horses are on holiday. Wiggy and I picked a Saturday in November, sent out invitations to our nearest and dearest and set up our marquee in the Channers' garden. As we're both Roman Catholics – me on my mother's side and Wiggy on her father's – we had the ceremony in St Aloysius, a lovely church on the Woodstock Road in north Oxford, which was conveniently located for the party in Godington. Neither of us is exactly devout: Wiggy went to a convent, but although my parents were married in a Catholic church, their open view of religion didn't include a Catholic education.

My stag night was organised by my best man, Daniel Hughes, with a lot of help from Justin Llewelyn. He'd worked in the champagne business for years, so he was able to get us into clubs and generally put the evening on the traditional track. We started with dinner for twelve in the Officers' Mess at Knightsbridge Barracks, but the numbers dwindled rapidly as the lightweights fell away. Towards the end of the night, we ended up in a club where you paid an escort to dance with you: as snogging a stranger has never been my thing, I opted for the hands-off tariff, though you could pay more for more. It was a great party, but the only thing I remember about the next day is having breakfast in my parents' house in Romney Street with Julian Dollar, Philip Clapham and Alec Lochore. My father's housekeeper, Tsang, was the most amazing cook so refusing her eggs was out of the question, but on this occasion, forcing them down was almost a bridge too far.

Our wedding day was glorious, a blaze of late autumn sunshine, and the elaborate plans unfolded without a hitch. Two hundred people came to the church and a further 200 joined us for a sit-down dinner and dancing afterwards. I can ride to a rhythm, but it deserts me the moment I step on the dance floor, making me particularly inept, but as I love it I never let that stop me, no matter how cruel the jokes. Everyone had a good time. That certainly included Alice Plunkett, an event and point-to-point rider I'd known since I was eighteen and she was fourteen. In those days when I first met her she'd seemed a 'sweet little girl', but somehow I ended up dancing with her at my wedding, earning a significant scowl from my new wife. In the short term, Wiggy needn't have worried, because Alice spent the rest of the evening with Daniel Hughes.

Wiggy and I went to the West Indies for our honeymoon, not a good choice as it turned out, though we got off to a relaxed start, spending a couple of days at home to recuperate from the festivities before we flew out on the Tuesday. Given Wiggy's fear of flying it may have been insensitive of me to organise a trip with four short flights in an eight-seater plane, in addition to the long-haul one from Britain, but no one can blame me for the resident iguana on Young Island, an off-shore hideaway with just one secluded hotel. All of the guests were told about him on arrival, not because he's dangerous, just so they wouldn't be surprised to see him. We never did, but his lurking presence meant that Wiggy could not go anywhere on her own.

I'd booked the lodge at the peak of the island, so our luggage had to be carried up a hundred steps, but our enjoyment of the fabulous views came to an abrupt end when our bedside fruit disappeared in the night. It was apparently eaten by a harmless tree rat, but Wiggy immediately negotiated a swap with another couple and a porter was summoned to drag all our bags down again. After a lazy few days, we moved on to Cobblers Cove on Barbados, a peaceful haven with a comforting absence of unacceptable wild life, but unfortunately Wiggy wasn't well so she didn't enjoy it as much as she might have done.

Back at home as a married couple, our impending move to Dorset was an on-going debate. My father's second cousin, Anthony Pitt Rivers, wanted me to take over his farm in Hinton St Mary near Sturminster Newton. He was the youngest of three brothers, none of whom had any children, so I was the closest relation. Anthony talked about it with my parents long before he mentioned it to me, aware that it would mean I'd never move back to Knowlton. Basically, it was my choice and I readily accepted Anthony's proposal, leaving Andrew to concentrate on Knowlton when he left the army. It was always on the radar and I was very excited about it.

I shall be forever grateful to Alex Van Tuyll. Not only as she is a key member of my staff, teaming up with Jackie to provide the discipline and attention to detail that makes Fox-Pitt Eventing work, but she inadvertently led me to Amazing Bob, my favourite horse of all time. Alex, a regular pupil at Stratton Audley, asked me to find her a fun horse that would give her confidence. Vere Phillipps recommended his current uneducated five-year-old, a dark bay part-bred Irish hunter, and we went off to Leicestershire to try him. He was at the wrong stage for Alex, but I liked him. As it turned out, he is very much like Steadfast, 17hh, with a regal look in a middleweight way and a big, white, honest face. When I rode him over some hedges, his jump was strong, flat and fast. He looked like a hunter and he had indeed been hunting, ten days out of fourteen, without ever threatening to settle down. As he wasn't a classic eventer type either, Vere was potentially stuck with him. When I rang him to say I'd take him, he thought I'd gone mad. He was very affordable, especially as Philip Channer wanted to go halves with me, and I had a funny feeling he was too good to miss. I don't often have hunches like that, but I always follow them up if I can. In the belief that I was over-estimating his horse, Vere insisted I have him on trial for two weeks and every time I rode him, he made me smile. As he was a bit of a joke on the yard we nicknamed him Bob the Cob. When people asked me how he was doing, I'd say, 'amazing' so he became Amazing Bob. He's a very shy, serious horse who always tries too hard, not the most talented horse I've ever had, but definitely the most endearing.

CHAPTER FOURTEEN

Amazing Bob

After the Olympic setback, the chance for the national team to get back on track came at the European Championships at Burghley in 1997. In an attempt to make it a global competition by including the Kiwis, Australians and Americans, the FEI offered team and individual Open European medals as well as European ones, a good idea in theory, but a fiasco in practice. By now, I knew Cosmo was a worthy replacement for Chaka. No one would ever describe him as a Ferrari, but he had many qualities. In the spring, he proved his well-being at his first Badminton. His dressage was gradually improving and a clear cross-country round within the time left him in fifth or sixth place. A show jumping clear, his forte, put him up to third, behind David O'Connor on Custom Made and Mary on Star Appeal, my best Badminton result to date. If I could come third, I hoped I could win; it was an exciting thought, as I felt my Badminton luck was finally beginning to change.

Following Atlanta, it was all change for Team GB. Giles Rowsell came in as the new *chef d'équipe*, having been promoted after many successful years as the Young Rider *chef*. Andy Bathe took over as the team vet, while Amanda Sutton retained her position as physio. Collectively they raised the level of support to squad riders, but sadly the benefits were short-lived.

Cosmo was the only Olympian on the Burghley team, but I rejoined Ian and Mary, now riding Arakai and Star Appeal, with Chris Bartle as the new addition on Word Perfect. As the event was on home turf, there were eight individuals, among them Pippa Funnell with Bits and Pieces. Considering the championships had been downgraded to three-star to make them more user friendly for less experienced nations, Mike Tucker's cross-country course was gratifyingly difficult. The two Mikes, Tucker and Etherington-Smith, had cornered the market in top-level cross-country design in Britain. Etherington-Smith has flair and style, producing elegant more predictable courses, but Tucker is braver, specialising in tough fences that conceal their secrets until you tackle them.

Mike Tucker delivered a genuine championship course and it did a lot of damage unfortunately, most relevantly to Chris, who came off Word Perfect early on, and to Pippa, whose first senior international ended in a nasty fall. After a good test, Cosmo went fourth for the team across country. Chris's fall meant we had to go well and we did, clear within the time. That put the team in the gold-medal position, with Cosmo third individually behind Mark Todd and Germany's Bettina Overesch (now Hoy) on Watermill Stream. He was a bit sore in the evening, so it was over to Andy and Amanda to do the best they could. Luckily Wiggy had struck up a good relationship with Andy at the Olympics, so there was no threat of the vet ban that had scuppered Chaka's chances at Badminton two years earlier. On Sunday, Cosmo though much better was held in the box after the trot up, along with Bettina's horse, Watermill Stream. Once he got the okay, I knew they'd have to pass Cosmo as well, especially as the crowd clapped and cheered him along during the second trot up.

The Kiwis and Aussies were up in arms at the decision and the Kiwis harassed me in the show jumping warm-up. They pretended they were helping Mark by changing the fence every time I approached, so that I couldn't jump it. Poor Wiggy and our show jumping trainer, Ken Clawson, were struggling, but they had no chance against the Kiwi helpers, until stewards came to sort it out. Mark wasn't involved – he's a great sportsman and he was going to win Open European gold. It was a pretty unpleasant experience, but it certainly added lustre to our double team gold (Open European and European) and my individual European silver and Open European bronze.

Back at Stratton Audley, Wiggy and I were in expansionist mode as we tried to develop good horses for the future. Amazing Bob lived up to his nickname by powering through his first season, progressing seamlessly from novice through intermediate to advanced. He gave it everything right from the start, never ducking a challenge or throwing a tantrum and I'd come back from every cross-country thinking that he'd been perfect at every fence. Pie in the Sky came on as well, winning his – and Judy's – first two-star three-day event at Blarney Castle. At Lion d'Angers the year before, he'd taken off outside the wings at the second steeplechase fence and crumpled into the ditch. It was a totally unpredictable fall at a two-foot fence, and we were lucky to walk away unscathed, particularly so as it was a week before my wedding.

By this time, Loch Alan had returned to Knowlton, Lismore Lord Charles had gone to Frederik Bergendorf and The Lord Chancellor had been sold to Holland. We were still finding our feet, learning the bitter lesson that you can waste a lot of time on horses that are never going to be good enough. Wiggy helped Jackie with veterinary issues and the stable management and continued to have big ambitions for her riding. However, she was never comfortable with her results. By now, we had our own company, Stratton Audley Park Stud, and money in the bank, but we didn't own many horses. We bought several hopefuls for Wiggy, but none worked out. As everyone who does the lottery knows, you've got to be in it to win it, which, in eventing terms, means finding a horse, getting out there, and going for it. That approach had little appeal for Wiggy. She often pulled out if she felt the ground or the horse wasn't quite right, and although she had reason, it was a discouragement for owners who felt they weren't having much fun.

I had found two schoolmasters for Carter Evans, an inexperienced American enthusiast who gave up his life at home to see how far he could get as an event rider in England. When he was back in America, he was happy for Wiggy to compete on them, but they were not totally suitable. Boom was a lovely generous horse, but he was effectively a middleweight hunter, while Riverspec, a solid achiever who she took to advanced level, didn't have the gallop for a three-day event.

Following Cosmo's great performance at Burghley, I was optimistic that the new season of 1998 would continue in the same way. The selectors gave him a bye for Badminton ahead of the World Championships in Pratoni, leaving me with Mostly Mischief for the big spring target. Bob's progress was continuing the right way, and I was looking forward to his first two-star. Among the rest of the team was a new ride, Chase the Melody, owned by former international rider Sue Benson. He was a talented but unpredictable thoroughbred – certainly there was no way I would have predicted that his routine novice run round Weston Park would end in the worst accident I've had off a horse. He tried to stop at a haycart spooking at the water beyond it, but his momentum meant he cartwheeled over it and landed on my left leg. My foot didn't come out of the stirrup, but when it did I stood up, thinking I'd got away with it. As it felt a bit dead, I stamped it on the ground to get the feeling back, then turned to remount the horse. To my horror my foot didn't turn with me. It was like standing on an oil slick, completely loose at the bottom of my leg and facing in the wrong direction. Not being a great warrior in such circumstances, I sat down quickly and soon passed out.

The prognosis at the John Radcliffe hospital wasn't good: two broken bones, tibia and fibia, and ligament damage, that would take a while to mend. Normally bubbles are burst by horses going lame, but being out of action myself was even more depressing. Once I'd had the operation, I took a more positive view, determined to keep the rest of my body in shape so that I could ride again as soon as possible. Initially, I felt excruciating pain every time I put my leg down, but once that went, I focused on my physio, keeping fit and swimming round the Channers' pool. It was all deadly boring, but I felt grateful I worked with horses, thinking through their brains and bodies as well as my own, rather than going it alone as most athletes do. Forced as I was to take a step back from the sport, I wondered why I risked my life to ride wonderful, but often quite stupid, animals over solid jumps at ridiculous speeds, but the wondering was short-lived and I was back in the saddle as soon as I was able.

My accident probably saved me from what would have at best been a good completion at Badminton. After a year dogged by lameness, interrupted only by a career high at Boekelo in 1996 when he came fifth, Mostly Mischief was ready to meet his major target. For Monika Hunt it was important he should go so I tried to persuade Toddy to take him to Badminton, but even the master of the chance ride turned him down. Wiggy rode Paul Ridgeon's Inchmickery in her first three-star at Bramham, a fairly traumatising experience, as she lost what little control she had and retired after he tried to take an unjumpable route through the water. I watched from the wings and enjoyed the lack of stress that comes with riding a quad bike rather than a horse. Normally I wake up on cross-country mornings feeling sick. Now I looked at the ashen-faced competitors and vowed I'd never let the hype get to me again. 'We're only here because we want to be, so what's with all the fuss?' I asked myself. Naturally that theory vanished as soon as I was back in action.

My physio and rehab went better than expected and as a result I was back in the saddle by the end of June. In late July, I opened Cosmo's World Championship campaign at Cornbury, a nerve-racking occasion after a three-month lay-off in which I'd had far too much time to think. In my early comeback events, I was far too cautious to be competitive. At Thirlestane, the final trial for Pratoni, I gave Cosmo his head and he responded enthusiastically, only to jump out of the leaf pit three from home and land hopping lame on three legs. That was the end of our World Championship dream and, as it turned out, the beginning of the end of Cosmo's career. Appropriately, it fell to Bob to give my season a little credibility with a solid three-day win at Necarne Castle in Northern Ireland.

I wouldn't say we'd earned a holiday, but we certainly needed one, so I persuaded Wiggy to return to Southern Africa. We stayed with Tara

Getty, my best mate from Wellesley House and the manager of the Phinda game reserve in Botswana, a Getty Foundation project set up to generate a viable way of life for the local people. Before we left, Wiggy had a premonition that the plane was going to crash. She was not worried about me going on it – she even suggested I take Jenny Record, a great friend who is now godmother to my son Oli – but there was no way she was going. On this occasion, I put my foot down and convinced her to come. She worked so hard for the long months of the season, I thought it was important for both of us to have some time away from the business together.

Tara arranged for us to spend a few nights in each of the Phinda resorts, one in the jungle, one on the coast and one on the plains, so that we could see different fauna in their natural habitat. The jungle element had glasshouses so you could open the curtains and be right there in it, an amazing experience. In fact, at one point the jungle wasn't just outside the glasshouse. To find a full-grown male baboon sitting on our bed when we got back from the communal dinner in the boma was always going to be disconcerting. He was pretty unhappy to see us and even more unhappy to be booted out.

The next day, we went tracking in the bush in the early morning, looking at prints and faeces to determine animal movements. Wiggy wouldn't leave the Jeep, but I was fascinated. Back at the lodge, I saw a lion's print just outside the breakfast area, so I asked the guard how long it had been there. There was a pregnant pause while he inspected it before coming up with a verdict: no more than three minutes. The result was pandemonium, with gongs sounding and voices raised in panic. Seemingly our visitor had walked straight through the lodge's communal parts unspotted.

After that, we moved into Tara's new house on the reserve. Our trips away at the end of each season were essential, the break helping to set us up for the next year. Eventing is a way of life and one that I wouldn't change, but the commitment leaves little time for anything else, so I relish any small windows of opportunity to experience another life.

CHAPTER FIFTEEN

The Star That Nearly Got Away

Parking your lorry at events is always random, so I had no sense of destiny when I drew up next to Toddy at Tidworth in April 1999. M W Guinness, a well-loved figure on the eventing scene, was trying to persuade him to take on a very naughty mare, but Toddy was shaking his head. 'He won't do it because he's giving up next year,' she said, turning to me. 'You've got long legs. Maybe you could give it a go?' On my way home, I dropped in to see the mare and agreed to take her on trial, an experiment that lasted barely a week. As I was leaving her yard, M W opened another stable door, showing me a little horse called Tamarillo, who was the pride and joy of the Guinnesses' breeding dynasty. 'You can look, but you can't touch,' she said firmly. 'Isn't he the most beautiful horse you've ever seen?' And, in his own Araby way, he was.

Two days later, I ran into him again, warming up for the show jumping at Bicton, with M W in close attendance. In drenching rain, he was giving his rider, Diana Burgess, a hard time, refusing repeatedly at the practice fence to the point she withdrew him and took him back to the lorry. The next day I got a phone call from M W. After she'd talked me through the fiasco, I suggested she bring him over. So there he was, a small Anglo-Arab who wouldn't jump. I looked at him dubiously and wondered what use he could ever be. I have been told that Arabs had sussed human beings after sharing their desert tents for centuries. As a result, they were too intelligent to go that extra inch: where other horses might die for you, Arabs would prefer you died instead. 'I cannot be seen riding an Arab,' I thought as I got on board. This one could certainly move and he had unbelievable presence, but when I tried to jump him, he stopped and stopped, displaying an implacable loathing for coloured fences, however small. 'He's lost it,' I said, as M W and her head groom Jo looked on disconsolately. That was undeniable. The question was whether he could be turned round. And was I prepared to try?

The Guinnesses had bred him, and Diana had produced him to win some Burghley young event horse classes and competed him up to intermediate level, but she knew she'd reached the end of the road. I remember thinking that I would be the laughing stock of the eventing world riding an Arab peacock who looks as though he should be in a show class at Wembley. Given that he was only 16.2hh and he'd lost his nerve, Wiggy was adamant I shouldn't take him, insisting that I could not expect to find a good horse if I always filled the yard up with rubbish. My counterpunch was that a horse as athletic as that couldn't possibly be useless. Also, Wiggy couldn't deny we needed liveries and the Guinnesses were potentially great owners. When M W asked me what I thought of the horse's prospects and I said, 'There's a twenty per cent chance of him coming right,' she looked at me as if I'd told her he'd lost his right foot. And yet he came. Negative vibes and all, Tamarillo was now part of my life.

Although he was a classier and more athletic horse than I had ever seen, Tam was hard to take seriously at first. He's never been friendly, and he's very suspicious of men. He loves Jackie, but there's no way I could walk up to him in a field, let alone catch him, except by bribing him with food. Like Cosmo, his jumping was an issue, but his problem was spooking and he would stop every time I altered the fence. I felt the best approach was a positive one, committing him to the point where he couldn't opt out at the last second, his favourite modus operandi. This is not a sensible way forward for either horse or rider, but Tam is as athletic as a cat and he has a lightning brain, so he'd always take off rather than risk hurting himself. After a month of endless repetition and quite a lot of encouragement, he began to make progress, but it was painfully slow.

By June, I hoped he was ready to tackle a novice class at Great Missenden. He led with a dressage score of twelve and a clear round show jumping as he went into the cross-country. My decision to go flat out came to a lightning halt at a twelve-inch log following two steps up out of a wood into open fields. I hurtled forward, landing with Tam's ears in my crotch, just managing not to fall off. He was scared witless as he shot around with me sitting on his head, but once I was back in the saddle, I gave him a healthy thump to re-establish that I was more of a threat than the fence.

After a further month of message reinforcement, we went to the prestigious novice event at Cornbury Park, a difficult cross-country track that asked plenty of questions. Tam behaved impeccably, flying round at a scary speed to finish second and, for the first time, I felt as though he was enjoying himself. He confirmed this with wins at Knaptoft and Hartpury, followed by a fourth in his first intermediate at Somerleyton Hall. He still had moments when he lost it, stopping at a practice fence for example, so I decided to take him hunting through the winter, a scheme he shot out of the water by getting a cough. No matter: I now knew that my little Arab was no joke.

Fate came in to play again when I next parked alongside Toddy at Chatsworth that May. He was discussing Stunning with George and Jayne Apter, among his most loyal owners during his years in Britain. The Apters had bought the New Zealand thoroughbred for Toddy in the hope he'd ride him at the Sydney Olympics in 2000, his swansong before he returned home. Toddy was explaining that, as his first Olympic choice would be Eye Spy, he'd fully understand if the Apters wanted to find a new rider for Stunning. At thirteen, the fiery chestnut had had a hard life, racing until he was seven, then putting in two years on the New Zealand show jumping circuit before taking up eventing. With Toddy, he'd developed a do or die spirit, coming second at Bramham, falling at Burghley and winning at Achselshwang in 1998, then falling again at Kentucky shortly before Chatsworth. With Cosmo sidelined for at least a year, I was short of top prospects, as George knew full well. When I chatted to Toddy about taking Stunning, he asked so eagerly when I was coming to get him that I assumed he wasn't going to miss him too much.

Riding him confirmed that he wasn't passing him on out of charity. I knew Stunning had issues, but the Apters were fantastic owners who were in the sport for the long haul, so I didn't want to turn him down. Even so, it was a tough call. Stunning was as difficult as they come, wooden, tense and hot-headed, but I saw him as a challenge. By the time Toddy had got him two years earlier, he was set in his ways and they were not ways that were easy to live with. He is a sweet horse and a lovely character, but he didn't have much natural talent and he didn't go eventing because he liked it. He wasn't brave, but he was generous and amazingly tough enough to go on until he was eighteen. As I faced up to his limitations, I consoled myself with his record. How bad could he be if Toddy had won three-stars and tried four-stars with him? The easiest way to find out was to take him to Burghley. He went very well until the last water jump, when he ground to a halt, his muscles so cramped they went into spasm. Was it dehydration, mineral imbalance or stress? Blood tests failed to provide answers, so we never got to the bottom of it, but the poor fellow probably did well to get so far.

Without Cosmo, I was in a bit of a dip, with no hope of going to the European Championships at Luhmühlen that year nor indeed to the Sydney Olympics in the next if he didn't recover in time. I was now out of the loop, isolated from my former team-mates, the champions at Luhmühlen, with Pippa, in her first year at the top of her game, winning individual gold with Supreme Rock.

Pippa has credited her breakthrough to Nicky Heath, the team sports psychologist who came to talk to us all about our approach to eventing. I never felt the need for that kind of help, but Nicky arrived at a time when Pippa would have tried anything, acupuncture, reflexology, whatever, and she grabbed it. Since then, she's presented psychology as a major element in her success, the way she learned how to deal with her nerves and worked out how she can compete best. I, however, feel she's being modest, because a rider with her talent was bound to rise to the top at some stage.

My main focus for the 1999 spring season was the three-star competition in Saumur where I rode River Dragon, Pie in the Sky and Western Reef, owned by Catherine Joice. River Dragon and Western Reef finished ninth and sixteenth, but Pie, a talented horse who led the dressage, pulled up lame after banging a joint on the third element of the coffin, so we couldn't present him at the vet's inspection the next day. Wiggy had a steady clear on Willy B Free. After his performance in Saumur, Pie got an exemption to join Stunning at Burghley. He lay fourth in the dressage but sadly pulled up lame after the steeplechase. He was an unlucky horse but he was not a galloping machine, and the speed of 690 metres per minute required on the chase proved too much for him.

If it had not been for Bob, the situation in 1999 would have been seriously depressing. Despite his type, Bob was finding the progression to advanced surprisingly easy, so Bramham seemed the natural place to go. At only eight years old, I was simply hoping for a solid all-round performance and once again he surpassed all expectations, proving to be precocious enough to finish seventh behind some experienced four-star horses who had rerouted from Badminton. Any thoughts of selling him on were firmly kicked into touch when he suddenly put himself into contention for the Sydney Olympics following a second place in the Achselshwang three-star in the autumn. He was narrowly beaten by Chris Bartle on Oscar and I could now enjoy the winter knowing that Badminton was a realistic target.

When the season ended, Wiggy and I flew to New Zealand, a snake free country, on an extended horse-buying spree, interrupted by Puhinui, the most important three-day event for home-based Kiwis. As an added attraction, they ran a three-day invitational international, with twelve riders on borrowed horses. As they paid our airfares and offered fantastic hospitality, the take-up was excellent, with Mary King, Bettina Hoy and Matt Ryan joining the New Zealanders, Toddy, Blyth and Andrew Nicholson. The horses were pulled out of a hat, making it all a bit of a lottery, but I was lucky enough to get Gimmick, owned by Andrew Scott, who'd produced Stunning. He was a hot little grey, but a good jumper who made nothing of the easy two-star track.

When Puhinui was over, Wiggy and I hired a car to tour the South Island, rejecting bungee jumping in Queenstown, but risking a bit of white water rafting. We also went whale watching and trekking in Milford Sound before heading back to Auckland to check out our purchases. We'd looked at a lot of very small racehorses, short of bone, uneducated and temperamental, but we made the mistake of finding three youngsters to ship home, one to bring on and sell, one for the Apters and one Wiggy bought from the Nicholsons.

The New Zealand trip was fantastic. I loved competing and exploring the country was fascinating. Although the horses we bought didn't turn out to be superstars, the experience was worthwhile. On the surface things were great, but Wiggy was not in good form. Although Willy B Free had gone well for her at Achselschwang, she wasn't enjoying her riding and she still didn't want to practise as a vet. I tried to encourage her to make more of her own life. Ironically she then persuaded me to buy Valhalla as a fun horse for her from Andrew and Jayne Nicholson. He was Jayne's favourite, but had issues so was cheap. By January 2000, we had two Nicholson horses; no coincidence as it turned out, though months would pass before I knew the reason why.

CHAPTER SIXTEEN

How Bad Can it Get?

As well as being a low year for me, 1999 was been one of the most traumatic in the history of the sport. The Coral Cove affair was never going to end well, but no one imagined it would end as badly as it did. The tragic tale had begun at the World Championships at Pratoni in 1998. With the 1997 team horses out of action, the selectors opted for Karen Dixon, Gary Parsonage, Nigel Taylor and Vere Phillipps's wife, Polly. Britain still needed to qualify for the Sydney Olympics and the team delivered, winning a bronze medal behind the Kiwis and the French, thanks in no small part to Polly's fine performance on Coral Cove. But, after he failed a dope test, the team was stripped of the medal and our Olympic participation was again in doubt.

We will never know what really happened, but Coral Cove had been stiff and sore, though not lame, after the cross-country at Pratoni. When he was tested, he was found to have seven times the permitted level of aspirin in his blood. Blame was fired in all directions, at Andy Bathe, the British team vet in Pratoni, at Vere and Polly, and at Giles Rowsell, the British *chef d'équipe*. The saddest aspect was that they didn't stick together and hold their hands up.

Polly had been a friend since our Pony Club days, but I knew Andy well through Wiggy and the British team, so I was torn between the two sides. When Andy had to express his point of view at a British Eventing tribunal, Wiggy got very fired up, preparing his case and giving him unstinting support throughout. Inevitably Andy was struck off as team vet, something he'd always wanted to do and did very well. With his reputation in tatters, he had a tough time, but he hung in there. He's now a partner in the renowned Rossdale practice in Newmarket and he's still my main vet.

With the affair only breaking as the 1999 season got under way, the scandal gradually built up a head of steam. There was a groundswell of opinion that Polly shouldn't be allowed to compete until the situation was resolved, but she hadn't been stood down, so she was perfectly entitled to ride at Badminton. She was a high energy person, living life at the double as she combined her veterinary degree course at Cambridge with being master of the university drag hunt and competing as a young rider, so it was predictable that she'd respond to the pressure by going on the attack. In atrocious conditions, she knew she could move right up the order if she really went for it, but her luck ran out at the dew pond. She took a horrendous fall when Coral Cove tried to jump the bounce combination in one but, miraculously, she emerged unscathed.

Polly then decided to go to Bramham where, despite general hostility from the riders, she finished third behind Leslie and Shear H2O. Giles Rowsell had been forced out at the same time as Andy, and Michael Allen, the chairman of British Eventing (BE), resigned immediately after Bramham. The highly respected Jane Holderness-Roddam was elected as the new chairman of BE, with the popular Mandy Stibbe as the chairman of selectors.

The worst spate of fatalities in British eventing history had already begun at Savernake a month earlier. I was in the start box on one of my three novice rides when the news came through: Peta Beckett, a young mother with two small children, had died at a simple bounce fence. After competing in Pratoni as an individual the year before, she was an emerging talent, a breath of fresh air and someone who always looked as if she was having fun. She operated on a shoestring, with no outside financial support, so it was tragic that she should have a fatal accident just as her years of hard work were coming to fruition. Her husband, Marvin, had no interest in horses, but he supported her to the nth degree. If it could happen to her, a true professional, it could happen to any of us. And it did, just six weeks later, while I was competing at Chantilly with Western Reef: again, grief mingled with a frisson of fear when we heard that the talented Australian, Robert Slade, had been killed at Wilton.

Thirlestane Castle is one of the highlights of the August calendar, but in 1999, it turned into one of the most awful weekends. All of us had been drawn into the Coral Cove affair and everyone had an opinion. Despite being cleared, Polly was still riding under huge pressure in the bitter aftermath. No one will ever know if this was a factor in her fatal fall. When the news filtered back to the lorry park, there was a stunned silence. Emotions ran high, disbelief and sadness mixed with a sense of guilt that we were all in some way responsible.

I was appalled. Minutes before, I'd met her as she rode down to the start when I was returning from my round on Stunning. We had a brief chat about how some of the fences were riding and I wished her luck. She always rode to win, but Lucinda, who saw the accident, said she wasn't going fast. We all live with horse-rider misunderstandings on a daily basis: this one occurred at a relatively simple fence, resulting in a somersaulting fall that killed Polly instantly.

Anyone who dared to hope the worst was over had their illusions shattered the next week at Burghley when Simon Long, an event rider and show jumper, had a fatal fall at the sunken road. It was a particularly difficult and complex fence and his horse, Springleaze Macaroo, stopped at the final rail after tripping on the step up to it. In the heat of the moment, Simon made one of those misjudgements that any of us can make at any time. Instead of giving his horse space to take off, he turned him and asked him to jump from a standstill. Unfortunately, Macaroo responded bravely, breasting the fence and coming down on top of Simon in a slow, rotational fall. A fortnight later, the nightmare reached its climax when the young Scottish rider, Peter McLean, died at Somerleyton Hall.

In the fifteen years I'd been eventing, there'd been occasional fatalities, among them Mark Davies, who'd died at Burghley in 1988, and David Foster, a popular Irish rider, who'd been killed just before

Badminton in 1998, but five deaths in five months was unprecedented and unacceptable. Any rational person might wonder how riders could set off round a cross-country course in the shadow of so much tragedy. I suddenly found that each time I got to the starting box, I'd be thinking that this could be it. It must have been the same for everybody, but I would go through the routine, telling myself that the odds were against it, convincing myself that my horse was more than capable and reminding myself just how much I loved doing it. By the time the starter said 'go', all the negative thoughts had disappeared and my focus was on the job in hand. In the long term, it has made me take a much more critical view of the horses I'm prepared to ride.

Given that the riders who died were competent professionals, it seemed reasonable to assume that the fences were to blame. The public outcry grew and with it the demand for a major review of the sport at all levels, with the emphasis on safer jumps and more stringent qualifications for horses and riders. Mike Tucker became the chairman of the new safety committee and Jackie Stewart was drafted in from Formula One to add an outside dimension to the discussions. The committee, which also included Lord Hartington and Ian Stark, looked at all the angles before recommending the safeguards that are now standard practice.

Their first concern was the fences themselves. If you fall when you're going fast, you have a good chance of landing clear, but if the horse takes off slowly and comes down steeply, you can easily be caught underneath him. One way to reduce the danger is to fit frangible pins, as developed by Transport Research Laboratory, into upright posts and rails. When a horse hits a fence in a way that triggers a rotational fall, there is point at which the pressure of his body on the rail deconstructs the pin, causing it to collapse. Naturally this suggestion raised questions as to whether riders would be more foolhardy if they knew the fence would come down, a worry that was offset to some degree by imposing automatic elimination on anyone who broke a pin. The technology has already saved lives, but the way the fences are built means that it is not practical to be used widely in Britain and it's not been adopted sufficiently in Europe, perhaps because they've never had accidents on the scale that we've had.

The obvious way to reduce risk is to build easier fences, with less imposing ditches, no true parallels and more user-friendly drops, but it's difficult to get the right balance between safety and dumbing down. In the long term, the 1999 death toll triggered the end of the traditional, long-format three-day event. With no steeplechase or roads and tracks, the short format, introduced internationally at the Athens Olympics in 2004, is cheaper to stage and, therefore, more profitable, a point duly noted by Badminton and Burghley when they eventually took it on board for 2006. One of the theories was that with a lower endurance factor horses would not get tired and the sport would become safer.

Nowadays, the imposing nature of the cross-country has also been sacrificed to the safety element, often leaving timing as the key factor in deciding the result. Ideally, the direct routes should tempt only the best horses and riders, but the designers can never control who takes them on. If the direct routes are so inviting that all the competitors attempt them, you're left with a dressage and show jumping competition.

The other revolution in that stormy pre-millennium year was the founding of PERA (Professional Event Riders' Association), a group designed to give competitors a long-overdue voice. It was started by some of the more political riders, among them Eddy Stibbe, Toddy, Blyth, Mary, Andrew (Nicholson) and me, and we appointed Robert Lemieux to run it. Eventing had always been a traditional sport, managed in an old school way. Decisions were made and riders were not expected to have opinions. Standards needed to be maintained, but now the officials had to put in the work required to build serious courses within the new restraints. As we were taking the risks, we wanted PERA to appoint rider representatives at events to voice any concerns we might have about courses or conditions.

Another major initiative concerned prize money, historically minimal in what started out as a very amateur sport. Our plan was to offer a

£5,000 prize for the PERA class at high-profile one-day events like Belton. Anyone could enter, but only those who paid the annual subscription could win the money. Our sponsors pledged £100,000 to get PERA running on the right lines but, stupidly, we failed to keep track of the accounts, so we ended up spending money we never actually had. Eddy generously kept it afloat for a while, but poor management won in the end: a predictable problem for an organisation run by competitors with insufficient time to check up thoroughly or follow matters through. Subsequently, PERA was replaced by ERA (Event Riders' Association) and we achieved our goal of rider representatives at the big events, a poisoned chalice if ever there was one, as we all discovered when our turns came up.

By the time we celebrated the millennium at Eddy and Mandy's fabulous party, we were all glad to see the back of 1999.

CHAPTER SEVENTEEN

One in a Million

B y the time I took Tamarillo to his first two-star three-day event at Blarney Castle in June, the new century wasn't looking much better than the old. Cosmo made a brief comeback in the spring, but his leg went again, a typical follow-up injury above the existing scar tissue. He never went lame, but it was obvious that he could no longer take the work, so we retired him. He was still growing in confidence and potentially he had several more years of top competition ahead of him. If I had him now, I'd enter him selectively, as I do Tam, so as to preserve him for as long as possible, but I didn't know as much about horse management then. Frank Andrew gave him to Alison Quinlan, his devoted groom from Atlanta, and he's the love of her life, still competing today at Riding Club level in his late teens. When he left, Cosmo took most of my Sydney hopes with him, though either Stunning or Bob had an outside chance of making the team if they did well at Badminton.

The weather was appalling, bitterly cold on the dressage days, then boiling hot for the cross-country, making the going soft and tacky. Bob was well placed after dressage, with Stunning back in the pack. On the cross-country, Stunning started out reluctantly, but little by little his confidence grew and by halfway he was going well. Unwisely, I got brave and decided to tackle the direct route at the Vicarage Vee. The result was exactly what Chaka had done; he veered left into the rail and ended up in the pigswill ditch. After he'd heaved himself out, he refused to jump back over the simple ditch and I retired him. By this time, Wiggy was at the start of her first Badminton cross-country, waiting for the saddle Stunning shared with Willy B Free. Knowing how desperate she'd be, I hurriedly unbuckled the girth, handed Stunning to a huntsman to lead back and hitched a lift to the ten-minute box. When George and Jayne Apter spotted me with a saddle but no horse, they panicked, reasonably assuming that Stunning had been badly injured, so they were very relieved to see him plodding back through the crowds a few minutes later.

Wiggy fell halfway round and retired, so things could only improve as I set out on Bob. He flew round to the second last fence, two angled tables on a turn, then out of the blue on the approach he ground to a halt. His time was good and he only had to gallop in front of the house, clear the last and pass the finishing line, but nothing would persuade him to go near the fence again. As soon as I led him away, he was as bright as a button and towed me back to the stables. For all his qualities, Bob is no hero. On one occasion, we poulticed his foot and he lay down for a day, resulting in colic that confirmed his belief that the end of the world had come. His lack of thoroughbred blood meant he was likely to struggle in four-star events, especially in mud and energy-sapping humidity, but it was hard to understand why he would give up so quickly. I wondered whether he'd got cramps or a stitch but it's hard to prove that theory.

So it was all up to Tam. He had the minimum qualifications for Blarney Castle and he'd done his best to put himself off games on the horse walker we had at Stratton Audley. He was playing the fool as usual when he fell on his knees on the concrete and trapped himself under the partition. The horse behind saw him as fair game and jumped on him, but somehow Tam emerged okay. Nowadays he can't sneeze without being blood-tested, but back then he was a real dobbin, so lazy that Mary Channer was happy to hack him out. No one was worried as it was 'only Tam'.

Blarney was a decent two-star track with lots of types of fences that he hadn't seen before and M W and I knew it was crunch time: if he didn't like it, we'd find out today. He led the dressage, but it rained non-stop on cross-country day and I felt his little feet and extravagant movement might make it tough for him to gallop through the mud. That morning M W was pacing around in a highly nervous state when she bumped into an Irish friend who said consolingly, 'Don't get your hopes up. A horse with movement like yours hasn't got a chance in this.' She came back to the stables all doom and gloom, saying he'd never cope with the steeplechase. But he did and he's always performed amazingly in wet conditions. With his light action and athletic ability, he's equally good in firm or soft conditions, though he thinks it's hard labour when it's muddy in the dressage arena.

At Blarney, he nipped round easily, making nothing of the going or the fences, and won comfortably from the front. He now felt like he loved cross-country, an impression he confirmed by winning the intermediate championship at Gatcombe on his next outing. Although he'd only done one advanced, coming fourth behind Stunning at Cornbury, I felt he was ready for his first three-star three-day at Blenheim that September. At the end of dressage, he was second, with Stunning third two points behind him. Again the going was very muddy and with Stunning going clear within the time, I was in the luxurious position of riding Tam to beat myself. I took him fairly easily, accounting for his lack of experience and clocked up 2.4 time faults, which put him a fraction behind his stable companion. If they both show jumped clear, Stunning would take the honours by a whisker.

And they did. Tam went first, so I'd already won when I went in on Stunning, a horse who very rarely left all the fences standing. Either of them could have had two fences down and still come second, which may explain why Stunning jumped his most relaxed round ever, never touching a fence rather than skimming them all as he usually did. This was my best victory with him and the highlight of 2000, a reward for the disappointments at Badminton and Burghley.

As for Tam, I was now beginning to realise that I had a superstar. He's so well balanced that he made Blenheim seem smooth and effortlessly easy, like getting on Minnie Monster as a child and popping round without a care in the world. Generally, I like big horses because I feel more comfortable on them and, being so tall, I certainly dwarf Tam, but he's never had a problem carrying me. Although you can get nimble giants, small horses are often a better bet, being more naturally in control of their bodies and Tam is exceptionally well coordinated. If I'd gone to see him with a view to buying him irrespective of his issues, I'd probably have said no, though his outright talent would have made him very hard to leave behind.

As it is, we have a partnership rather than a relationship: I'm very fond of him and we have a mutual respect. Well, I think we do. Sometimes he's happy to see me, sometimes I can't get near him in the stable, let alone the field, and sometimes he acts as if he's never seen a human being in his life. One day you can put the saddle on as if he was a pony, the next he can be a rodeo horse, bucking and lashing out. At Stratton Audley he once went berserk and took out a wall when one of the girls tried to get on him after his holiday. At the time, we didn't worry; he was a spooky unpredictable Arab with a mind of his own, but nowadays we take every precaution. In 2005, aged thirteen, it took us ten days to rebreak him to the saddle after his post-Badminton holiday. As he was on the horse walker, it didn't really matter, but we know we have to factor in the time he needs to readjust.

His unpredictability is at its most frustrating in dressage. He very rarely does a whole test without a glitch – a spook, a buck or a kick – losing the marks that should put him in the lead. He'd have won both the Badmintons he came second in if he'd done half of what he can do in dressage, but he makes out he's terrified by the smallest things in the arena, then goes fearlessly round the most demanding cross-country track. In 2000, he progressed from novice to top contender for my next Olympic horse. If it hadn't been for Tam, it would have been a bleak year. Relations between Wiggy and I had been difficult, but my marriage was in much more trouble than I ever imagined.

As ERA got into its stride, I had to take my turn as the rider representative at Burghley 2000, a no-win situation at a time when the competitors were flexing their muscles and the officials were resisting the new system. The riders would tell me their concerns and I'd present them to the officials, who took everything I said as if it came directly from me. The riders were unhappy with the going, the length of the steeplechase and a couple of fences, including the sunken road where Simon Long had been killed the previous year, but the officials refused to consider the changes I requested, leaving me stranded between a rock and a hard place. To make things worse, I had another disappointing experience with Bob, who stopped at the last water. This time I wasn't going to let him get away with it, so I turned him round and gave him a good smack, at which point he flew the fence and galloped home full of running, his chance completely gone.

The next day I watched Wiggy show jumping with Lucinda Green. 'Are you all right?' she asked with some concern. 'Fine,' I replied, thinking she was referring to the rider rep fiasco, but a few weeks later, Sheila Cotter left me with less room to hide my head in the sand. She is one of the most special people I've known, and treated me like the son she never had.

On this occasion, Wiggy was abroad staying with friends, so I stopped off to have lunch with Sheila. It was normally a relaxed occasion with horses as the main topic of conversation, but she was obviously concerned about something when she asked me if I was all right. 'Absolutely fine,' I replied without hesitation. 'The horses are well, everything's great.' 'I'm sorry,' she said. 'I've got to tell you that I've heard Wiggy's having an affair with Andrew Nicholson.' 'Of course she's not,' I said. 'Why would she be doing that?' 'Oh, I'm so relieved,' said Sheila. 'I've been meaning to ask you for ages, but I was never able to pluck up the courage. I thought you'd come to lunch to tell me you were in trouble.'

That night I spoke to Wiggy, who was on holiday in Greece. 'You're never going to believe what I was told today,' I said, roaring with laughter. 'There's a rumour going around that you're having an affair with Andrew Nicholson. Have you ever heard anything so ridiculous?' Characteristically, she believed that attack was the best means of defence, so I was subjected to a torrent of hostile comments about people jumping to unjustifiable conclusions. 'Whatever are they going to invent next?' I said as I put the phone down, thinking no more of it.

However, when we returned to New Zealand at the end of the season, I felt she was behaving oddly. During our time out there, we always seemed to be doing different things and she was becoming increasingly distant. Even so, it took a massive row to persuade me to confront her about our marriage. I was probably about two years too late, but at least I was decisive when I told her something would have to happen if we had a future together.

All in all, the New Zealand trip wasn't a lot of fun and no sooner had we landed than the rumour machine was back on our case. This time it was Judy Skinner who asked me if Wiggy and I were still together. 'Absolutely,' I said, but crunch time had arrived. I confronted her again, asking for the truth, and this time I got it. She and Andrew had been having an affair for a year and, as is often the case, everyone knew apart from me. At that moment I knew my marriage was over.

CHAPTER EIGHTEEN

A Happy Bachelor

I remember the date well, 21 December 2000, the start of my new life. The next few weeks were a torment. I didn't tell my parents and I wouldn't let Wiggy tell hers. That made her cross, but I was in the driver's seat for the first time in a long while and it was my turn to call the shots. As usual, Christmas had been the subject of discussion. Before I found out about the affair, I'd said I was going to Knowlton and Wiggy had said she wasn't, expecting me to stay at Stratton Audley with her. When I prepared to leave, she said she was coming too, but there was no way that was going to happen.

Spending time away allowed me to put things into perspective. At the age of thirty-one, the worst thing that had happened to me was losing my grandmother. Now my world was thrown upside down. I'd always taken marriage very seriously. I knew mine wasn't easy, but I didn't see it as bad and I always believed Wiggy and I had a future together. We'd been very lucky, with a roof over our heads, supportive parents and a good business. There'd been no financial issues, no tragedies, no disasters and fortunately, as it turned out, we hadn't tried to have children.

Starting out on my own was a daunting prospect. Wiggy had managed the business side of the yard herself, often coming down hard on me for not taking enough interest in the bottom line. We rented the yard together and lived in her mother's bungalow. If we were going to split up, all that would change. I wondered if I could cope and I can't deny I had moments of vacillation. After all, couples do survive unfaithfulness.

From my perspective, Wiggy had done something irreversible, leaving me with a simple choice: accept it or walk away. We could try again, but what if we came unstuck ten years down the line? I arrived at Knowlton exhausted and slept for hours, waking up with my brain in turmoil and my energy in overdrive. I realised I had options that had been closed to me over my decade with Wiggy, an exciting prospect. Christmas passed in a blur of mental exhaustion, an emotional whirlwind of highs and lows that I'd never experienced before. I fobbed my parents off with excuses, saying Wiggy had to stay at Stratton Audley because we didn't have enough help. I doubt they were convinced, but they were tactful enough not to ask too many questions.

Back at Stratton Audley, Wiggy had revealed all to her parents on the grounds that she couldn't pretend to be jolly any longer. The Channers were sad, but supportive, accepting the situation and helping us both to move on. On 16 January, eight years to the day since I'd left Knowlton, I moved into Well Cottage, next to the yard. We'd argued over all our joint possessions except Basil, our severely epileptic dog who was better off in the care of the vet. We stumbled along for a while with our horses in the same yard, but there was a limit as to how long that could last.

At Well Cottage, new horizons soon opened up and my social life blossomed, partly because friends were quick to rally round and partly because I was a newly made bachelor. Soon after my move, I went down to Knowlton to talk to my mother, confirming that all her suspicions were true as we did our customary round of the horses. To her credit, she managed to say how sorry she was, before suggesting it would all work itself out for the best in the long run. I agreed, but explained that Wiggy had been the only one for me and I couldn't imagine fancying anyone else or falling in love again. Naturally my mother was quick to reply, 'Don't worry, darling, you will.'

I'd been behaving like a married man since I was twenty-one so it was great to be newly single and on the loose. Better still, I was free to go where I wanted when I wanted and I did, feeling more alive than I had in years. I really appreciated my supportive friends, though

I dread to think how much I took advantage of their patience with my tales of woe.

In normal circumstances, I'd have been throwing myself into my horses, determined to prove that I could go it alone, but the spring eventing season had been cancelled throughout Britain due to foot-and-mouth disease, leaving me with lots of unaccustomed party time to fill. When the epidemic first broke out, I was taken off by two good friends, Rob Stevens and Mark Corbett, for a week's skiing in a chalet in La Tania, near Courchevel. We shared it with an extraordinarily varied bunch of people, but we had a common purpose, an enjoyably debauched holiday with no strings attached, and this we achieved with a huge amount of laughter and fun.

Getting divorced did me the world of good, though I wouldn't recommend the process to anyone. Wiggy would agree with me now, but at the time she was adamant we should go to counselling. As a counsellor's job is to get people back together again, I couldn't see the point.

Foot-and-mouth was a disaster for both the farming and eventing communities, but if it had to happen, the timing worked for me. Normally our split would have been the talk of the lorry parks, but with no events, we escaped a lot of that. I still see getting divorced as a failure and the experience left me bruised and vulnerable. However, dealing with the press interest was another matter. Neither Wiggy nor I was interested in speaking to the press, though a *Daily Mail* reporter tried to interview me. 'This is your chance to set the record straight,' he said, 'and if you don't, we'll fill in the gaps ourselves.' 'You'll do that whatever I say,' I replied in the course of telling him to get lost. He said he'd reveal the intimate details of Wiggy's affair with Andrew if I didn't cooperate, an empty threat, because I knew he'd do it anyway if he needed to. I warned my mother and Anthony that it might be in the paper the next day and took great pleasure in telling Wiggy that I'd sold my whole story. She went to newsagent at 6 a.m., found there was nothing in the paper and rang me immediately to tell me what a bastard I was. In that instance, she was probably right.

Andrew admitted his affair with Wiggy. I tried to communicate with Jayne, but it soon became obvious that we were coming from completely different angles. At that time, Wiggy stayed on near her parents. They always supported her no matter what, but they'd also taken a great interest in the horses, with Mary riding out regularly and Philip doing a lot to help, so our split marked a huge change in their lives.

Given that I still had my horses, owners and team, my life changed very little when I left Wiggy. Looking back, I can see she and Andrew did me a huge favour. I have no regrets and have learned a lot from the experience. My father had always been concerned about me marrying Wiggy, but he may not have felt able to express himself as forcefully as he could have done. My divorce brought us closer together and he was very keen to send Andrew a crate of champagne, though he resisted the temptation in the end.

In the summer, I collected Pippa to go to Tina Gifford and Phil Cook's wedding, triggering a whirlwind of speculation that we were having an affair. Pippa and her husband, William, were separated at the time, so we were going through the same kind of emotional turmoil, but she was still trying to make her marriage work and they're now happily back together again. If she hadn't been, who knows what might have happened, and we often laugh about it now. If Wiggy and I managed to be competitive over our very different eventing careers, imagine how it would have been for Pippa and me.

Tina's wedding was both happy and in a way weird. Pippa and I sat together feeling very cynical about the whole concept of marriage but thrilled to see our best mate looking so beautiful and happy. Tina and I go back to junior days, and in fact our mothers competed against each other in the 1960s and 70s. Although we haven't shared our luck, we've always been very supportive of one another's careers. She's one of my most loyal friends, and one of the most talented and professional event riders there is. Recently she has been short of a really good horse, but I wouldn't be surprised to see her back on the team for Beijing or London.

With eventing on the back burner and Wiggy out of the organisational loop, horses kept flooding into the yard. At one stage I had thirty-three, twenty-nine of them ready to compete, and me as the only rider. It was a crazy, cathartic year anyway, so I accepted any ride I was offered, provided it was safe. I looked at every horse as an opportunity rather than a potential disaster. I took more risks, pushed the horses a bit more than I normally did and ran the yard in a more relaxed way. The team responded with real energy, working themselves to death, but laughing a lot.

There weren't enough stables to go round at Stratton Audley, so we developed a hot bunking system, with horses going in and out in shifts throughout the day. Jackie relished the challenge of being totally in charge and we took on two amazing girls, Victoria Fry, known as Posh, and Malin Fex, from Sweden. Victoria, a cook who wanted to get into horses, was recommended by my great friend, Jenny Record, but I remember wondering if she was working pupil material as she strode confidently into the yard. I tried her out on a livery horse and she was soon galloping round the school as if she was on the wall of death. 'William, help, I can't stop,' she yelled. I wondered what she expected me to do, but managed to deflect the horse until he slowed enough for her to get him under control. Despite the riding issue, she seemed keen and a really great person to have around, so I agreed to give it a go. She formed a strong bond with Malin and they made a cheerful team when we went to events.

On the administration front, I was lucky enough to find Becky Elvin to help me keep the show on the road. I'd met her at Pratoni in 1995, when she was grooming for Lucy Jennings, and also through her good friend, Alison Quinlan, Cosmo's groom at Atlanta. Becky, a bubbly blonde habitually dressed as a beach bum in Bermudas and shades, never seemed like groom material and she soon moved up to Stoneleigh to run the Pony Club office. She's an incredible organiser and very good at paperwork, so my lucky number came up when she took over my life.

With the home circuit dead until mid-May, I went a bit mad, travelling to international one-day events in France, Belgium and

Ireland at every opportunity. Jackie made sure things ran smoothly at Stratton Audley, letting me loose in foreign parts with Victoria and Malin, and we had a load of laughs. I felt Stunning knew enough to compete at Saumur without a previous run and he justified my faith by coming fourth. That, combined with his victory at Blenheim the year before, was enough to get us selected for the European Championships at Pau, much to my delight as I hadn't been on a team since 1997. At nine, Tam was too inexperienced to go to a three-day event without a preparatory competition, but the selectors put him on the list in case something went wrong with Stunning.

It was with mixed emotions that I accepted the four-star ride of Springleaze Macaroo in June. In the tragic year of 1999 he had fallen on his rider Simon Long and fatally injured him. Realistically it was not his fault, but the association remained with him. He'd been ridden by Katie Parker in the four-star in Kentucky, but she had broken her pelvis during a ride on a novice, so his owner Ben Walden offered him to me – potentially a great opportunity as Burghley was his next target.

The first domestic three-day event was at Burgie in Scotland in mid-June. I had four entries, headed by Highland Lad – the winner, as it turned out – who'd been sent to me by Carol Hudson when her rider, Owen Moore, decided to take time out.

The shake-up was doing me the world of good. The horses went well, the business looked up and the support I had from my family brought us closer together again.

CHAPTER NINETEEN

The Team Game

————

The Scottish Open Championships at Thirlestane in August 2001 is a perfect illustration of the frenzied diversity that marked my belated gap year. Pippa won on Supreme Rock, leaving me to take the minor placings with Stunning, Springleaze Macaroo, Tam and Bob, who finished second, third, fourth and fifth respectively. Every month *Horse & Hound* identified a Balvennie Moment, presenting a bottle of the sponsor's whisky for an outstanding achievement. This was mine, a prize for trying so hard on so many horses and not winning!

There was no chance to rest; no sooner had we made the long trip back south than it was off to Northern Ireland for the international at Alfie and Vina Buller's Scarvagh Stud. I had four rides, and as I had to be back the following Monday to compete at Highclere before going to Burghley on the Tuesday, my mother had offered to help with the driving. It was a brilliant event and the horses went well, with Western Reef winning the two-star. Unfortunately, this came with the enjoyable problem of having to wait for the prize-giving, so suddenly we were cutting it very fine to make the flight home. Loaded with saddles and kit, Alfie drove Catherine, Joice and me at breakneck speed to the airport, leaving my mother, Malin and Posh to deal with getting the horses home. I changed in the car, only to discover that I had no footwear other than my riding boots, so barefoot I legged it to the check-in and we made the flight by seconds. I fell into bed at Well Cottage around midnight, but Jackie had everything sorted so we could set off with a new team of five to Highclere at six o'clock the next morning.

Predictably, back in Northern Ireland the horses missed their boat so my mother rerouted to stay the night with Jessica Harrington, a long-time friend and leading National Hunt trainer. Despite the last-minute notice, Jessie was happy to help, but the only problem was that all her stables were full. Undeterred, my mother found an empty paddock in the dark and turned the four horses out together. Posh and Malin were horrified at the prospect of their four precious charges surviving the night, but they needn't have worried as they all made it home the next day in one piece.

From Highclere it was on to Burghley, where Macaroo finished ninth and Bob thirteenth. Macaroo led the dressage but then lost out with a few time faults on the cross-country. His top-ten placing firmly established him as an exciting addition to my growing team of top horses. Bob's result was a major landmark in his career, his first clear at four-star level re-establishing my belief in him. Then it was on to Blenheim with Highland Lad and River Dragon, the daughter of Hirola, a hot, homebred, chestnut mare I had ridden in Pony Club when I was twelve. Highland Lad ended up a respectable fifteenth, but River Dragon was all set for her career high, doing the test of her life and going clear within the time cross-country. Unfortunately, she hit the last fence, bruising her stifle so badly that we had to pull her out, a real shame as she was lying fifth and the result would have done her credentials as a brood mare no end of good. As her dressage was too inconsistent for four-star, she competed at three-star level with Alicia before fulfilling her destiny as a Knowlton brood mare, producing some lovely foals that I will probably be too old to compete.

I always seem to have had issues with handbrakes. On one occasion, I was standing in a shop when I saw my car rolling down the road towards me. I watched transfixed as it turned into the kerb and came to a miraculous stop right outside. The next incident was potentially much, much worse. I was at Tidworth and a Swedish girl I had been training was also there. She'd loaded her horses on to the lorry to go home, only to discover that it wouldn't start. She asked me to help, so I took the handbrake off to try to jump-start it. It wouldn't move, so I went to find a tractor, only to turn around and see it trundling down the hill. We watched in horror as it found a clear path through two lines of parked lorries and impaled itself on a tree. The branches peeled back the roof like a can of sardines, leaving the horses out in the open, delighted by their new perspective on the world and miraculously unflustered.

Maybe I should have thought of these incidents when I parked behind Pippa on the ferry to Calais, the start of the road to Pau. Lorries are always chained down for the crossing, and the back ramps are left open so the horses get plenty of air. On arrival the ferry master ordered the unchaining in preparation for landing. Simple really, so how come my lorry was three-quarters of the way up Pippa's ramp when I came down to collect it? Yes, you guessed it. I'd left a lorry containing three of the most valuable event horses in England on a boat with the handbrake off. Worse still, the guy who did the unchaining had to sprint clear to avoid being squashed. It was a deeply embarrassing moment, and not one my team-mates have allowed me to forget.

Given Stunning's chequered career, I wasn't expecting to be in the team, but when Rodney Powell's horse went lame shortly before the competition, I joined Pippa, Jeanette Brakewell and Leslie Law. Tina Cook and Caroline Pratt, who was competing in her first European Championships, were selected as individuals. Before we left I was allowed to choose whether to take Stunning, an outside chance at this level, or Tam, who I didn't feel was quite ready. This was my first experience of the open, rider-friendly politics introduced by Yogi Breisner, when he became team manager in 1999, and backed by the chairman of selectors, Mandy Stibbe.

The team included a new training system, with Tracie Robinson on the flat and Kenneth Clawson, who had been brought on board as the show jumping trainer. Tracie is a wonderful enthusiast, passionate about what she does. Her background was with leading British dressage rider Carl Hester, but later she had trained Toddy in his last few seasons. She is a true team player and a great pair of eyes on the ground, especially in the final warm-up before a Championship test. Kenneth has been instrumental in the overall improvement of Team GB's show jumping; he's dedicated to the job and never misses a trick. With him, Yogi and Tracie in place, there could be no more excuses for underperformance.

In the end I opted for Stunning mainly because of his experience, but also because I wanted to save Tam for the World Equestrian Games in Jerez the following season. Stunning was a complicated horse. He was difficult to get to peak fitness because his muscles were prone to cramping or 'tying up' and he generally lacked confidence. Toddy often got a very good test out of him, but initially I struggled to find the right buttons. However, he improved slowly as he got less tense. After fairly good performances at Blenheim and Saumur, he did his best test at Pau, well in contention in sixth or seventh place. My preparation had been to work him little and often under Yogi and Tracie's supervision, getting him to relax without making him stiff, and it turned out well.

So far so good, but as the anchor man, I wasn't relishing the pressure. What on earth was I going to do if one of the other three came to grief? Jeanette sailed round first, but my worst fears were realised when Leslie and Shear H20 tripped coming out of the water and refused. When Pippa put in a brilliant clear round, the chips were down. If the team was to get a medal, Stunning would have to go well. Given that he's an ex-racehorse, I reckoned I could take the long routes at both the water complexes and still do the time, so I rolled my sleeves up and set out, determined to give it my best shot. Stunning certainly gave it his, flying round inside the time to take the individual silver position behind Pippa. We were ecstatic, particularly so the Apters, whose faith in him had never wavered. The enthusiastic French crowds sit very close to the show jumping at Pau, a disadvantage for Stunning who froze in the highly charged atmosphere. Show jumping has never been his strong point and he had two down, though it could easily have been more. Annoyingly I dropped to sixth, but the team – and Pippa – collected golds.

It was a big moment for Team Stunning, a credit to Jackie's management and to the Apters, who'd never had a horse represent Great Britain before. The selectors saw me as a team player rather than as an individual winner and they'd relied on Stunning to do well, so I was thrilled that we'd delivered and that our score had counted towards the gold medal. Most importantly, it was great to be back on the team again and Pippa, Leslie and Jeanette, who'd been together in Sydney, made me feel very welcome. There was a good spirit, all of us out to do our best individually, but very supportive of each other. By this time everyone expected Pippa to take gold, as she would have done in Sydney had she been in the individual competition, and Jeanette had established herself as an ultra-consistent performer. Leslie was on a roll, though he was always quick to put himself down.

With Tam waiting in the wings, I dared to hope this team would find a winning formula over the next few years, with Yogi providing the overall strategy. At this early stage, we were learning and respecting each other's foibles. We all know the risk we take whenever we ride across country and we react in different ways. I get sleepy. Pippa retreats into herself to focus, Leslie and Tina need company and Jeanette vanishes.

It was a fantastic end to an extraordinary season. I had pushed myself and my team very hard, but I had moved on from my divorce in the only way I knew how. I had proved to myself I could do it on my own and in fact was enjoying life more than ever. The 2001 season over, I took myself off to Australia for some time out. Three months earlier, Lucinda Green, supportive as ever, came to dinner at Well Cottage and the conversation predictably moved onto girls. 'Alice Plunkett is the perfect girl for you,' she announced firmly. 'Think about it and you'll see she's the obvious choice.' I replied that she was way out of my league, completely crazy and she wouldn't want to get involved with a boring divorced man. 'Don't dismiss it,' said Lucinda, and we left it at that. I ran into Alice before I left and we realised we'd be in Australia at the same time. 'We must get together,' we said, chatting politely about nothing and thinking it would never happen, not least because I'd been invited to compete in a three-day event in Adelaide while she was covering the Melbourne Cup for television.

As always my prime purpose was finding more horses, so I joined up with my good friend and agent, Sharon Ridgeway, a regular source of quality eventers. The first horse she found me was Coastal Ties, bought for me by Lady Kelvedon. On this occasion, Sharon and I were driving around together when I spotted a newspaper ad for an unbroken two-year-old Arab colt called All That Jazz. 'Perfect for M W,' I said half jokingly. 'You're an idiot,' said Sharon. 'We're in Australia remember, he could be two thousand miles away!' but when I read out the phone number she said, 'Oh my God, that's right here.' We dropped in to see him and I rang M W immediately, 'He's the most gorgeous-looking horse and he'll put some size onto your Arabs. He's cheap and even if he's useless you'll love looking at him.' I now wish I'd kept a leg in him because he's potentially an amazing horse and he's already taking his double duty, eventing with me and going home to the Guinnesses to cover mares, in his stride.

Away from horses I planned to join up with Ginny Loisel, a Kiwi friend who was going out with my great Belgian mate, Constantin Van Rijckevorsel (Tintin). The plan was for us to meet some other friends and join up with Alice when she wasn't working on television coverage of the Melbourne Cup. The Cup was an experience like no other. It really is 'The race that stops the nation'. Predictably, although she got us tickets for Flemington, we didn't see much of Alice. We met up with some of the English racing gang, headed by Andrew Balding, and hit the town. It now transpires that I thought Alice was interested in Andrew and Alice thought I was interested in Ginny, so at the end of a great night we went our separate ways, each privately dismissing the likelihood of a relationship.

CHAPTER TWENTY

Mission Accomplished

Alice's birthday is on 5 January, three days after mine, so we had excuses to keep in touch over the Christmas period. I had a party in London, which she couldn't come to, but I made sure I went to hers the next day. She put me between two gorgeous girls, Emma Ramsden and Chloe Gardener, but I failed to last the night and went home early, the worse for wear from the night before.

The next time I saw Alice she was in Florence Nightingale mode after I dislocated my collarbone in a fall off a young horse. Her work as a racing journalist meant she often went to Newmarket and her route took her past Well Cottage, so she dropped in during my convalescence. On one occasion the conversation turned on to my New Year's resolutions. Mine was obviously to win more prizes and jump more jumps, while hers was to kiss more frogs and to have no more thunderbolt city experiences. After two or three visits she invited me to supper in her cottage, which was just twenty minutes away.

The rest is history. I was slow off the mark and it took a lot of hints for me to realise that she might be interested in me; after all, she does flirt with all men. 'Was I a frog then?' I asked some time later. I didn't get an answer, but I knew this wasn't going to be a casual fling. As good friends we didn't need to take the risk of having a relationship if there wasn't a good reason.

By chance, we had both been asked to go on the same ski trip in a group with Tintin, Ginny Loisel, Piia Pantsu and her partner Fred, Dan Jocelyn, Tanya Cleverly, Blyth Tait and Paul O'Brien. I had to cry off at the last moment due to my collarbone. Who did they ask to replace me? Ginny's best friend, Wiggy. They left two days later, Alice vaguely panicking and desperate to keep our early relationship under wraps for a bit longer. Bizarrely, Wiggy spent some time on the holiday trying to convince Alice she'd be perfect for me.

Alice lives her life at a speed which makes anyone else's look motionless. She is the only woman to have completed both Aintree and Badminton, a real feather in her cap and a typically daredevil Plunkett achievement. She was brought up to pack as much as possible into every day, just as I was. We have similar values relating to hard work and achievement. Like me she went to university to carry on riding and to defer decisions about her future. She studied Eastern Religion at Bristol, putting in the minimum of hours to get her degree and combining her studies with eventing and racing. She started point-to-pointing in her gap year and rode eight winners, but her highlight came on the appropriately named Bold King's Hussar in the Foxhunter's Chase at Aintree. The horse was bred by her grandfather, who had written in his will that he imagined its white face landing over Becher's. And it did, with Alice in the saddle.

She started eventing in the Pony Club, and was a budding star through junior and young riders, competing in the European Championships in Compiegne. She secured a lucrative sponsorship deal with the clothing company, Racing Green, so she was able to make it her business after university. At her first Burghley, in 1999, she was held on the course for ages due to Simon Long's accident, so she pulled up. The next spring she jumped clear round Badminton, but her result gave her pause for thought. 'If I'm really pleased with just going clear then it must be time to give up.' A week on her own on Pabbay, an island in the Outer Hebrides, crystallised her decision to put her horses on the market and not to renew her sponsorship deal.

If she wasn't going to make it to the top as an event rider, she felt she'd be better off developing her budding career as a racing journalist. She can be very self-deprecating, very hard on herself at times, dwelling excessively on her mistakes. In eventing it's important to move on when things go wrong. If you spend too much time on introspective analysis the only way is down. When she can fit it in, Alice still jumps and schools the horses and she's still furious if she gets it wrong. Eventing is a tough sport for an ambitious person and Alice lacked the confidence she might have developed had she had a really good horse.

She had dipped her toe into journalism while still riding, working regularly for the Racing Channel and things went better and better once she focused on it full time. Within the year she had secured the contract to co-present the World Racing Series, travelling to the twelve $1,000,000 races around the globe. She was taken on by Channel Four to host their lunchtime racing show and moved on from there to the *Morning Line*, their flagship Saturday programme. She has definitely found her niche there, keeping the likes of John McCririck, who quickly dubbed her 'The Saucy Minx', and John Francome under control.

At thirty-two, I saw myself as a miserable and cynical old divorcee, not a label I'd ever imagined I'd have, but one that made me aware that I was second-hand goods, unlikely to be seen as a dream ticket by any prospective parents-in-law. If the Plunketts felt that way, they certainly never gave any hint of it and I felt totally at home with them from the start. Alice and I had parallel track childhoods, going to school in London during the week – in her case the French Lycée – and spending the weekends in the country. She was the eldest of three daughters, followed by Eloise and Katie. David and Celia had inherited their love of horses from their own parents and they hunted, point-to-pointed and rode in team chases with great passion and success. The children were brought up in a free and easy way with horses as the main focus: like me, Alice had a grey pony called Minnie. Her greatest childhood triumph came on The Boss Man at the Pony Club Dressage Championships when she was fourteen and I was eighteen. It was a victory for her team over mine and she has the picture to prove it, she with her prize rug, and me with my best boy trophy.

At this stage I was definitely not looking for another wife. I was enjoying my freedom and had no intention of settling down too soon. I was on an emotional rollercoaster, not sure how I'd be feeling from one day to the next. Was I still on the rebound? This question tormented me, because I didn't want to enter into a relationship with Alice and then hurt her if we weren't thinking along the same lines. The more I got to know her the more I admired her. Katie, her little sister, had died from leukaemia when she was sixteen in 1996, so Alice had had to come to terms with tragedy when she was barely out of her teens. Shortly before we got together, Eloise was diagnosed with a malignant melanoma, yet Alice was always on good form, the life and soul of any situation, with loads of energy and enthusiasm. How she did it I really don't know, but she did it with great courage.

Right from the start my feelings for Alice were totally different from any I'd previously experienced. Of course, I was ten yeas older and more mature, but I noticed straight away how much we laughed. Teaching me to laugh at myself is one of the best things Alice has done for me. With her, I was relaxed and comfortable. We enjoy winding each other up, but we have mutual respect for each other.

As our relationship developed during 2002 I discovered how much easier life can be when you find your soul mate. With Alice I enjoyed being more social. I have a few very good friends and Alice enthusiastically added them to the hundreds she had already. She never finds it an effort to entertain or go out. There are occasions when I try to revert and take the easy option and stay in. After a busy day with the horses I am usually exhausted, but when we get out we have a great time.

By hook or by crook, I was determined to be in Dorset by the end of 2002. My cousin Anthony had been waiting for me to move for ages. At times he must have despaired at my procrastination, though it turned out to be time well spent. I landed on my feet when I found a suitable yard at Fontmel Parva, just three miles from Hinton St Mary, where Anthony lives. It was owned by Henry Woodruff, the son-in-law of Ben Walden, who owned Springleaze Macaroo. I'd been at Stratton Audley for nine years and I was still very comfortable there, so leaving would be a massive upheaval. However, I knew the time had come. Ben put in a huge amount of work to get the stables and accommodation ready for us. We agreed to move in May, so he only had a few months to sort the place out. He knew what we had at Stratton Audley and did his best to reproduce the essentials.

I'd made my decision to go to Dorset before Alice and I got together and I had to go, with or without her – at that stage I dared not hope it would be with her. She was characteristically enthusiastic about it, coming with me for recces and meetings whenever she was free. We were driving down one day when she got a phone call from Eloise to say that the chemo she'd had for her cancer hadn't worked and that there was nothing more the doctors could do. The two sisters were very close and before that phone call there'd been some hope, but now we were totally distraught.

Eloise was twenty-seven, an engineer with a fantastic career and a wonderful boyfriend in Andy Fleming. She had loads of friends and everything to live for. Her illness came out of nowhere, a single mole she'd had removed turned into rampant melanoma. She deteriorated very quickly through the summer of 2002 and died on 24 July. Alice, Andy and her parents lived through a desperate time, nursing her at home right until the end. I tried to be there for Alice, but I also knew I had to give her space to be with Eloise when she needed to be. Seeing how bravely they all coped gave me huge respect for the Plunkett family, but it made me wonder if I was the right person to help Alice at such a time.

She would never have come to Dorset when Eloise was still alive and I would never have suggested it. Even after Eloise's death, I assumed Alice would stay in Oxfordshire where she'd always lived and that we would be spending most of our time charging up and down the A303. She has a close attachment to the area, a huge local network of supportive friends and it's a much more convenient base for racecourses all over the country. The last thing I wanted was to ask her to come with me, forcing an answer that might be no, so I decided to keep quiet and see how things worked out. Luckily Alice decided herself, saying, with characteristic enthusiasm, that she was determined to come. I knew leaving her parents and mates at such a vulnerable time was a big sacrifice, but we were committed to each other now and we'd become incredibly close in highly emotional circumstances, so it was an opportunity to put down our roots together.

We moved into a lovely stone farmhouse in the middle of the village and Alice made sure it was decorated and furnished when we arrived on 1 December. I was unbelievably lucky to have her with me. She is a brilliant homemaker and responded to the warm welcome we received by making friends with everyone she met. Mean as I am, I refused to hire a removal company, so we transported everything from Stratton Audley, Well Cottage and Alice's cottage in horseboxes. After some understandable hesitation, Jackie agreed to come with me, along with Alex Van Tuyll, the groom who'd joined the team at the end of 2001. They worked like slaves with Tim Jennings, my maintenance man, to organise fifteen lorry loads of horses, tack and equipment for delivery at the new yard. Mission accomplished, I was in Dorset at last.

CHAPTER TWENTY-ONE

On Top of the World

I know now that 2002 was my watershed year, the division between my past disappointments and my present happiness. By the end of it, I had a new home, a new partner and a new record: the first British rider to head the world rankings. In most sports, that would put your name up in lights, but not in eventing. The FEI used to make a big thing of it, with Land Rover giving a worthwhile five-figure prize to the winner, but nowadays the reward is a little cup and a magnum of champagne presented at an ERA dinner.

The FEI spends endless time trying to devise a fair scoring system, as yet without success. Four-star events count for much more than three-star ones, but they're easier to win in, say, America because there are fewer entries. As a result the world rankings are biased in favour of riders based on the other side of the world, so a leading eventing nation like Britain is very poorly represented on the roll of honour. Nevertheless, my victory was a welcome boost for my owners and sponsors.

With a quartet of potential four-star winners in my string, more than I'd ever had before, I started my spring campaign with cautious optimism. My first target was Lexington in Kentucky, America's premier three-day event. The competition was sponsored by Rolex and they were introducing a $250,000 prize for any rider who could win Kentucky, Badminton and Burghley back to back. In eventing terms, that's serious money, so I took Springleaze Macaroo and Stunning to Kentucky, with Tam and Bob earmarked for Badminton two weeks later.

Kentucky comes the week before Badminton in the calendar adding to the huge logistical challenge of flying fit competition horses across the Atlantic ready to land and perform at the highest level. The flight itself is eight hours but there is a lot that goes with it that makes the journey a marathon. The horses have to leave home at least five or six hours before they're due to fly to allow time for all the necessary paperwork at the airport. It is amazing how well they travel in the modified cargo planes, but there is always a vet on hand for any emergency. Once landed they have to be put in quarantine, standing in a stable for thirty-six hours before a further sixteen-hour road trip to the Kentucky Horse Park. Jackie accompanied the two boys on their journey and thankfully everything went as well as we could have hoped with the horses arriving in good shape.

Macaroo led the dressage, ahead of Kim Vinoski (now Severson) and Winsome Adante, with Stunning well in touch. Stunning was my first ride and he powered round the cross-country within the time on a glorious morning, but by the time Macaroo was due to go, a lunchtime deluge had turned what had been perfect going into a bottomless bog. When he had sixteen time faults on the steeplechase I wanted to withdraw him, but it was not that simple. We were there thanks in no inconsiderable way to Lottery funding, so to withdraw without a serious reason could well be looked upon as bad form. Even so, I didn't want to put unnecessary mileage on him when his chance had gone and, after some discussion, Yogi agreed with me, but it was a miserable experience for the owners, who'd flown over to see him. Then again, it could have been worse, because at best he would have incurred another twenty time penalties on the cross-country and in the conditions there was an increased risk of injury.

Stunning was in second place behind Winsome Andante overnight, but his shoe had come off during his round, aggravating a corn problem, so it was over to Jackie and Jenny Hall, the team vet who'd replaced Andy Bathe, to do their best to get him sound for the vet's inspection. They achieved this on hard ground with the help of a special shoe which covered two-thirds of his foot, but he wasn't as comfortable on the soft so he jumped even more economically than usual, getting worse and worse the further he went. I'd been carrying a niggling groin strain throughout the spring, but without any great anxiety because it would warm up and the pain would go away once I was in the saddle. That all changed during Stunning's round. He was never a smooth jumper and he would often twist his body in the air. This action rotated my pelvis, something I could usually deal with, but on this occasion I finished in agony. Miraculously, he only knocked two fences down to finish fourth, but I was in so much pain I couldn't canter the lap of honour. At that point I realised that riding at Badminton the next week was going to be difficult, potentially jeopardising Tam's World Games prospects.

On the plane home I grabbed a line of seats and slept throughout the flight, but there was no improvement when I woke up. I could walk and pick my leg up, but I had no inward strength, which was a major concern. My physio was going to have to work a miracle if I was going to be able to ride at Badminton, which was due to start in three days. The physio diagnosed a strained groin ligament, an injury I'd always thought overrated until I had it myself. For the first time I sympathised with injured footballers.

Having not ridden Tam and Bob for a week, it was crucial that I should get some training in on Monday and Tuesday. On Monday, I physically couldn't sit on a horse and, on Tuesday, I managed to ride at the walk. Realising that no amount of physio was going to get me to Badminton, I went to see the team doctor Peter Whitehead in Gloucester. It was now Wednesday and I needed to be able to ride properly for Bob's dressage in twenty-four hours' time. I also had to be able to work Tam properly if he was to perform at all respectably on Friday. With the help of injections into the ligament I was able to ride through the pain and I survived the two days of dressage. On Friday night, the pain worsened and I accepted that I wouldn't be able to start both horses on Saturday.

Exit Bob, who was lying twelfth, leaving the way clear for Tam, who was my more realistic World Championship horse. After more injections on Saturday morning, I trussed myself up in a vetwrap figure-of-eight bandage through the crotch, Roman-warrior style and completed the roads and tracks and the steeplechase without mishap. By the time I got to the ten-minute box, my makeshift wrapping had worked loose, so I pulled down my breeches while Alice rebandaged me in front of rows of curious spectators. Normally the Badminton ten-minute box is a very tense and serious time. I was so focused on getting my bandage sorted that I lost all self-consciousness about undressing there until Pippa and all the other riders waiting to go started laughing their heads off at what was going on. No doubt they wondered what kind of treatment I was having, but when I set off, still in agony, it turned out to be the least nerve-racking Badminton cross-country I've ever ridden. It was Tam's first four-star, yet I was more worried about myself, being prepared to stop at any stage especially if I felt I was damaging him by sitting crooked on his back. With no power in my right leg, I could only point him at the jumps and pray. I was grateful for every one he cleared, counting them off, not worrying about the time and just calculating how many more drops I had to survive. Not many horses would carry a lopsided rider with one functioning leg round the most challenging track in the world, but Tam didn't care, galloping effortlessly without a single false stride.

Clear within the time, he moved up to third, behind Pippa on Supreme Rock and Andrew Hoy on Darien Powers, who later dropped down in the show jumping. For some reason the pain was more manageable on the Sunday, and I was able to run him up in front of the vets and jump the faultless round that took us into second place. It would have been nice if Supreme Rock had provided me with a fairytale ending by knocking a couple down, but he had a good start in the dressage and Pippa thoroughly deserved her win. On the plus side, I now knew I had a true champion. He is so quick and agile and he travels so easily within himself that I often wish the four-star courses were that bit harder to test his rivals to the limit. I've had great horses, like Chaka and Cosmo, but Tam is in a class of his own. He's never been under pressure and he's never used all his gears: five years later, I've come to believe he never will.

After Badminton, I took a month off to get my ligament sorted out, resuming at Bramham on Highland Lad – Monty. If I'd required a horse to test my recuperation to the limit, he was the one to choose. When his owner, Carol Hudson, wanted an eventer, she spotted a picture of Mary King's Star Appeal on the wall at Goresbridge Sales in Ireland and decided she was going to buy one like that. She duly did. Monty was a boisterous brute, talented but very difficult, with zero respect for anyone, and I'd be lying if I said I bonded with him, yet he did the job at Bramham, coming sixth in his first three-star, with my second ride, Judy Skinner's Just a Sovereign, in eighth.

Two months later, Monty was about 500–1 to win Burghley, yet he did, one of my greatest flukes ever. He'd never won a major event and he wasn't ready for this one, so I had no intimation of success. If I had, it wouldn't have survived for long because he behaved like a lunatic from the moment we arrived, galloping sideways, sweating and jumping around like an over-excited two-year-old racehorse. Tails flapping on his back always sent him berserk, so I tried to get him used to them by wearing them whenever I rode out in the park. Daisy Dick, a fellow competitor, still laughs at the memory of me, coat-tails flying, trying to calm a runaway bay horse covered in white foamy sweat as he charged towards her two hours before our test.

Heading back to get ready, I was so frustrated that I set him a tongue-in-cheek challenge, 'If you can walk back to your stable from here on a loose rein without jogging for a single stride, you'll win.' This challenge had a one in a million chance of success, but when I dropped my reins, he walked every step of the way. I then forgot about the challenge, only recalling it later when it became significant. Meanwhile, Carol and her husband, David, had been checking out the course. 'I can see Monty's name on a plaque listing previous winners at the end of the Hall of Fame avenue,' said David firmly. I looked at him curiously, wondering if he was having a laugh, but he wasn't joking. Then again, he wasn't a horse person, so I forgave his optimism. Omens, omens? At the time, I thought no more of it, but later it all seemed a little spooky.

Despite his preparations, Monty delivered the test of his life, finishing a couple of marks ahead of Bob in a fairly competitive position. It wouldn't have been good enough if the cross-country hadn't caused a lot of trouble, but Monty delivered where others failed. Although he was a really good jumper, I was concerned about his speed and stamina at this level, but he kept going, ending the day with a couple of time faults in fourth place, with Bob one place behind. Frustratingly, Bob knocked two show jumps on Sunday, dropping to seventh, but Monty was clear. Polly Stockton, who was in the lead, had one down on Word for Word, a horse that didn't have the best show jumping record. Leslie, on Shear l'Eau, held it together almost to the end, but unbelievably he hit the last fence and victory was ours, leaving Alice, Alex and me in total shock. My second four-star win had come totally out of the blue and even now I can't quite believe the horse pulled it off.

With the World Championships in Jerez a fortnight away, I just had time to take Ballincoola, nicknamed Max, to the three-star competition at Blenheim before I left for Spain. I'd persuaded Judy Skinner to buy him in the spring of 2002 after Andrew Hazeltine had produced him to intermediate level. Judy wanted a horse to run with Just a Sovereign and I'd been looking for one for ages, but Max wasn't an obvious choice. He's an Irish worrier, a plain, ordinary chestnut with average dressage ability, but he had an incredible jump. It was a difficult call for me, but he was eight years old, ready to go and relatively inexpensive, so he was at a useful stage. Judy was away when I went to try him and, as usual, the sellers had people queuing up for him, so we had to make a quick decision. I knew she wouldn't love Max at first sight, but I had a good gut feeling about him.

She agreed to buy him, but when she came to Gatcombe two weeks later to watch him, her heart sank through her boots. What was she doing with this string-necked hunter? It didn't help that he's a pretty unfriendly and suspicious character, as Irish horses often are. 'He looks better under saddle,' I said hopefully. That was true, but even after he did a reasonable test and jumped two clear rounds, she wasn't convinced. She warmed to him a bit when he won Burgie, his first two-star, on his dressage score, but what I hadn't realised was how much it would take to raise his flatwork to the standard required for higher level competition. He's a sensitive horse, hot-headed, tense and mentally complex and he was not keen to improve.

He wasn't really ready for Blenheim, but I didn't want to do another two-star, so we went for it. His test was pretty average, with a mark in the low sixties, and he jumped round the cross-country with a couple of time faults, finishing fourteenth. Job done, not inspiringly, but efficiently enough; I'd learned more about him and Max gained some good experience.

After Blenheim, I realised I couldn't make head or tail of his dressage and I came to believe I never would, so I persuaded Judy to send him to Lizzie Murray to have a go. As the daughter of Jennie Loriston-Clark, a stalwart of the British dressage team, Lizzie has an incredible dressage talent and several top riders send her their more difficult charges. At the start she was so conservative and guarded in her assessment that we weren't sure she could see any light at the end of the tunnel, but gradually she made an impact and Max now goes to her regularly in the winter to work on his dressage.

With the team riders unchanged from the victorious expedition to Pau the year before, I arrived in Jerez, the sherry capital in the south of Spain, for my first World Championships in a buoyant mood. Team GB was undoubtedly one of the favourites to take gold and Jerez is a city that celebrates the horse. Every May, a huge festival takes over with the regional Andalusian breed paraded in their hundreds through the centre ridden by women dressed in colourful flamenco dresses. That colour and enthusiasm rubbed off on the Games with the opening ceremony proudly showing off the tradition and variety of horses in that region.

The setting wasn't ideal for the three-day event. It was in the middle of town, with the cross-country a good half an hour drive away. The temperatures were in the mid-thirties and the facilities were limited but none of this fazed us like it had in Atlanta, as we had a hierarchy in place that believed we could win.

Tam performed fairly well in the dressage, ending up seventh or eighth. Walking the cross-country course I was encouraged as it was clear this was not going to be a dressage competition. It was built by Mike Tucker and was tough, but the going was inconsistent, having been sewn from scratch just a few years earlier in very shallow soil. The Spaniards watered heavily in an attempt to improve it, but succeeded only in making it green and very slippery.

By the time I went as anchorman, Jeanette had done a good clear, but unbelievably both Pippa and Leslie each had a stop which left it up to me to put the team in a medal-winning position. Yogi warned me about the bogey combination at the first water, but left me to make my own decision as to how to tackle it. I approached the log too fast, landed on a bank that was now so loose it was like a moving carpet and slipped. Tam then jumped down into the water totally off balance, tripped up on to the bank and refused at the house at the top. Another refusal and the team ended the cross-country in a dispiriting fourth place.

Tina Cook and Polly Stockton, the individual riders, also had a competition to forget, so morale was at rock bottom. The next day we were rooting for Jeanette, still in the hunt for individual honours, and Yogi did his best to convince us that it was not over yet – but it was hard to believe we had any chance of retrieving a team medal. Tam did a brilliant clear on Sunday, Jeanette was also faultless and Pippa had one down, so the team miraculously moved up to bronze position behind the French and Jeanette took individual silver, her best-ever result. By battling to the end, we salvaged our Olympic qualification, but Jerez has to go down as a lost opportunity. With the exception of Jeanette, we had not performed to our best, and as we headed home we felt we had let everyone down.

As the season wound down in Britain, I made two final continental forays, finishing fourth with Stunning at Boekelo and introducing Coastal Ties and Wallow to three-star competition at Pau before our focus turned to the long-awaited move to Dorset.

CHAPTER TWENTY-TWO

Business Basics

I had been looking forward to going to Dorset, but such a major change was bound to be disruptive and worrying. In the end it worked and moving with Alice, with her inexhaustible energy and enthusiasm, made it exciting. It was our first place together and the chance to create a future. Both my grandfathers rode in point-to-points and if I hadn't taken up eventing, I could well have got into training. Adding a racing element was always a priority, especially given Alice's background. The downside of racing, as far as I'm concerned, is that there's nothing you can do to influence the outcome once the jockey's in the saddle. If I get it wrong in a competition, it's my fault, but in a race, it might be someone else's. I find that hard to come to terms with, though I'll certainly have to if we move into racing full time when I retire from eventing.

Our rented yard at Fontmell Parva worked well from the start but it was always our long-term plan to design our own yard on the farm at Hinton. A traditional brick yard with outdoor stables might have been ideal, but the cost was prohibitive, roughly three times as much as a multi-purpose unit under one roof. The modern system creates a compact workspace, making it easier to look after the horses, so our main challenge was to simulate an outdoor yard in an inside building. We got the green light for the stables fairly easily, but the planners baulked at the relatively tiny on-site accommodation, two Finnish pre-fabricated wooden chalets, one for Jackie and one for the pupils. The only way we could get permission was to agree that we would take them down if we stopped trading.

Patrick Hoare, who I had met through Alice, masterminded the project. Paddy helped us design the complex, rationalising our sometimes far-fetched ideas. He is a good draughtsman, with a keen eye for detail, and he did the initial designs himself before the architect did the fine-tuning. Inevitably there were a few complaints when we put in our planning application, but overall we were welcomed warmly into the village.

Our intention was to construct a unique eventing establishment, two blocks of twelve boxes, divided by a tack room, a drying room, a shoeing area and a garage for the lorry. For maximum flexibility, the boxes could also be let in separate blocks of six. We set up a trust with Anthony to finance the stables, but eventing economics are very individual. My hope is to compete at least until the London Olympics in 2012, and then move on to train racehorses or I might become more involved in teaching, taking pupils with their horses for training. If we opt for racing, we might need to expand, but I don't want to go into it in the all-consuming way I'm in eventing. We'd be more than happy with thirty horses in training which in racing terms is a very modest number.

Initially we were adamant we didn't need an indoor school as well as an outdoor one but we eventually decided the extra expense was worth it. That was a good call because it has already been invaluable for teaching in winter months months and for loose schooling. We also put in a horse walker and a half-mile all-weather gallop from the riverbank to the top of the hill.

At the moment, racing is a hobby, restricted to a few point-to-pointers, whereas Fox-Pitt Eventing pays its way. I was incredibly lucky to find Hackett at a time I needed the security that comes with a sponsor. Over the eleven years we worked together, the deal worked well for both of us but, by 2003, they felt they'd exhausted my potential and pulled out to employ Jonny Wilkinson in the aftermath of his Rugby World Cup triumph. I had no chance in that competition; it was a good commercial decision on their part and our association ended amicably.

Rather than put all my eggs in one basket, I now aim to have five major sponsors plus several smaller product endorsements. The products are diverse, lawn mowers and quad bikes, stables, probiotic diet supplements and vibrating massage blankets as well as clothes. Clinics and lecture demos are another source of income. I will do more individual teaching in time, but it's riding horses that gets me up in the morning and they are my priority. I also buy and sell the odd horse, but I am a hopeless dealer and hate selling. Pippa concentrates on a string of about twelve, but I have double that number, which means I keep my options open at every level from novice to advanced.

My father's financial acumen comes naturally to him, but I've had to learn that you can only maximise your potential if you know your value. He gave me an allowance until I left university at the age of twenty-three, but I'm so frugal, I saved most of it. My early sponsorship money from Smirnoff and Hackett was absorbed into the Knowlton horse pool. We had our own stables, fields, facilities and forage, so it was hard to appreciate what the real cost was.

The first time I managed my own finances was when Wiggy and I moved to the Channers, but again we didn't have to pay for accommodation and there were stables and a field we could use. As I didn't have to give the Hackett cheque to my mother, I felt much richer, but the reality was that I had the money to run one horse and develop the business. Jackie was paid for, but there was no income until Chaka came. I remember feeling massively responsible as I wrote out my first invoices by hand in one of those little booklets with carbons, but I always felt it would work out okay, provided we knuckled down. The rent for Stratton Audley Park Stud was daunting at first, but I had the naivety and optimism of youth, plus an inbuilt ability not to worry about anything until I had to, so the possibility that it could be a disaster never crossed my mind.

I knew I would have to earn a proper living one day, and I was aware that competing wasn't the easiest way to do it. If you want to get to the top, riding has to be all consuming rather than a sideline and, even if you are good, eventing provides little in the way of income.

Livery is now a large part of my turnover and I've been lucky to find ten or twelve loyal enthusiastic owners with the same goals. Veronica and Nikko Ward were my first owners, then Michael Turner, who owned Chaka, got me off to a good start, reinforcing my belief in plain speaking. I had to put myself in the marketplace when Chaka retired, initially with Frank Andrew, who owned Cosmo, and Monica Hunt, who bought Mostly Mischief for me to ride. I looked at my fellow competitors and saw how they came and went, depending on the quality of their horses. As there are only so many good eventers, I had to make it clear I was available and keen.

I always present an open picture of the horses I have and the priorities I give them, with newcomers and youngsters giving way to advanced horses. As both trainer and rider, I never have much spare time, but the owners are part of the team, good friends who I enjoy keeping informed. I dread the inevitable competitiveness between them, but the best horses always rise to the top, so the decisions are usually made for us.

Over the years, I've built up a rapport with people who love eventing, for example Judy Skinner, who is on the same wavelength as me, and Paul Ridgeon, one of my early patrons. George and Jayne Apter have similar dedication, but it took a while to get them in my corner. When they were looking for a new rider to replace Robert Lemieux on a horse called Kayem, they asked Owen Moore and me to try him. Owen got the nod, but when he injured himself, the horse went to Mark Todd. George and Jayne had fun with Mark, so they bought Stunning for him to ride at the Sydney Olympics, hoping that his swansong would bring them a gold medal. By the time they offered Stunning to me, he had baggage and I thought I'd be unlikely to win anything major with him – how wrong I was! However, I knew I'd be crazy to turn down such great owners.

The next three-day event of the season was Le Lion d'Angers where I was looking forward to riding a new exciting horse called Idalgo (Frog). The Apters had bought Idalgo as an up and coming prospect. He'd been produced by the leading French rider Nicolas Touzaint and was presented to me by an agent as a horse Nicolas would like to keep, but had to sell because none of his owners would buy him. He is the most amazing-looking animal, 17.1hh and athletic, though in reality he is physically weak. As a seven-year-old, he'd been fast-tracked by his owner, then sent to Nicolas so that he could be sold on. He was amenable when I tried him in a calm environment, so I thought I'd find the right buttons and learn to ride him.

By the time I got him home, he had fire coming out of his nostrils. However, he settled down by the autumn enough to finish fifth in the seven-year-old championships at Le Lion d'Angers in France. There he certainly caught a lot of people's eyes and for the first time showed me the true star potential he has.

With eventing and racing, we have a lot going on and are very often away. I am very lucky to have Jackie still at the helm after thirteen years and now Alex Van Tuyll as a very able second in command. They each have their own strengths, but they combine to run the yard to perfection, not always an easy task for two ambitious, successful people. There's a certain amount of banter between them, but they appreciate that the job would be too much for one person. Ultimately the buck stops with Jackie. She always travels with Tam and Alex with Max, but otherwise they take it in turns to go to events, the upside of a sometimes very tough job.

Working with horses is very hard on the body and leaves very little time for anything else so you've got to love it to stick with it. Jackie and Alex are as ambitious for the horses as I am and as disappointed when things go wrong. Alice always jokes about the way Jackie and I bicker and wind each other up, just like an old married couple. We're so much on the same wavelength that we often open our mouths and the same thing comes out. That can be good, but sometimes we get our wires crossed by assuming we've read each other's minds rather than spelling out what needs to be done. It would be nightmare without them – they are invaluable.

I also have a back-up rider, Ibby Macpherson, and three working pupils who come for between six months and a year to learn all aspects of eventing. Before we take them on, they are always invited on a two-week trial to see how they fit in. It's difficult to find enthusiastic youngsters who are keen to learn and prepared to work hard in return. Some think they should be walking in Jackie or Alex's shoes within a week. Others are under the illusion that they are the next Mark Todd. Nevertheless, we've had wonderful people from all over the world who over the years have been a great part of the team in their own different ways. If only I could persuade Jackie to write a book about her experiences, what tales she could tell.

CHAPTER TWENTY-THREE

Win Some, Lose Some

With plans in the pipeline and horses in the yard, we prepared for our first season in Fontmell Parva. We were buoyed up by the feeling of anticipation that comes with a clean break and a new start but, after nine years near Bicester, ideally located in the centre of the motorway system, I was worried about the logistics of getting to the events and how the extra hours on the road would affect the horses. The only way of driving out of Dorset is to leave huge amounts of time, something I'm not very good at, but I learned to cope and event horses are well travelled from a young age, so it didn't affect them. We enlarged some of the stables at Fontmell Parva, bought a new horse walker and improved the arena, but the greatest drawback was using gallops at Amesbury, a five-hour round trip we sometimes had to make three or four times a week.

I took no chances with my advanced horses, ferrying them to Newmarket to see Andy Bathe as and when needed, and paying Sam Head, our faithful farrier, to come down to shoe them. It was all crazily impractical, expensive and time-consuming, but in the period of transition, I needed to stay with the people I had confidence in. I'm a great believer in physiotherapy, so Amanda Sutton was another key member of the team, making sure the horses – the real athletes in eventing – were on top of their game when it mattered.

With six advanced contenders in the yard, the vibes were good. Bob was heading for Kentucky, Tam and Highland Lad for Badminton and Ballincoola (Max) for Bramham, with Coastal Ties and Wallow on track for Saumur. After a good win in the advanced class at Weston Park, I had high hopes for Bob on his first transatlantic expedition, especially when he was second behind Pippa and Primmore's Pride after dressage. He went brilliantly cross-country, but Primmore's Pride held on to his lead.

Unusually he clocked up a few time faults in the show jumping and ended on exactly the same score as Polly Stockton, emerging as the winner only because he was closer to the optimum cross-country time. If Bob had jumped clear, he would have won. A bitter pill for me because I was to blame for the mistake that put him down to third. I vividly remember letting him flatten towards a simple parallel, something Tam would have sorted for himself, but Bob couldn't. It was frustrating because he jumped well and I felt he deserved to win a four-star event. A lot of people don't share that view but, on his day, he is a four-star horse.

Badminton dawned clear, cold and blustery, conditions designed to reduce Highland Lad's dressage from Burghley winner to riding club also-ran. I'd tried to calm him throughout his spring preparation but without much success. Carol Hudson is a very hands-on owner and is devoted to Monty, but she's a small lady and he's a massive brute of a horse. In racing, the owners give their horses a quick pat as they leave the parade ring, but in eventing, some like to be more hands-on. Like children who play up in front of their parents, horses often behave better when they're outside their comfort zone. For Monty, seeing Carol meant running riot and that's exactly what he did. I knew I'd somehow got away with it at Burghley but at Badminton Monty reverted to his old ways. refusing to settle at all.

Tam provided his customary mixture of brilliance with some freestyle, so I suppose sixth could have been worse. Pippa and Supreme Rock were well in the lead, but at least we were in touch. By Saturday, the gale had been replaced by a downpour, a horrible day that suggested trouble ahead. Nor was it long in revealing itself. When we took the horses out in the morning, Tam was lame. He'd banged his splint and there was a lot of soreness where it aggravated the suspensory ligament. There was no way I could run him, but I couldn't withdraw him until I'd told M W.

As was her custom on Tam's big days, she'd gone AWOL and she wasn't answering her mobile, which left me in a bit of a dilemma as I set off on Monty. I hadn't been able to see the point in running him cross-country from such an uncompetitive position, but the Hudsons were determined he should, saying that he was only ten and Badminton would set us up for a brilliant future together. He started out very well, but the further we went in the mud, the more his lack of quality told. His stride got longer and longer until he was almost impossible to do anything with in front of a fence, sprawling all over the place. By the time we got to the lake, a slippery downhill take-off into a long bounce, he was running on empty. As I couldn't influence his approach, he hit the first rail chest high and slithered over the second with his legs vertically above him and me clinging on for dear life. He threw himself into the water from an impossible position, but somehow managed to stand up and put in three curving strides to the next combination, coming into the final arrowhead at forty-five degrees showing why he was a four-star horse. Although I had no reins, he jumped it as if it was a Pony Club fence, his immense bravery counterbalanced by a total lack of brain.

'Why on earth am I riding him?' I asked myself, even as I patted him to thank him for saving my bacon. He finished very tired with eight time faults, then turned into a raging bull as he tipped over the edge from mania to full nervous breakdown. After three of us had manhandled him back to the stable, he raced round for a hour, refusing to eat or drink and trying to crush Alex against the wall whenever she went in. The next day he had one down in the show jumping and finished a mediocre twenty-second. We let him eat grass for an hour afterwards to calm him down and the vets gave him tranquillisers so he'd be happier for his return to the Hudsons' yard.

Carol had already decided to take him home after Badminton, but I was expecting him back for the autumn season so I was unimpressed when she rang two weeks later to say he wouldn't be coming. If she'd been up front with me before the Badminton cross-country, I'd never have agreed to ride him, as she knew very well, and I felt it was wrong of her to pressurise me under false pretences, especially in such testing conditions. As it happened, I wasn't too sad to see the back of Monty.

Meanwhile, Pippa had set the season alight by winning Badminton on Supreme Rock by a single point over Finland's Piia Pantsu and Karuso. Her back-to-back victories in four-star events set her up for the Rolex Challenge, meaning that she'd win the $250,000 prize if she could complete the treble at Burghley. Supreme Rock was a very impressive, trainable horse, but his jumping technique was famously average and not many riders would have done as well with him as Pippa did. At the start of his career he was apt to run out cross-country and he'd often knock two or three show jumps, but Pippa and her husband, William Funnell, gradually taught him to go a bit higher. Even so, he regularly had one down, but with such good dressage, he could usually afford to.

It's never great to tell an owner her horse is lame when it's lying sixth at Badminton, but M W understands the eventing game and she takes the knocks in a very pragmatic way. She was relieved we'd noticed before the start and was happy to put Tam away for the rest of the year so as to give him the best possible shot at the 2004 Olympics. He went home for his holiday, a decision that nearly ended in disaster when the hunt went through their property and Tam escaped through an open gate. He was found sometime later in a neighbouring field grazing peacefully, but the potential for damage on the roads meant that all future home leave has been cancelled until he retires. The pressure of having Tam at home isn't something that M W relishes.

I was hoping that Coastal Ties or Wallow would emerge as potential winners at Saumur following their satisfactory introduction to three-star level at Pau at the end of the previous season. Coastal Ties gave me some cause for hope, with a decent dressage and a double clear, give or take a few time faults. He finished seventh, his best-ever three-star result, but his basic fragility meant that the more you trained him, the less likely he was to make it to the competition.

Wallow had an off day which was disappointing as I was always convinced he'd be good, but I was still waiting for him to be lucky. He had come from Ireland as a four-year-old in 1997. Breaking him in was a challenge because he was totally uncooperative, although we got there in the end. He was the softest pussycat in the stable, but once you were on him, he wanted you off, though there were days when he was angelic. He was a red bay like Tam, with a white star, a very athletic, smooth operator, tricky mentally, but not a worrier. From day one, riding him was like water skiing, gliding along from one fence to the next, with just his opinionated ifs and buts to spoil a perfect picture. At nine, he had the ability to do better dressage than Tam. When he let us believe the penny was dropping, he became a very exciting prospect.

After his moderate test at Saumur, I withdrew him and rerouted him to Bramham with Max. Wallow hadn't liked Saumur, but he was on a high at Bramham, right behind Pippa on Jurassic Rising in the dressage. Max had also improved to finish fifteen marks higher than he'd been at Blenheim the year before, thanks in part to Lizzie's winter training. Pippa was still in the lead after the cross-country, with Wallow second and Max third. By the end of the competition, we'd improved on that, taking advantage of a not so good round by Jurassic Rising to finish first and second. I was delighted, not only for myself, but for Judy Skinner, who owned shares in both horses. She'd had a lot of bad luck, so this was a well-deserved reward for her support and tolerance. Wallow had delivered at last and Max, who had been close to the transfer list six months earlier, had sealed his place in our team. Although he was tough and sound, we'd wondered if he'd be trainable, let alone world-class. We now knew he was progressive, even though fractious and mentally fragile, and we were prepared to live with that.

In the familiar 'win some, lose some' equation, mad Highland Lad had now been replaced by ultra-sensible Tom Cruise II, following a phone call from his owner, Sue Somner. She'd kept him with Andrew Hoy, but they'd reached the end of the line, perhaps because Sue has an obsessive attitude towards her horses. Tom Cruise had completed his first advanced at Chatsworth and been placed in his first two-star three-day, but if I'd known how he'd performed on these occasions, I'd have thought twice about taking him on. Andrew was honest enough to suggest he wouldn't be sorry to see the back of him, but I didn't know why until I started riding him. A beautiful quality horse by Cruise Missile, he was very well schooled on the flat and he wasn't about to hit a fence if he could help it, but his jump was disappointing and lacked scope.

Sue was determined he should go to Luhmühlen four weeks later, but first I had to qualify him by completing the advanced at Rolleston. As a prep, I thought I'd have an easy pop round Longleat Open Intermediate. All was going well until I came down the hill to a simple post and rails. A photograph later revealed that he hit it above the knee and in fact managed to cut his right stifle with his left front stud. Somehow we survived to complete. On to Rolleston where he led the dressage, show jumped clear and completed the cross-country with twenty time faults because I made sure he went clear by taking several long routes. In that context, seventh didn't seem too bad and I thought there was nothing to lose by going to Luhmühlen. It was a championship venue with a big track that I'd never attempted and there wasn't much of a British entry after our crowded spring season at home, but I shut out Andrew's words of warning and headed for Germany.

I had very little idea of what to expect, but the competition started well with a good test that put us in fourth. On the cross-country the first crisis came at the quarry, where he left a leg on the hanging log on the way in. The reins dropped over his head onto the ground as I tried to sit far enough back to stay on, but he forged ahead up two steps to an arrowhead without putting a leg through them and bounced out with me hanging onto the neck strap. I kept on pulling on the neck strap and we stopped just in front of the crowd so I could grab the reins back. I didn't feel he was the bravest of horses so the second water, a narrow log in, a table in the middle and a fence on the hill going out, was also a cause for concern. Rightly, as it turned out, when he slithered over the log, put in an extra stride at the table and chested it. 'Damn it, I've thrown it away,' I thought, whereupon he clambered it in a scissors movement, leg by agonising leg. One of them went the wrong side of the flag, but his head was on the right side, so we were able to continue up the bank out of the water, unfortunately in the wrong direction.

I then had to turn him back into the water, where he lost his footing, went down on his knees and disappeared. 'This has to be the end,' I thought, but up he came again. Rather unsympathetically, I gave him a good kick as I pointed him at the third element and we were back on track and somehow completed clear inside the time. By the end of the day, our clear round put us second to Zara on Toytown and when she knocked three show jumps to my one, Tom had won a three-star event. We stood there in stunned silence, with Sue Somner ecstatic. When you get the right result, you tend to forget how lucky you were and how easily it might not have been, but Tom was a winner because he was amenable and very genuine. Luhmühlen has to go down as one of the luckiest wins of my career.

Bramham and Luhmühlen marked the start of a golden patch, the run up to a great Gatcombe where Stunning, who'd retired from three-day events after Boekelo 2002, and Bob took first and second in the British National Championships and Tom won the intermediate championship. Thinking his hairy Luhmühlen might have scared him, I took him to a two-star event at Lulworth first, only to discover that I'd entered for the wrong class. I revised the advanced test in five minutes flat, but there was no way I wanted to tackle the cross-country in a three-star international, so I asked the Italian Technical Delegate, Guiseppe Della Chiesa, if I could go *hors concours* (run, but not compete) at the lower level. There was a lot of discussion about it, suggestions that it was unfair and inconvenient, but I'm not proud, I knew what Tom needed and I was prepared to beg. This was my first run-in with Signor Della Chiesa, but it wouldn't be my last.

Coastal Ties was my number one for Burghley, but when he came out in large itchy welts, I was left with Max. He wasn't really ready for the challenge of a four-star but it would have been a waste to have done another three-star. He proved us right with a mediocre performance, a dressage in the sixties, eight cross-country time faults and two show jumps down. Once more Judy and I considered the transfer list because we both wanted a top-class horse and he wasn't looking like being one. However, he'd gained valuable experience and jumped clear round his first four-star, so he wouldn't be easy to replace. At nine, I felt there was scope for improvement and Lizzie was prepared to go on struggling with his flat work, so once again he narrowly made the cut.

After my mediocre dressage, my personal prospects of a Burghley title were minimal, leaving me free to watch Pippa make her historic attempt on the Rolex crown. In the months since Badminton, the pressure had built steadily, especially when injuries to Supreme Rock and Cornerman shortly before the event left her relying on Primmore's Pride. Outwardly she appeared calm, but when we chatted in her lorry on the Tuesday evening, she said, 'I've had the worse three months of my career.' Primmore's Pride is a difficult ride and it was hard for him to gallop over Burghley's undulating terrain, so she imagined the ultimate prize slipping through her fingers, even before the competition began. My view was that, barring accidents, she'd win by a margin, given that her main challengers, Zara and Toytown, were unknown and inexperienced.

How wrong I was. Primmore's Pride didn't produce his best test and his time faults put him behind Toytown at the end of cross-country. As Zara had had three show jumps down at Luhmühlen, Pippa was still in with a shout, but Sunday afternoon developed into a real cliffhanger. When Primmore's Pride delivered an immaculate clear round, it was up to Zara to win or lose her first four-star event. I watched her warming up for her round, so relaxed and casual that you'd have thought she was at a local pre-novice. Earlier, when her mother (Princess Anne) came up to say, 'It's time to get ready,' she replied, 'No, I'm not there yet.' She was totally in control, no sign of nerves or dither, and she went into the arena with nothing to lose.

The gods were certainly in Pippa's corner because Toytown jumped much better than he had in Germany, keeping everyone on tenterhooks with a faultless performance until the second last fence. When that fell, the crowd gasped and Pippa had won the Grand Slam. At the celebrations afterwards, I'm sure she felt overwhelming relief more so than ecstatic pleasure, but it was an incredible achievement.

For me, Burghley was the start of an autumn spiral that bottomed out at Blenheim. There I was with Wallow and Tom, both red-hot favourites after victories in their previous three-day events and both well capable of winning this one. After Bramham, Judy and I were offered a tempting sum for Wallow to go to the States, but Yogi helped us resist it by introducing Brook and Sally Johnson as potential shareholders. They agreed to buy a third of him but, so as not to put all their eggs in one basket and in the hope of having more fun, they came in as part owners of Bob as well.

At Blenheim, Tom boiled over in the dressage, a strange performance for a horse who'd never been naughty, but on this occasion he arrived with his eyes on stalks and refused point blank to concentrate. The result was a mediocre fifty, some way behind Pippa and Jurassic Rising on thirty-six, but at least Wallow was well in the hunt with thirty-eight. On the cross-country I had a fall with Tom Cruise and a run-out with Wallow at the same fence. Tom left a leg at the second of a double of corners and dumped me as he nearly turned over. When I tried to set up Wallow by checking at the first element, he cocked his jaw and ran out. I retired on Tom, but Wallow went round the rest clear. Pippa won, comfortably reversing the Bramham form after producing a polished show jumping round.

Would my downward spiral continue at the European Championships in Punchestown? In Tam's absence, Bob had been recruited for the team. I took him to Blenheim so I could ride him in the run-up to the competition and he was in fantastic form, but as soon as we got to Punchestown, he didn't feel the same. The cross-country was difficult, which was perfect for him, but he clearly thought Blenheim was the main event. His test at Punchestown was there or thereabouts, but he nearly came to grief on the cross-country at a hanging rail drop off a steep bank into water, only to save himself miraculously and go round clear with a few time faults. The downside was he lost an overreach boot and arrived at the finish sore. Pippa and Leslie had gone well, so we were in gold medal position, but if we were to win it, Bob had to be fit to jump, because Jeanette had retired at the second water after a fall.

Unsurprisingly, he was still sore the next morning so I trotted him past the kennels, to liven him up enough to pass the vet and jump round with two fences down to finish eighth. Leslie dropped out of the individual medals with a rail down, but Pippa took bronze and we won another team gold, an excuse for a fine Irish party before we went home. In his early days, I had a dream that Bob would be my horse for the Sydney Olympics, but he was never quite that calibre and I certainly had reservations before Punchestown. In fact, it turned out to be his finest hour. He really dug deep and gave his all, and it was great to have Sally and Brook supporting him and being there as part of Team GB.

Tom redeemed himself at Boekelo, where he was a late acceptance off the waiting list. His dressage was the best I've ever done in a three-star event and he capitalised on an easy cross-country, giving me a really encouraging ride to finish inside the time. Horses tend to go clear when you show jump with several fences in hand and Tom was no exception, completing a flawless all-round performance that earned a well-deserved victory by over twenty points. I was very glad to have fallen off at Blenheim.

After Boekelo, we dared to hope he'd develop into a four-star champion, though I had doubts as to whether I'd ever see him again after he returned to Sue Somner's yard for the winter. Most of the pleasure she got was through looking after Tom at home. For me it is not a control thing having the horses on my yard, but I have a system and team that works for me. I cannot risk competing on a horse at three-star level and above that I haven't prepared myself. Getting horses fit in the right way is one of the most important things in eventing and I feel very strongly that it's my responsibility. Do it incorrectly, and you not only don't win, you put yourself and your horse at risk.

Taken as a whole, our first year in Dorset was a success. I hadn't won a four-star, but with a hat-trick of three-stars and second place behind Pippa in the world rankings, I could look towards Athens with some confidence. Tam would be back in action, possibly with Tom Cruise as my second string. As the Olympic cross-country has to be user friendly, taking into account the heat and the less experienced nations, Yogi was looking for horses with excellent dressage and reliable show jumping. Trained to perfection by Andrew and Bettina, Tom was able to score highly for his spectacular extensions and flying changes and, although sometimes hairy cross-country, he was jumping clears more often than not in the show jumping.

CHAPTER TWENTY-FOUR

Get Me to the Church on Time

By the time I made my first visit to Pabbay in June 2003, I'd decided to go for it. Getting engaged seemed like a natural progression.

The Plunketts have co-owned Pabbay, an island near Harris, since 1974. As it was otherwise uninhabited, it had always been a great escape, an annual break from the real world, with very special memories for the whole family. In Alice's childhood, the only accommodation was a bothy, a simple one-storey one-bedroom shepherd's house. Initially, they cooked on a camp stove, bathed in an outdoor tin tub and used water from the burn, but later they added a four-bedroom open-plan log cabin, so it was very comfortable by the time I came on the scene. The only preparation I made for my proposal was a bottle of champagne, which I slipped into the back of the fridge as soon as we arrived. Inevitably Alice spotted it immediately and opened it to drink a toast to being on Pabbay with her godson, Barney, his parents, Candida and George Baker, and her good friend, Chloe Gardiner.

We spent the next three days doing traditional Pabbay things. Alice went into manic mode, organising activities that included lobster potting from the small white boat, *The Maggot*, shrimping, hikes and fishing. It was tricky to find a suitable moment to propose. A barefoot walk at midnight ended with us both in stitches, brilliant fun, but not the greatest ambiance for a declaration of undying love. By the final day of our holiday I was getting pretty desperate, so I couldn't believe my luck when Chloe decided to stay home and chill rather than come out on the boat. 'Hang on, I'll see if Candida and George want to come,' said Alice, running towards the house. 'No,' I said, 'I want it just to be us.'

Collecting lobsters is a bit of a balancing act for the person who has to stand up and pull the pots out of the sea, so it would have been best to get that out of the way first, but it didn't work out like that. 'Will you marry me?' I said in a moment of reckless spontaneity. 'Yes,' yelled Alice, letting go of the steering as she leapt up to hug me. Our brief euphoric interlude ended abruptly as *The Maggot* headed for the rocks. I grabbed the tiller and steered it to safety in the nick of time: its starring role in our romance has been preserved for posterity in a cherished wedding gift from David and Barbara Ogilvy Watson, who share the island – a painting of two passionate seagulls perched on the dinghy.

As old habits die hard, I wanted to ask Alice's father for her hand in person, rather than on the phone. She found that very hard to accept, especially as it meant hiding the news from her friends. To make it worse, the Plunketts were arriving on Pabbay the day after I left, so she'd have to keep the secret for the days she'd be there with them. Well, that's what I wanted, but I should have known better. I'd hardly driven out of Bristol airport before she was on the phone: 'Hi, babe, I'm sorry, but you're going to have to talk to Dad.' 'Okay,' I replied, 'but let me phone from home so I don't get cut off in the middle.' Positioning is key if you need a mobile signal on Pabbay and Alice could hardly keep her father in the same spot for the next hour, so she was back within moments. 'Dad's right here,' she said, passing the phone to him and adding, 'Will's got something he wants to ask you.'

I screeched to a halt on the verge as David nobly pretended he hadn't a clue what was going on. 'I've asked Alice to marry me and she's accepted,' I babbled. 'I'd like you to give us your blessing.' He said he was thrilled, sounding as if he meant it. As for my parents, they were delighted. Second time around, they couldn't believe their luck.

As the end of the season approached, we planned our November wedding. With Plunketts and Fox-Pitts in the mix, the guest list was going to be interesting. Weddings are about families as much as they are about couples and although Alice and I aren't particularly religious, it felt right to get married in the church in Great Tew where Katie and Eloise are buried. David would have liked a Roman Catholic ceremony, but the priest didn't want to know, so we were lucky to have Reverend Conway, a Canadian Protestant minister, and Cannon Strong, both with a more relaxed view of divorce.

I wasn't allowed to have Julian Dollar as my best man for my first wedding, but he more than made up for it at my second. He decided that Knowlton was the best place for the stag, not least because it ruled out clubbing, and he made sure that everything ran like clockwork. In the afternoon, we played boys' games, with go-karting, shooting, both clay pigeons and real ones, and a sumo-wrestling tournament, with everyone dressed in fat suits. As I'd tried it the year before, I knew I wouldn't be a contender, but the pulsating black eye I got from Philip Clapham during my second-round annihilation was a massive source of amusement.

General behaviour deteriorated through a delicious dinner, but luckily order returned in time for the magician and a stripper. I was completely caught by surprise because I'd specifically forbidden Julian to book one. When she came in pretending to be a waitress, I thought, 'Uh, uh, here's trouble.' She put me in a wig and glasses, then sat on my knee and took her kit off, but I wasn't allowed to touch much. By the time we let off a box of rockets at 3 a.m., everyone was too far gone to appreciate the danger of aiming the biggest one straight at Knowlton's historic chimneys. Luckily it missed by millimetres, exploding in the garden outside my parents' bedroom, a wake-up call they took very well.

I had three weeks to recover, which turned out to be just enough time for the black eye to disappear. Alice had a typically Plunkett idea that we should both go hunting on the morning of our wedding day, though not together, because traditionally we weren't allowed to see each other until we arrived at the church. After a big dinner party at Cradle Farm the previous evening, I'd spent the night with the Magnays who are good family friends. I woke up to torrential rain, triggering alarming thoughts as to whether my bride-to-be would make it to the church at all...

Despite her Aintree record, Alice is known for excessive courage and an ability to over-estimate her horse's talent on the hunting field, miscalculations that can result in anything up to three falls a day. I knew this could happen even when she was riding George, the faithful family horse who'd taken Eloise safely round the challenging Melton Hunt Cup course. The Heythrop Hunt generously brought the meet forward to 10 a.m. so that Alice had time to hunt for a couple of hours before she went home to change. You can imagine how relieved I was to get a phone call saying it was my turn. I rode Hector, on loan from Georgia Bale for the hunting season. He could be unpredictable, but luckily he was on his best behaviour on my big day. It's still hard to believe that the hunting plan came off, but lots of friends made the effort to come out with us and we had great fun.

The rain stopped and the weak November sun was shining as we arrived at the church, positive vibes that were confirmed when I saw my family and friends assembled in flickering candlelight inside. The ceremony was intensely emotional. Alice looked incredible and so relaxed that I didn't feel at all nervous. If things had gone wrong, we'd have laughed it off, but everything went very smoothly. By the time Alice and I walked down a long pathway lit with flares as man and wife, I was on top of the world.

There are no better hosts than the Plunketts and they put on a wonderful party in a marquee at Cradle Farm, a delicious sit-down dinner followed by dancing till dawn. Dave Gilmour, Pink Floyd's lead guitarist, is one of my owners and I persuaded him to play a couple of tunes with the band. It was the high point of a magical night and I'm really grateful to him for doing it, because I know he'd have preferred not to. Alice was thrilled and so were the musicians, not surprisingly, as they don't often get a chance to sing alongside a rock legend. After that, everyone partied like mad and the night passed far too quickly.

Reality was quick to strike back when we arrived at the Bear in Woodstock at 4 a.m. for our wedding night. 'I'm sorry, sir, but we need proof of payment,' said the night porter, barring the door. I explained that Becky had pre-paid with a credit card over the phone, but he was adamant. 'You can't come in without ID,' he said firmly. 'We're wearing a wedding dress and a morning suit. Do we look as if we're going to do a runner?' asked Alice indignantly. Our taxi had left and he was dying to throw us out, but he reluctantly let us in after we'd promised we wouldn't leave until we'd paid. As usual, Becky came to our rescue the next morning. The celebrations continued through the day, with lunch in the marquee, another amazing feast that passed in a bit of a blur. It was an excuse to keep on partying and see more friends. All too soon, lunch and dancing merged into supper and bed.

We had Monday to relax before we flew out to Bangkok for a honeymoon that combined work and play. I refused to tell Alice where we were going until we got to the airport, but she's fascinated by history, so I knew she'd love Angkor Wat, Cambodia's celebrated ancient ruined city. We stayed in the Grand Hotel d'Angkor in Siam Reap, a luxurious French colonial palace that proved the ideal base for two sick people to visit the magnificent temples. Alice got flu first and then I caught it. 'Is it particularly hot today?' I asked, pouring with sweat and aching in every limb as I walked round the ruins. Even so, we spent five amazing days, setting out early every morning with our guide before the crowds arrived. He was on a mission to show us as much as possible, so we climbed mountains to visit remote antiquities that few tourists ever reach. I'm not normally the best of sightseers, preferring a quick two-hour fix to a whole day on the job, but in a place like Angkor, you really do want to understand everything.

Alice had television commitments in Hong Kong and, as I'm not a great shopper, particularly not on my own, I agreed to do some teaching. Her assignment was to cover the Hong Kong Cup at Shatin, part of a highly enjoyable party week at the races. As it turned out, her schedule was more relaxed than she'd anticipated, so she had a great time with her mates, while I taught at a centre run by Gina Porter, one of my mentors in the Pony Club.

Alice and I spent two nights in the Mandarin Hotel, an inspired and hugely generous wedding present from the Keswich family, before returning to Thailand for a week of complete relaxation at the Banyan Tree in Phuket. All in all, we had a brilliant time, arriving back in Britain for Christmas.

CHAPTER TWENTY-FIVE

The Ecstasy...

After missing the Sydney Olympics, I was determined to focus on Athens for 2004. With six potential Olympic horses in my yard, I was in a positive mood, but the reality was that Bob would find it too hot, Max wouldn't cope with the dressage and Coastal Ties would probably be lame, leaving me with Tam and two genuine reserves, Tom Cruise and Wallow. Ironically, due to his absence from competition for the previous eighteen months, Tam was the only one of the six who wasn't qualified for the Games. After surviving his holiday with the Guinnesses, he'd come back into work in great shape, but inclusion in Team GB, who had already qualified following the bronze medal in Jerez in 2002, depended on a good result at either Badminton or Saumur. In theory, I could have taken Wallow or Tom Cruise to the Olympics, but if I was to have a realistic shot at an individual medal, it had to be Tam.

When the entries went in, I earmarked Wallow and Max for Kentucky and Tam and Bob for Badminton, with Coastal Ties as a floater: as it turned out, he replaced Wallow on the transatlantic flight. Lexington, the designated host for the 2010 World Championships, is a fabulous event, held on a permanent showground, with massive numbers of stables, a great course running through mature parkland and excellent going. In other words, it's as far removed from the Olympic venue at Atlanta as it's possible to be, but it had become clear that getting there was a huge ordeal. The US Immigration authorities are convinced that our horses will introduce diseases they haven't got, so they have to be quarantined for thirty-six hours as soon as they land. The deal is they're fed and left without rugs, a potential source of contamination, in a temperature-controlled barn. All human contact is forbidden and they have to stand in without exercise for the duration.

Such treatment can have an impact on super-fit horses and, on this occasion, both of mine came down with travel sickness. As I understand it, they got hot coming into land, then freezing cold waiting on the tarmac at the airport in New York. When Alex finally took over for the trip to the quarantine stables, having flown out separately, she found both horses covered in dry sweat. We had them tested for viruses, but they were clear, so the likelihood is that it was a management-induced problem.

After the quarantine period, they had to spend a further sixteen hours on the road, a hell of a journey for any horse. It was touch and go whether mine would be able to compete but, miraculously, they bounced back, thanks to Jenny Hall and Alex's careful management. Once again Max had spent part of the winter doing dressage training with Lizzie Murray, a programme that resulted in a respectable score of forty-seven. As he added nothing to it in the jumping phases, it was good enough to put him in fourth place behind Kim Severson and Winsome Adante. Coastal Ties was right behind him at the end of the cross-country day, but I knew the show jumping would be a problem because the time was very tight. He had two fences down and eleven time faults, earning me some merciless teasing for what everyone saw as an absurd miscalculation. Two fences down would have put him in fifth rather than eleventh so my time faults cost me £1,000 a second, but I consoled myself with the thought that he'd probably have hit several more if I'd hurried him.

As soon as I was back in Britain, I headed rather apprehensively for Badminton. Olympic qualification, a top half dressage mark, no more than one refusal across country and no more than four show jumps down, should be a formality for a horse like Tam, but an unlucky slip would bring my Olympic dreams crashing to the ground. My preparation had been limited to one slow, clear round in an open intermediate at Tweseldown seven weeks earlier, followed by withdrawals at Fontainebleau and Weston Park, because I thought the conditions were unsuitable. Better to get to Badminton underprepared than not at all, but good as Tam is and as much as I trust him, I knew it was asking a lot to tackle an event of that calibre after more than a year without a proper cross-country run. As I was nearly out of Olympic options, I crossed my fingers and hoped the steeplechase would focus his attention on the greater challenge to come.

In the dressage he scored 40.8, a pretty good test but not his best, and he ended up sharing second place with Pippa on Cornerman, behind Andrew Nicholson and Lord Killinghurst. I knew Andrew wouldn't relinquish his position easily. As fast as I'd go cross-country, he'd go faster. Then again, Lord Killinghurst isn't the most reliable show jumper, so if I could stay in touch, I might be able to tighten the screw on the final day. It was raining hard on Saturday morning when I set out on Bob, still a contender after a nice test. He usually goes easily through mud, but the going on the steeplechase was terrible, so he accumulated a couple of time faults. He then perked up on the cross-country, flying round until the lights went out at the quarry three from home. 'Not another inch,' he said and he meant it, so that was that.

Should I run Tam or not? I spent the next few hours discussing this dilemma with Yogi, M W, Lucinda Green, the chairman of selectors, and Alice, eventually deciding not to start unless the technical delegate modified the time on the chase. As the officials had ignored us when we mentioned our concerns at the rider meeting the night before, this didn't seem likely, but when the early horses came back exhausted, they were persuaded to review the situation. Eventually they extended the optimum time for the steeplechase and deducted any penalties accumulated earlier in the day, but that wasn't much consolation for the riders whose tired horses had refused or fallen on the cross-country. As is often the case, the officials only acted when they absolutely had to, doing too little too late. In slippery conditions in 2003, they'd taken out some of the jumps halfway through the competition, an unsatisfactory solution, but better than nothing.

As Tam still had a last-gasp chance of Olympic qualification at Saumur, I didn't want to risk him unless I thought I could win. Then again, no one was even close to making the time and I knew he operated exceptionally well in mud. I agonised back and forth, but finally decided to go for it. Thank God I did, because he nipped round, galloping effortlessly, taking all the direct routes and jumping out of his skin. The Wexford Lady, ridden by Sarah Cutteridge (now Cohen), was one of the fastest and she'd finished well, but most horses were running out of steam by the end, so I held Tam back and tried to persuade him to save some energy. Once we were through the lake, I let him go on a bit and he finished so enthusiastically that I realised he could have gone a lot quicker. Of course I couldn't have justified the risk, but I didn't need to, because twenty-one penalties, the third fastest time of the day, put him well in the lead. After victories in the two previous years, Pippa's luck ran out with falls off both her horses at the gate out of Huntsman's Close and Lord Killinghurst's speed was blunted by the ground.

As Tam had never had two rails down in his life, or even one in a three-day event, I was optimistic, especially after he trotted up sound at the vet's inspection, but that was before I got on him. He could have been stiff, but he gave no sign of it, coming out on top of the world and far too full of opinions for our joint good. He jumped the practice fence very well, but otherwise refused to concentrate, arguing and shooting all over the place at the slightest excuse. By the time we went into the ring, I could have had three down and still won, but I didn't know that. It turned out to be a round I'd like to forget, one of the most tense and spooky he's ever done. After he had the third fence down and rattled several more, my confidence plummeted. I couldn't believe we were about to throw it all away, but when he ran at the last and knocked that too, I was convinced I'd blown it. I can't express my relief when the announcer said, 'Eight jumping faults for William Fox-Pitt so he's our winner for 2004.'

Victory at Badminton was my lifelong ambition, way ahead of an Olympic gold medal, so it was a wonderful moment. I could have wished for a better finale, but I had won Badminton and that was what counted. When Clare Balding came up to interview me for the BBC, the first thing I said was, 'My God, that was just awful,' which surprised her a bit. The general media reaction was 'William Fox-Pitt wins Badminton at last'. I hadn't thought of it like that, but if you first complete aged twenty, winning at thirty-five could sound a bit 'finally'. Not that I cared, because I'd always been haunted by the fear that I'd never win, so I was proud and very relieved to end my long, bumpy courtship with the world's premier event. Victory only brought my completion tally up to nine, two each on Chaka and Steadfast, one on Cosmo, one on Highland Lad, plus Tam's three, which isn't all that much to show for fifteen years of trying. All the more reason I saw it as the highlight in my career and a defining moment for an exceptional horse.

Andrew Nicholson, in second place, and I managed to exchange congratulations as we stood next to one another at the prize-giving ceremony, but a week later he tried to get me disqualified at Chatsworth, a less-welcome career first.

Stunning had won the international section in 2003, a victory he had a good chance of repeating in 2004, but I had four horses in the other classes, so my timetable was complex. To cut a long story short, I arrived late at the start of the cross-country on Stunning and Andrew decided I'd engineered it so that I would go after him. That would mean I'd know how fast I needed to go to beat him. Alice, who was interviewing the riders for Eurosport as they finished, was the first to confront his fury.

She barely got a word in before he let rip about how I should be disqualified for cheating and how unfair it was that I had missed my time. When he insisted everything he said should go on air, Eurosport couldn't believe their luck, but I didn't think anything more about it as I set off on Stunning. After all, I wasn't going to get any kind of advantage by missing my start time. Meanwhile Andrew was in the secretary's tent, putting down £70 to appeal to the ground jury to eliminate me. As I went through the finish, there was an announcement on the public address system: 'Will William Fox-Pitt go to the secretary's tent immediately.' If I had difficulty believing a fellow competitor was trying to get me thrown out on a technicality, I was even more surprised that the stewards were taking his objection seriously.

When they interviewed him, he said I'd conspired to go late so I'd know how many time faults he'd had before I started. As the Chatsworth time is impossible to get, everyone has penalties, but Stunning, an ex-racehorse and one of the fastest in the game at the time, had been closest to the optimum the year before, a performance he might well repeat. Andrew also claimed that I'd positioned my mother at the water jump so she could phone his split time through to me so I'd know exactly what I needed to do to beat him. The plot was so surreal that I had trouble grasping it and I was surprised that the officials were investigating it, though I later learned they were obliged to once the money had been put down. In the end, the stewards and the ground jury overruled the objection and allowed me to show jump, but it was an unbelievable waste of everyone's time.

At the end of the cross-country, I was lying in third, one place ahead of Andrew, but as I pointed out to him, Stunning was likely to have one down anyway. Annoyingly, my prediction came true and I ended up behind him. Looked at dispassionately, it was all rather pathetic, but everyone thought it was hilariously funny, especially when Jayne Apter, mortified that anyone would try to get her beloved Stunning eliminated in the twilight of his career, took Andrew to task.

Chatsworth also marked my first public appearance on Mr Dumbledore, a magnificent eight-year-old bay that had arrived from Sharon Ridgeway in Australia a month earlier. As he'd shivered in his summer coat through a typically chilly spring, I'd have preferred to have given him a gentler introduction to British eventing, but he needed to complete the intermediate novice at Chatsworth to start his qualifications for his first two-star at Burgie in mid-June. I'd originally bought him for Biotel, one of my sponsors, and they'd been very excited when he'd passed the vet in Australia, but there was an ominous silence after that and it turned out they'd lost interest. Sharon rated him very highly, a horse with potential who was ready to go places fast, so I asked Judy Skinner if she'd like him. She wasn't looking, but after she saw the video, she persuaded her great friends, Margie and David Hall, to come in with her.

Dumble is a lovely character, but like them all he has his little quirks, not least that he's calm one moment and full of it the next. After his initiation in Australia, where events typically take place in a field in front of a handful of spectators and a herd of cows, the razzmatazz and the public address system at Chatsworth freaked him out. We had no problem with the dressage, which took place in a field just as it had done for him back home, but his eyes were out on stalks when he went into the show jumping arena and he was out again before I could stop him. All things considered, he jumped pretty well and had just one fence down. The cross-country was fine and we finished third, but I felt he had a long way to go.

I gave him a bit of a break before the journey to Scotland for Burgie but, once I got there, I realised he had three issues which I'd have to sort out if he was to complete the event at all. The first was the pig farm on the first set of roads and tracks, a no go for him throughout the week unless he was with other horses. As I couldn't afford to wait for four minutes for the next rider to give me a lead, I stationed Alex in the bushes and told her to emerge bellowing as he passed, ensuring he'd take off past the pigs at high speed. My second problem was his non-existent steering on the steeplechase, a legitimate cause for concern as he nearly took out a line of spectators when I lost control. As they were regulars watching friends and relations, they were alert enough to avoid annihilation by jumping out of the way.

The third issue was a section of the cross-country course smothered by seagulls. I knew they'd move before Dumble ploughed through them, but I had to convince him that galloping into a flock of birds was a good idea. In the end, he was persuaded and went clear inside the time, taking the jumps effortlessly, but causing problems in between. On the Sunday, he could have had four show jumps down and still come second behind Caroline Powell, but he only needed two. It was a good result, but I called a halt to plans for another three-day event until he had got a bit more mileage under his belt. He stayed in work until the end of August, completing the two advanced events he needed for his 2005 campaign, and then took an early holiday to relax and digest everything he had learned. At the time it was a frustrating decision, particularly for his owners, but it paid off in the long run.

As Judy thought she had too many horses, she put Dumble on the market and sold him very easily to Liz Halliday, an American girl who'd been based with me at Stratton Audley a few years earlier. She'd tried him twice and he was just about to be vetted, when Judy rang me up at 7 a.m. at Fairyhouse where Alice and I were looking at racehorses. 'I haven't slept a wink all night,' she said, 'but I've realised he'll be very difficult to replace, so I'm not selling him.' Although I felt we'd have to pay Liz some compensation, I was very happy to keep him, because I knew he had it in him to be a winner if everything came together. Fortunately, Liz was very understanding.

Next up after Chatsworth was Saumur with Tom Cruise, another successful outing, because he finished on his dressage score, completing a hat-trick of three-star wins which I'd never done before. He made the tight time at Saumur very easily, but just as I was beginning to see him as realistic Olympic back-up for Tam, the routine scan I run on all my horses after every three-day event revealed some minor tendon damage. He stayed in my yard to do his rehab in the new spa I'd bought with Tam's Badminton winnings, then returned to Sue Somner in East Sussex while I went to Athens on the understanding he'd be back for the autumn events. I thought she was strangely unenthusiastic at Saumur, but I didn't realise why until I got a letter after the Olympics saying she was keeping him at home. At the time it felt like a shame but I'm a true believer in fate.

Was someone up there looking after me? Certainly I wasn't relishing the prospect of riding Tom round the twisty undulating Burghley track later in the year. After Saumur, I'd received lots of messages of congratulation, but it was Tina Cook who hit the nail on the head. 'Bad luck, mate,' she said. 'You can't dodge a four-star next time.'

After his Badminton fiasco, I reckoned Bob needed to go back to three-star level, so we went to Bramham, where he led the dressage. He'd been seventh there as an eight-year-old several years earlier and I knew the cross-country was a walk in the park for a horse of his experience. Sure enough, he cruised round effortlessly until he shut up shop at the third last fence. When he started stopping ten strides before it, I tried to set him up a bit, but he just felt as if he was running out of petrol and that was that. We checked him from head to foot and found nothing. I think it all stems from his memory of his first Badminton as a nine-year-old when he stopped because he was genuinely exhausted. Who knows, but maybe I took him a year too soon.

I don't get many spare rides nowadays, but that year I was offered Parkmore Ed by Philip Adkins, an ambitious amateur who hopes to take him to the 2010 World Games in Kentucky. Philip hadn't qualified to ride at three-star level, so he wanted me to give Ed some experience. For my part, I got a highly talented horse to ride for the season and one that I missed when he went back to Philip. At Bramham, he raised my morale after Bob's debacle with a solid, all-round performance, finishing second behind Terry Boon on the highly rated Foreign Exchange.

At the end of June, I went to Pabbay with Alice and three other couples for a badly needed pre-Olympic break. We had a great time but, with the Games just two months away, I found it impossible to relax. Instead I ran round frantically trying to keep fit while thinking I really shouldn't be there at all. I managed just five days before I left, eager to get back to the job in hand.

CHAPTER TWENTY-SIX

... And the Agony

B ack in Dorset, my six potential Olympic contenders had been reduced to two. Coastal Ties wasn't fully fit, Tom was side-lined, Bob was in disgrace after Bramham and Wallow hadn't got to an event during the spring season. Knowing that Tam isn't the luckiest horse, it looked as if I might end up riding Max in the Olympics. Tam went fantastically well in the final team run at Aston-le-Walls at the end of July, beating a top-class international field to lead the dressage, and jumping clear round a big track. I clocked up   a lot of time faults on the cross-country, but he would have won easily if it had mattered, so it was a real boost. The selectors had given the team riders the option of competing at Gatcombe in August, but I decided to give up my rides on Stunning and Bob to concentrate on the big one.

The team, announced after the spring three-day events, was pretty much as expected: Pippa, Leslie, Jeanette and me, with Sarah Cutteridge getting the nod over Mary King, the travelling reserve. Under Lucinda Green, the selection policy is to choose the team early, an approach that has been ridiculed by other countries who believe riders should fight for their places till the last possible moment. Yogi shares the credit for the new transparency, a total turnaround from my early experiences in the 1990s when everything was more regimented. He is employed to keep an eye on us and to report back if things go wrong, but he expects us to tell him if we have any worries, trusting us to be honest. As a result, we operate as a close unit with parallel goals and none of us would want to take a horse that wasn't one hundred per cent to a team competition.

Once again, there were new Olympic regulations, three riders to count out of teams of five and no separate individual competition. Athens was the first short-format Olympics, which is cheaper to stage because there are no roads and tracks or steeplechase and requires less space. As the International Olympic Committee had a big issue with competitors getting two medals for a single performance, they decided the top twenty horses should jump a second time at night to decide the individual placings, putting the greatest emphasis on the show jumping.

Our final squad training was organised by Yogi and Will Connell, our world-class performance manager (a post created under the Lottery deal), at Waresley Park. They left no stone unturned to give us the best shot at gold – at this stage, we didn't want any old medal – and they went to amazing lengths to simulate show jumping under lights, a first-time requirement for all of us. We needed to know how our horses would react to the shadows and reflections before they did it for real in front of the Athens crowds. We jumped the course under massive floodlights set up round Eddy Stibbe's school, then put our horses away for several hours, as would happen between the two rounds in Athens. That was key because they'd have to jump for the second time late at night, when they might reasonably think their day's work was done. As it turned out, the test was all the more challenging because it took place in torrential rain, thunder and lightning in an arena that resembled a bed of fireworks. Predictably Tam was even more spooky than usual, but he still coped well.

In the run-up to the Games, we were all aware the weather could be unbearably hot, so we trained our horses in fleece rugs that covered them from head to tail. The idea was to make them sweat to help them acclimatise, like the human athletes training in a heat chamber, a difficult process with Tam because his Arab blood made him exceptionally slow to break out. The longer it takes you to sweat, the hotter you get, so he'd sigh deeply whenever I put on the rug. I hope he realised that I shared his ordeal, sweating it out with him in many more clothes than I felt comfortable in. Abandoning all the extra kit when we arrived in Athens was a relief for both of us, but the plan worked because he sweated freely and coped well with the heat throughout the competition. It would have been easy not to have gone to all the work with the floodlights or to think the horses wouldn't need to be as fit for a short-format event, but everyone was focused on our quest for victory. The horses were on top form and there had been no setbacks in the build-up so sights were set on the gold medal that had eluded Great Britain since Richard Meade's individual gold in 1972.

As soon as we saw the cross-country course, we realised that to win was a lot easier said than done. The Olympics have to cater for nations that don't have the infrastructure we take for granted, but this creates the as yet unsolved problem of building fences that are difficult enough to test the best, without tempting inexperienced combinations to tackle direct routes that they are not capable of. Even a remote chance of winning an Olympic medal would tempt some riders to take such a risk. In Athens, the result was a joke, a course that I'd have been happy to take a first-time three-star horse round.

I set out on the first course walk, my heart pounding with excitement and hoping for a decent enough test. At the second fence, I passed Tintin walking the other way with the Belgian team. He put his hand to the ground and said, 'Grasshoppers could jump it.' And he was right. We were all completely deflated. If it had been a one-day event in England, I'd have walked it once, but we studied it exhaustively, trying to spot non-existent horrors. Atlanta was the last decent four-star Olympic track, with Sydney much smaller and Athens taking dumbing down to new depths.

Team GB is very lucky to be able to prepare so well, but we ride horses bred to gallop and jump rather than be dressage specialists. When a journalist said, 'The Germans think it's a good strong course. What do you think?' I replied, 'I think the Germans will win.' Given their horses and strengths, the competition played into their hands. The weather was below the threatened forty degrees Celsius, the humidity was low and there was a decent breeze. On a pretty flat course with going on top of the ground, our horses finished hot but not tired, with neither their courage nor their stamina tested. Brazil provided an accurate yardstick to the degree of difficulty when their five riders all went clear, a great credit to their trainer, Ian Stark, but still a surprise for an inexperienced eventing nation. Obviously the track has to be user-friendly if our sport is to retain its Olympic status, but we need to chose our horses carefully in the future with a real emphasis on dressage and show jumping strengths.

Athens delivered on the facilities, with immaculate stables in big barns cooled with fans and lots of training arenas, although the hacking was limited. We also had the benefit of a team lodge where family and friends could stay. Once again we were advised not to go to the opening ceremony due to our early start, but we had comfortable accommodation in new apartments in the Olympic Village. The synchronised divers, who were staying on the floor above us, raised morale by winning a silver medal before our own competition started. Back at the stables, it was Cutty's turn to draw the short straw when her horse, The Wexford Lady, went lame two days before the dressage. She was immediately substituted by Mary, summoned from the rat-infested reserve stabling: she'd been clattering bin lids together to disperse them whenever she went in to see King Solomon.

Solly is a very consistent horse and he always goes clear, but he's never inspired confidence in the selectors because his cross-country can be very deliberate. However, Mary is impervious to pressure and a real team player. As she'd always believed she'd be in the team, even dreaming about Yogi's call-up the night before disaster hit The Wexford Lady, she arrived in a very positive mood. Back in Dorset, Max, who could still be summoned up to two days before the vetting, was still keeping fit, a very generous call on Judy's part, because he was putting in the mileage and taking the risks for an event we were hoping he'd never compete in.

Nor did he, because Tam was sound and working well. When Yogi decided the running order, we all fell into our natural slots, with

Jeanette, who'd fallen at Punchestown when she went second, reverting to her trailblazer's role and Mary filling Cutty's slot. Leslie opened the proceedings for us on the second dressage day, followed by Pippa, with me as anchorman. By the time I went in, Leslie had achieved a personal best on Shear l'Eau and Pippa was in third place, behind France's Nicolas Touzaint and Germany's Bettina Hoy. Tam had been brilliant in the morning and, although I knew he'd react to the buzz around the arena, I was very optimistic, until I got back on him for the final warm-up. After a long siesta period in the heat of the day, our test was quite late and in between times a strong wind had got up. As a result, he came out wild. Because he'd been so good through the previous week, I hadn't allowed enough time in his warm up to accommodate this dramatic change of mood. Normally he's bone idle, standing like a police horse if he's not asked to move, but he was still on edge when I changed into my top hat and tails with only fifteen minutes to go and I knew my number was coming up way too fast.

As we trotted round, he was on fire, so elevated his feet hardly touched the ground, as he reacted angrily to my tails flapping in the wind. 'Jolly good,' said Tracie loyally, while I thought, 'I'm absolutely not in control of this horse.' I couldn't practise the movements because he was spooking and rebelling and shooting sideways all over the place, so I said to myself, 'Relax and ignore him.' When the crowd clapped as the horse ahead of me went in, he went mad and I got that freezing feeling through my whole body, just as I did during school exams when the time was running out. 'Keep calm, he will settle,' I told myself, realising that the last applause he'd heard had been his lap of honour at Badminton. Was it payback time? Please God, not here!

At the last moment, my prayer was answered. Tam took a deep breath and relaxed, just as if I'd switched off a light. I wouldn't say I'd got him back totally, but he was over his manic phase and I knew he'd be all right. Of course, he used the clapping that greeted him in the arena as an excuse to explode again, but after that he settled and did a very good test, marred by a couple of mistakes, an early change in a counter-canter and bucks in the flying changes, which invariably lead to low submission marks. His score of 38.6 left him in about eleventh place, seven marks behind Pippa and a little bit ahead of Leslie, okay, but not what I'd hoped for. As a team, we sneaked a narrow lead, but with the cross-country counting for so little, we still had it all to do if we were to win the gold medal. We couldn't afford to give an inch.

Strangely enough the size of the fences worked against us because we felt we couldn't attack in case we made a stupid mistake. Jeanette, who is normally a banker, decided not to risk the narrow Grecian Urn and went the long way round, accumulating four time faults. Mary, the cunning old pro, made the time, but Leslie had a hairy moment in the water, with Shear l'Eau clambering over the second boat during an otherwise very fluent round, and he too had a couple of time penalties. The hard-pulling, long-striding Primmore's Pride showed complete disdain for the fences, so much so that Pippa had to set him up more than she would have liked to prevent them tripping him up, a time-consuming exercise that resulted in eleven costly penalties. As she dropped out of the individual medal positions, the press moved in for the kill, asking how she could have been selected on a horse who was so obviously unsuited to a small twisty course. Poor Pippa was very knocked back and I set out in a cloud of gloom, with Team GB down to fourth. 'Go for it,' said Yogi. 'We've nothing to lose, so take your chance, for the team and yourself.'

Tam doesn't need to be impressed by the fences to jump well. He's just as good over two foot as four, a rare quality among advanced horses and a big bonus on this occasion. It was a privilege to ride him as he cruised round without a care in the world. I never have to hurry him and he's so mentally and physically alert that I barely have to think about the next fence before he's over it. As he finished comfortably inside time, everyone looked happy and relieved, so I assumed I'd done our chances some good. 'Well done,' said Yogi. 'You've moved us up to third place.' Going clear was a relief, but it was depressing beyond belief that five clear rounds had put us down to third. The time faults had been critical.

Tam seemed fine once he'd cooled off, charging breezily back to his stable with Jackie. I was cornered by the press, cheerfully talking them through a round that had left me the leading British rider and in fifth place overall. The prospects for the next day were pored over by journalist after journalist until at last I managed to extricate myself and head back to the stables with Alice, both of us relaxed and elated by Tam's performance and the fact that we were still in the hunt. As soon as I walked into the barn I knew something was wrong: Jackie's face said it all. Sure enough Tam was in his stable, looking reluctant to move and extremely sorry for himself. I couldn't remember him hitting a fence with his stifle, but Jackie said he had obviously banged it. Maybe he had the kind of pain you get when you clip your knee cap at an odd angle, and there was the chance that it might be gone by morning if we iced it through the night. Such hopes were blighted as soon as Jenny Hall saw him: he could walk a bit, but he didn't look as though he could trot – and if he was to pass the vet, let alone jump, he had to be able to trot.

Rather than put him through a night of treatment for nothing, we X-rayed him and learned the worst there and then. With three loose bone chips in the joint affecting flexion and movement, we had no choice but to withdraw him immediately. My Olympic dream was over for another four years. Lucinda, Yogi and Jenny were as supportive as they could be, but I had to return to the Olympic Village and break the news to my team-mates: 'Sorry, guys, you're on your own.' As I'd been in fifth place, one mark off an individual medal, with Pippa ninth and Leslie twelfth, it was a devastating blow to all our hopes, but I was also agonising over the bigger picture. Tam is my horse of a lifetime and, although his injury wasn't life-threatening, it could easily have put an end to his career. He needed an operation to remove the chips, and if he'd suffered ligament damage, he'd never compete again. I then had to break this news to M W and Finn, and to Alice's and my parents.

My absence put Team GB back to fourth, behind the French, Germans and Americans, but it was still tight at the top and I knew

I had to put aside my depression and encourage the others to fight back. We all felt very beaten up and flat, but we had to salvage whatever we could when the competition climaxed the next day. At the vet's inspection, the four British survivors looked outstanding, but some of the other horses were very lucky to pass, not least Ingrid Klimke's Sleep Late, who was so lame after falling on the flat that he had to be withdrawn before the jumping anyway.

Even though we didn't have a realistic crack at team gold, the tension was enormous as the horses came out for the final test. Pippa and Leslie jumped copybook clear rounds, moving up to fifth and sixth respectively. With Mary's two down, that was good enough for bronze, less than a fence ahead of the Americans, but far better than we'd thought possible a few hours before. I felt so proud of them coming back after so much disappointment. If Tam had been okay, we'd have won team gold by miles. As it was, there was a bitter battle for the top of the podium between the Germans and the French. Bettina, still in second place individually behind Nicolas Touzaint, had jumped with immaculate cool to give Germany gold, but everyone in the crowd realised she'd circled after going through the start before she presented Ringwood Cockatoo at the first fence. It was unbelievable that she could have made such a simple mistake at the Olympic Games and particularly as the medal was within her reach. No one could believe their eyes and wondered how the judges would react, and as her round progressed, the whispering in the stands reached a crescendo. Even before she had finished jumping, calls were coming in from home wanting to know what was going on – there was total dismay that she had not been eliminated. The reality in Athens was not so clear-cut, but the media outcry in the UK snowballed through the night giving the sport of eventing more coverage than it could ever have anticipated.

Following a French objection, the ground jury withheld the result while they studied the video. Everyone knows you're automatically eliminated if you go through the start twice, but on this occasion the situation was complicated, because one of the jurors had told the timekeeper to restart the clock when she passed the jump. He admitted the mistake, but did that mean Bettina should be disqualified, penalised for a refusal, given extra time faults or presented with a team gold medal? By the time the top twenty-five riders walked the course for the second round, the ground jury's decision was up there on the scoreboard: twelve penalties for the time she took making the circle, giving France gold, Britain silver and America bronze. It didn't last: even before Bettina started the second round that could win her individual gold as well, Germany's counter-objection had been upheld, and they were back on top.

Even in such a rollercoaster situation, Mary was too far off the pace to have a chance of a medal but, characteristically, she gave it her all. As is customary, the horses went in reverse order, so Leslie's second clear round put the pressure on the five world-class riders ahead of him. Shear l'Eau, a good jumper but prone to a single error, certainly picked his moment of glory and the roof nearly lifted off the Team GB part of the stadium as he went through the finish. Pippa was next up, jumping beautifully until she hit the planks to fall below Leslie. Kim also had one down, so Leslie was guaranteed a bronze by the time Bettina and Nicolas went in.

Despite tremendous pressure, Bettina held it together, retaining her lead with a single error and a couple of time faults. The spotlight then turned to Nicolas, a near cert for gold with a two-fence cushion, but his lovely, young, grey horse had nothing left to give and he knocked down four poles. So that was that: gold for Bettina, silver for Leslie, bronze for Kim and nothing for Pippa. As in Jerez, we'd have been disappointed if we'd known we'd finish in these positions at the outset, but clawing our way back from the depths triggered massive celebrations.

We were delighted for Leslie, who'd performed brilliantly in all three disciplines, and were optimistic he could rise higher still. The French, Brits and Americans had been quick to appeal to the Athens Olympic Committee about Bettina's reinstatement and their lawyers were preparing to present their case to the Court of Arbitration for

Sport. Feelings ran high at the press conference, with the French sitting mutinously silent and the Brits looking bemused while the journalists laid savagely into poor Bettina. She defended her right to her medals fiercely, as anyone would, but she must have known she would never get away with it. Harsh though it was, the rules would be upheld in the end.

Meanwhile, we had a medal ceremony to attend. The German team were on the top step of the podium, with the French second and the Brits third. As all team members get medals, regardless of whether they complete or not, I was there too, my olive wreath on my head. I felt a bit of a fraud, but it was a very special moment and I was happy to be there with the rest of them. Jaroslav Hatla, the lone Czech rider, lent me his horse for the lap of honour, a generous gesture, but nearly a disaster, as he was a challenging ride. Bettina was next up to receive her gold medal, ahead of Leslie and Kim. We looked on in disbelief, all bemused by the debacle that had unfolded and certain that the result could not stand.

By the time Yogi called me to say we'd won team silver and individual gold, with a bronze for Pippa as well, I was competing in Scotland. The team silver made little impact on me, apart from a fleeting thought that it would be a great boost for the sport's funding, but Leslie's gold was incredible. It was a shame he missed his moment of glory in Athens, but he's had a lot of bad luck and this break was well overdue. He's a quiet, understated guy, someone I've grown closer to through all the highs and lows we've shared, and I miss his easy companionship now he's moved to America.

A couple of months later, Princess Anne presented Leslie's gold and our silver medals at a reception at Buckingham Palace organised by the British Olympic Association. It was the climax of a day of celebration for the whole of Team GB, following record successes in the Games. We met in a hotel opposite Harrods, all in our Olympic uniforms, to get onto our designated tumbrel-style open carts for the victory parade. At the outset, our bizarre procession attracted the odd spectator standing in bemusement at the roadside, but embarrassment turned to elation when we were greeted by cheering crowds in Trafalgar Square. Clare Balding jumped from cart to cart interviewing the winners, including Leslie, who finally got his due recognition on the huge television screen that dominated the square. After our medal ceremony with Princess Anne, Leslie and Pippa had to rush off to Pau for the Eventing World Cup final, while Alice and I took the opportunity to go out in London.

Tam, having landed at Stanstead from Athens, went straight to Newmarket for his operation the next day. We wanted to get it done quickly because we were worried sick about giving him an anaesthetic. When horses go under, they fall to the ground and two out of a hundred never get up again, so it's a high-risk procedure under any circumstances. Surely the odds would be much worse than that for the most accident-prone animal ever, but we were lucky and Tam came through fine. Ian Wright, the vet, removed the chips cleanly and there was no ligament damage, so the prognosis was good. Given that the fragments were right in the joint, he was surprised Tam hadn't been sorer in Athens. After a two-week convalescence, we worked him to make sure he was okay, then put him in the field. From now on, it would be damage limitation all the way.

CHAPTER TWENTY-SEVEN

If Only They'd Listened

My owners had been very patient with my Olympic quest, but that was over now. In other sports, competitors get quality recovery time after the Games, but I had a string of horses at home waiting to tackle the big autumn competitions. Even before the closing ceremony took place in Athens, I was at Thirlestane Castle for the Scottish Open Championships with Stunning, Bob and Max. After Stunning won at Lulworth before the Olympics, we announced that Thirlestane would be his final competition. At eighteen, he'd competed in nineteen three-day events and he had over 1,000 points, a great record for a horse who never found life easy. He owed me nothing, but I knew I'd always want to continue entering him while he was fit and winning and so would the Apters. Then again, we wanted to retire him before he retired himself, and in order for us not to be tempted to carry on we decided to make the announcement in advance.

From the start, his swansong went like clockwork. He did a much better dressage than he usually did and we romped happily round the cross-country in a marginally faster time than Ruth Friend (Edge), who was in the lead. Show jumping second last, he had one fence down, so Ruth needed to hit two to lose. She knocked one early on, but I had to wait until the last for the second – and a fairytale ending to Stunning's long and wavy career. Given this performance, I'd have predictably dearly loved to revise my call, but Thirlestane had embraced the idea of giving him a traditional retirement ceremony, so there was no way back.

After the prize-giving, they read out his achievements, then we took off his saddle and walked him out without it, an emotional moment at what has always been one of his best events. He was a great grafter with a huge heart. As I led him round with a lump in my throat, something I'd never have expected when I first took the ride, it dawned on me how much I was going to miss him. George and Jayne Apter still own him, but effectively they gave him to Jackie, who's always adored him. She does dressage, hunts a bit and lends him to me for lecture demos. At the age of twenty-one, he looks as well as ever and I still find myself missing riding him.

At Max's second Burghley in early September, it was a similar story to Badminton, with too much rain creating sticky going and causing a big rift between officials and competitors. Wolfgang Feld had built a decent track, using the undulating ground to create interesting challenges, but the four-and-a-half minute steeplechase was a cause for concern. Before the event starts, the technical delegate, an independent expert who oversees the smooth running of the competition with special emphasis on the courses, is the ultimate authority as to whether or not there should be changes. On this occasion, the TD was Guiseppe Della Chiesa, the Italian I'd had a bit of a run-in with when I entered the wrong class at Lulworth a year earlier. I asked him if he'd consider shortening the steeplechase, triggering a response that I will never forget. 'William,' he said, patting me patronisingly on the knee. 'You must remember that your opinion is just one out of a hundred.' He'd been round the course on Tuesday, but he'd never ridden at this level and he no longer competed, so it was difficult for him to assess how far the horses would dig in and how much the patchy ground would take out of them. If a horse had galloped round in advance, there would have been hoofprints a foot deep in some parts, but without this information, he couldn't see there was a problem.

Several riders discussed possible course modifications with the rider representative, Eric Smiley, pinpointing the second last, a double of skinny picnic tables with a hairpin bend in between, as a potential hazard. Could the tables be treated as two fences, giving riders the option of crossing their tracks without penalty, rather than imposing the difficult right-angled bend? As it didn't make the jumps any smaller, it seemed a reasonable suggestion, but when we proposed it, along with some other adjustments, at the well-attended riders' meeting on Friday evening, we ran into a brick wall at every turn. The ground jury, who assume control of the competition once it starts, claimed it was their duty to maintain the proper standards. As I was in the lead after dressage, it was implied that I wanted modifications so I'd find it easier to win. Eventually I stood up and said, 'At the briefing you always tell us we're responsible for our horses, for looking after them and making sure we don't push them too far, but when we express legitimate concerns, you don't respect our opinions. As you're asking us to compete in unfair conditions, I'm passing that responsibility back to you. If anything happens to any rider tomorrow, on your head be it.' Total silence. What could they say?

Caroline Pratt turned to me and said, 'Good on you, William.' Less than twenty-four hours later, she was dead. I knew her well, especially since she'd ridden for the British team in the European Championships at Pau in 2001. She was always good for a gossip and a laugh, an unpretentious, hard-working woman who'd struggled for fifteen years to find the back-up she needed. Shortly before she died, she'd struck lucky with the Kinseys, brilliant owners who supported her and found her some nice horses, so she had everything to look forward to. She deserved it too, because she was a brave, accurate rider. After the meeting, we had a chat and her comment became a bit of a joke. After all we were riding good, experienced horses and we didn't have any particular fear of imminent disaster, so I thought nothing more of it after we parted.

Should we have protested more? If half a dozen top riders had pulled out before the cross-country, the officials would probably have had to listen, but Burghley is one of the year's big targets and we all have owners who are paying a lot of money to support an expensive sport. I believe Judy, among others, would have backed a boycott, but it would have been difficult to justify not running Max because the going was too soft when he was in the lead.

By Saturday, the ground was drying out and the weather had turned drainingly hot. The cross-country caused trouble all day, with the horses finishing exhausted and no one getting round inside the time. Max went brilliantly, until I took a pull at the water near the end instead of being positive. He had no stride and ended up standing flat-footed under the jetty. Thank God, he didn't take off, but his refusal was entirely my fault. When I presented him again, he jumped it fine, finishing in a good time in eleventh place. I was gutted at my mistake, for Judy, Max and myself, so I was in a negative mood when I went into the tent to watch the last few horses complete the course. Caroline had gone clear in the morning on Call Again Cavalier but, as I walked in, I saw her second horse, Primitive Streak, hit the fence I'd stopped at and flip over into the water. She was underneath him and I was later told she died instantly. I can't begin to imagine how the newspaper editors justified the horrific pictures they used the next day. Caroline's mother hadn't been at Burghley and she certainly didn't need to see them, no one did: yet there they were, exposed to the whole world. Just thinking about it makes me want to break their necks.

I can't say that Caroline died because her horse was exhausted because he had been going well, and the verdict at the inquest was a freak accident, but after a number of close moments throughout the day, there was a groundswell of opinion that we were lucky she was the only one. Eric Smiley also felt he'd failed us, because he hadn't been able to persuade the officials to listen to our concerns. On the plus side, Carl Bouckaert, an ERA member who is now the rider representative on the FEI committee, flew overnight from America for the meeting after the vets' inspection on Sunday morning. He showed enormous solidarity, dropping everything to come so quickly, and it was good to have someone objective to take the chair.

The proceedings were acrimonious enough in any case, with some riders calling for a boycott of the show jumping, but realistically that was never going to happen. Andrew Nicholson, lying close behind the leader Andrew Hoy, was notably out of sync with the general mood, claiming that the conditions had been perfect. Instead, the riders stood in the arena before the parade on Sunday to observe a minute's silence for Caroline. Once the show jumping started, the focus shifted to Andrew Hoy, who completed a remarkable Burghley with victory on Moonfleet and fourth place on Master Monarch.

At least Caroline's death concentrated our minds on the need to take control of the sport, a situation we spelled out at another meeting at Blenheim the next weekend in the presence of the chairman of the FEI committee, Wayne Roycroft. We wanted to develop a situation where the officials were obliged to listen if a certain number of riders protested. Officials are terrified of that kind of rider power, but it's our necks that are at risk. The deaths in 1999 made us aware that we had to ride more responsibly, but we also needed knowledgeable, more open-minded officials to make fair judgement calls. In nine cases out of ten, course and ground are fine so there are no contentious decisions to be made, but we have to convince the authorities that the time has come for riders to have more power of veto when the conditions are dangerous.

As yet, that hasn't happened. But after the Blenheim meeting, the FEI brought in some modifications as a compromise whereby if a certain number of riders objected, a mediator would be appointed to decide if the concerns should be upheld. We also proposed having the rider meeting on Wednesday rather than Friday to allow more time for negotiation, and that has now been approved. For the time being the situation has been smoothed over, but should we find ourselves in a similar position again, I feel we will take a more forceful stance. The BBC covers Badminton and Burghley on the understanding that the top riders will be there, so the organisers would find it hard to explain why eight out of ten of the dressage leaders failed to show up for the cross-country. Obviously we don't want to because it's not good for our sport, but when the FEI ignore us, we're not left with a lot of options.

Far from being asked to stand down or even explain his decisions, Signor Della Chiesa reappeared as technical delegate at Burghley 2005. On the whole it would have to be said that he doesn't do a bad job, but the riders thought it showed a lack of sensitivity and respect to appoint him again so soon. On that occasion, the competition ran smoothly in optimum conditions, but we also saw his return as a kick in the teeth.

From my point of view, Blenheim the following week was as dismal competitively as it was emotionally. In preparation for hosting the 2005 European Championships, it was a short-format event, which I assumed would suit Bob. He was up there after dressage, so he had it all to go for in the cross-country. When I was held up after four minutes, I thought, 'This must be my lucky day because he'll make the distance easily after a nice rest.' A quarter of an hour later, he set off enthusiastically, sailing through the water and galloping up the hill, but within three minutes he'd done another Bob. This time there were no excuses, no time limit, no exhaustion: he was just being a bugger, which was depressing.

My bleak campaign moved on to Boekelo. I was riding Parkmore Ed, a horse I liked a lot, especially after we came second to Terry Boon at Bramham. Ed's double clear showed me just how good a horse he could be, but I knew that if he ever reached his potential, it wouldn't be with me, because his owner, Philip Adkins, had always planned to take him back once I'd established him at a higher level. Philip competed on him in the autumn, but he felt they weren't quite ready as a partnership so he decided I should take him to Boekelo. He led the dressage and jumped the first part of the cross-country very fluently before switching abruptly and bizarrely into one-pace mode. He was still clearing the fences, but almost in slow motion. 'What on earth has happened?' I wondered as we laboured on. It's always difficult to pull up when you're in the lead and I probably allowed optimism to rule for too long before I stopped. The vet diagnosed heart fibrillation, caused by the onset of a virus, a condition that responded rapidly to treatment but one that is impossible to anticipate.

My final competition of the year was at Le Lion d'Angers where I had the ride on a Hungarian mare. The Hungarian experience had been a fascinating one. The previous winter I had a call out of the blue from a vet in Hungary saying he had a breeder who wanted to meet me with a view to riding his horses; I arranged for them to come over knowing that great horses can potentially pop up from anywhere. Andrew and Sandor arrived from Budapest with videos and books determined to convince me that the traditional Hungarian Gidran breed was the sport horse of the future. Hungary has a great equestrian tradition but since the war, and with the onset of communism, times have been very tough. I was buoyed along by the enthusiasm of these guys who, against the odds, were breeding nice horses that seemed to jump and move but had yet to prove they could really gallop. During the war the breed had been dispersed and almost made extinct but Sandor had gathered together a band of foundation mares from Romania and across Eastern Europe whose bloodlines could be traced right back and was trying to get the breed going again. Their flagship horse was a smallish chestnut mare called Sohaj and having seen her on the video competing, I was intrigued enough to agree to travel to the stud just outside Budapest to have a sit on her and make my final decision.

The week after Badminton, Alice and I set out on what felt like a real adventure. The stud was extraordinary, lush and green in the heart of the plains. It was home to nearly two hundred horses, all chestnut who roamed in large herds in one-hundred-acre paddocks. The facilities were basic but the intentions and aims absolutely right. Sandor had his own system for assessing the horses from foals. He graded each one at each stage in terms of conformation, movement and jump and was refreshingly critical and realistic of each one's prospects. Sohaj was on the small side and not the best mover, but she did jump so I agreed to take her on. It was clear she wasn't going to win Badminton but the Hungarians really felt I could make a difference.

I came away very keen to give their breed some international exposure and the scheme and their enthusiasm my support. Within two weeks she arrived at the yard, Sandor and Andrew having driven her across Europe themselves. It was a gruelling thirty-six-hour journey in a small trailer, but she showed just how tough she was by jumping clean out of her paddock within ten minutes. Sohaj never proved to be more than I originally anticipated, but she progressed through the season and finished a respectable twelfth at the seven-year-old championship in Le Lion D'Anger before returning to the breed in Hungary. I've maintained contact with the stud, and Sandor has generously given me a Gidran foal as thanks which he named Smile in honour of the experience.

Back in Hinton St Mary, the bulldozers had finally moved in six months late, but the old dairy was gradually being reborn as our new stable yard. Meanwhile, the horses stayed on at Fontmell Parva. While I was hacking out one crisp, winter morning, Alice called from London. 'Guess what, I'm pregnant,' she squeaked in a state of high excitement. 'Oh my God, here we go,' I thought as I matched her mood of elation. It was something we'd planned and it was definitely something we had both been hoping for.

I wanted us to enjoy it privately for a while, but Alice is particularly hopeless at keeping secrets – her record is probably about ten seconds – so I wasn't optimistic. She stopped smoking and drinking alcohol, ensuring that anyone she forgot to tell guessed immediately. No matter. The time was right for our life to be turned upside down for the best possible reason.

CHAPTER TWENTY-EIGHT

Out With the Old

Athens heralded the short-format era, a watershed in the sport that will affect the way we all choose and prepare our horses from now on. The thinking behind it is costs and logistics, making it more user-friendly. As with everything, there are pros and cons. I won't miss riding the steeplechase because of the wear and tear it puts on the horses. On the other hand, it did get your blood up helping you to ride positively and in a rhythm by the time you reached the cross-country. It also wakes up a lazy horse and helps focus attention and, if something goes wrong, as it did with Max at Badminton in 2005, it's better it should happen over more forgiving fences. Although it might seem the three-day event is a less-demanding test without the chase, I believe that the horses still need to be as fit as they ever did.

Despite all of this, I had to concentrate on my last-ever long-format four-star events at Badminton and Burghley. After his long post-Athens lay-off, Tam arrived at Badminton in a state of high excitement following a single, quiet, preparatory run at Aldon the previous month. Normally he looks around and eats grass, showing scant regard for other horses, but on this occasion he got very attached to Max, whinnying for him whenever they were parted. Max was indifferent to his overtures, but Tam would lap his box whenever he was left alone. Badminton is a place he knows, an exciting place for a horse who competes as little as he does, and the stress definitely got to him. I'm slightly superstitious so I'd asked Brian Higham, the Duke of Beaufort's stud groom, for the same stables I'd had in 2004. They are quietly tucked away in the farmyard and there is a useful spare one for kit in between the two, excellent for Jackie and Alex, who bring all bar the kitchen sink to three-day events! On this occasion, I wondered if Tam might have been less tense in a new spot.

A good dressage was going to be my biggest challenge. Given the threat to Tam's career after Athens, I felt very lucky to be riding him at all, but he was on his toes during the warm-up. As Pippa, riding Primmore's Pride, went in two ahead of me, her score, which was bound to be good, was read out as Tam came into the ring. I tried to delay for a moment to miss the main clap for Pippa but I got it wrong and Tam, as ever sensitive to applause, shot around snorting and skittering. The bell went far too soon and I thought, 'We've had it, he just isn't on the case,' but once I'd persuaded him to go into the arena, he gradually settled and performed reasonably well, give or take the usual white-knuckle moments. He ended up in second place, a few marks behind Pippa, with Max in fifth, so I had a strong hand for Saturday.

Traditionally the direction of the cross-country is reversed each year, but this time Hugh Thomas broke the mould and left the course much as it had been in 2004. The difference was that conditions were perfect, so, barring accidents, the competition was between Pippa and me. Max felt great as he started on the chase but, after two fences, I realised something was wrong. I kept going, just as I had on Ed at Boekelo the year before, wanting to believe it was a temporary blip, but after he'd struggled over another fence and continued at one pace, I had no option but to pull him up. Like Ed, he had a heart fibrillation, presumably caused by a virus, though it was never diagnosed because it didn't show up in the blood tests. He's been fine ever since after treatment which restored the heart rhythm, but that was the end of his Badminton.

Tam gave me a superb ride, finishing comfortably within the time with minimal effort. He always keeps me on the ball as he looks for gremlins, but basically it's very straightforward for him. I had one hairy moment at the third last fence, a steep bank to a pheasant feeder coming out of the quarry. My heart stopped as I realised we were on the wrong stride, but Tam used his feline instincts to make the necessary adjustments, taking off, touching down and taking off again before I had time to address the problem. As Pippa was a little behind the pace, we closed the gap to 1.2 marks at the end of the day and naturally I was hoping she might have a fence down or a couple of time faults on Sunday. Then again, Primmore's Pride is the best jumper in the business and he wasn't tired after the cross-country, so if Tam went clear, he'd probably go clear as well.

And that's exactly what happened: Tam performed faultlessly and I waited with resignation for Primmore's Pride to do the same. Would it have been different if Pippa hadn't deprived me of the black cat? While we were chatting that morning on the way to grab breakfast in the groom's canteen, she'd peered under my armpit and spotted it behind me. For a split second, she considered telling me to turn round and have a look, then she thought better of it. When we finished first and second, she said, 'Just so you know, there was a black cat behind you this morning. I was about to tell you, but I decided not to.' 'You deserve to fall off for that!' I replied.

Like most event riders, we can be superstitious, she even more than me. We enjoy friendly banter, winding each other up as much as we can, but basically we have totally different approaches. She's extremely disciplined and well organised, whereas I tend to go with the flow. A couple of years earlier in Kentucky, I'd left my breeches in the hotel, not normally a problem if you can borrow from a mate, but tricky when you're my size. I managed to squeeze into Leslie's spares, which were more like ballet pants, and wedged myself onto Bob to complete a clear cross-country round. Pippa would probably never be in that position, but if she was, she certainly would wait for her own kit rather than risk riding round in someone else's. At the European Championships in Pau, I barricaded the warm-up sand arena and let Stunning loose so that he could wander round and unwind. He had a canter round, then rolled and came in looking much happier, but Pippa thought I'd gone bonkers, taking such a risk mid-competition.

She's very into psychology and visualisation, whereas I believe that whatever will be will be, especially cross-country, where I trust my horse and let him get on with it. She rides in a more regimented way, analysing each stride, which may explain why she often beats me in dressage and perhaps I should do something about it. If the cross-country time is tight, we end up pretty much level, as we did on this occasion, with just fractions between us at the finish. Tam's a winner, so I feel to be second is a waste, but the competition didn't play into his hands and Primmore's Pride emerged the better on the day. Given their respective sizes, Pippa and I often joke about swapping, but Primmore's Pride would be a challenge for me whereas Tam is a man's horse, despite his size. He has respect for me most of the time, but he always pushes the boundaries and his confidence means that he would do anything to help me out if we got into trouble jumping.

When we returned to Dorset after Badminton, Tam and Max went straight to their new stables in Hinton St Mary. Work on the new yard had been progressing steadily through the winter with Paddy, wearing his project manager's hat, coming down at least once a week to supervise it. He buffered all the mundane nightmares, the problems with plumbers, builders, steel workers and, above all, with Monarch Stables. Inevitably, deadlines were missed and the move was delayed but only by three months and, considering the size of the project, that would be deemed a miracle in the building business. The day after Badminton, we shuttled the other horses and the kit over from Fontmell Parva, though the grooms had to stay there a bit longer until the lodges were ready.

I'd been planning to take Wallow to Kentucky's first short-format event a fortnight before Badminton, but had to pull him out when he fractured a splint bone at the start of the season, so the spotlight now turned to Idalgo (Frog), Dumble and Birthday Night (Barney) for Bramham. Frog had had a chequered 2004, flying round Chatsworth in the spring and then developing a water phobia at Lulworth in the summer. He wasn't a chicken, just unruly to the point of being unmanageable, so it was back to the drawing board in the autumn. He is a hot-blooded chestnut and he became feral to the point where the Apters considered cutting their losses. As a three-day event was an obvious waste of time, I took him to a few easy one-days and put him away early. He's a very powerful, athletic horse, but with a weak frame, so Dolly Maude, a good friend of Alice's who runs a very good pre-training and rehab yard, put him on her treadmill on his return to strengthen his back end before he joined Max at Lizzie Murray's for dressage training. By the spring, he was a different horse and I dared to hope he'd conform rather than rebel at Bramham.

Once Judy decided to keep Dumble, I'd taken him regularly to the Irish show jumper, Pete Charles, at his Basingstoke yard. When Lars moved back to Sweden he recommended I had help from Pete. Dumble was competitive in dressage, with an amenable temperament and regular paces, though less extravagant and expressive than Tam, but his show jumping needed work. Pete did a great job, setting up the kind of grids that improved his focus, keeping his mind on the job in the face of the inevitable disturbances, and I hoped that too would pay off at Bramham.

Barney belonged to Michael Turner, who gave me my first big break with Chaka, and Jane Walter, who lives near us in Dorset. He came to me as an eight-year-old in 2003 and I took him to Germany for his first three-day event at the end of that season. Jane and I landed in Munich and made good time as we drove towards the stables in Kreuth. As we approached the town, I called Jackie to say, 'Tack him up, we'll be with you in five,' but 100km later, we still hadn't found the venue. The directions didn't stack up, but it still took us ages to realise we were in the wrong Kreuth. 'Okay, Jackie, untack him and we'll see you in the morning,' I said as I headed across Germany towards the right one, five hours away in the opposite direction. As Jane, who hates both driving on the right and being a passenger, squealed whenever I exceeded 60kph, we arrived in a state of total exhaustion in the middle of the night. Barney redeemed the situation with an honourable tenth, following up with a third at Windsor in

2004, and he too had benefited from Pete Charles's training in his run-up to Bramham.

I wasn't sure if I'd be accepted at Bramham on three horses, but as they were ready and qualified after a good spring, it was worth pitching for it, rather than going solo with Barney to Saumur. They were all nine-year-olds doing their first three-stars, so I didn't know which would be best, but the dressage gave me cause for optimism, with Dumble in the lead, a couple of marks ahead of Bettina and Diamond Magic, Frog fifth or sixth and Barney in the top third, a solid result for him.

Bramham is one of my favourite events. The Lane Foxes are great hosts and embrace the competition with real enthusiasm and the course is built by Sue Benson, who has broken the mould to become Britain's only significant woman designer. She puts a lot into her work, constructing horse-friendly tracks that are imaginative and challenging, but always very fair. Her tight times make for a real contest, giving bold horses and riders a chance to catch up the dressage specialists. Bramham's inaugural short-format course was very decent, a bit twisty and plenty difficult enough, so the pressure was on, but I had no idea how my three would handle it. I knew Frog was fast across country, but I had never put my foot down on Dumble. He was in a position to win, but I was worried for him because some of the tight turns might not be to his liking. Starting early, Barney went as well as I could have hoped, but he jumped into the water crooked and ran out at the next element when I over-corrected.

Would I cock up on all of them? Happily not. Dumble devoured the cross-country, surprising me with his speed and finishing comfortably inside the time. With his amazing stride, Frog was at least as impressive, but he was so far up on the clock that I relaxed and got a fraction of a time fault, more than good enough though for second place. As he jumped clear on Sunday, I'd won before I went in last on Dumble, who could have had four fences down and still come second. He also had a fence in hand over Frog but, with so many distractions around the arena, I was not hedging my bets. Even in such a no-pressure situation, I went in expecting him to have a couple down but, give or take the odd spook, he was foot perfect. A triumph like that seems so easy that I wonder why it can't happen all the time, but experience has taught me that such moments must be treasured.

The next week it was on to Burgie in Scotland with another three. The logistics of getting three home and three on to Scotland is only possible because of my amazing back-up team. We made the change-over at Bramham on the Monday morning, with Jackie and Ibby driving the two-star horses up in the small lorry and Alex taking the three-star horses back in it. This time they were even more unknown quantities, two seven-year-olds, Macchiato and Silver Dollar, plus Diamond Manati, owned by Nick and Lyn Howe, who runs the Spinal Injuries charity. When they asked me to take him, I wondered if I had room for a fourteen-year-old who'd never progressed beyond two-star, but Lyn is such a great enthusiast it was hard to say no. When I tried him, I thought he'd be a lot of fun, a useful potential replacement for Stunning at competitions where I didn't have a major player. When he started having sideways tantrums halfway through his tests, I felt I might have made the wrong call but, after a lot of persuasion from Lyn not to give up, the nightmare ended at Burgie, where he won the long-format three-day event on a competitive dressage score.

As you would expect of such amazing event organisers as Hamish and Polly Lochore, there was also a short-format three-day which was perfect for Macchiato (Mac), another import from Sharon Ridgeway. When he'd arrived two years before, he'd been a cheap horse, not outwardly a world-beater, but consistent and a good jumper and he'd progressed unexpectedly well. With a respectable sixth at Burgie and advanced points, I could have got a good price for him on the open market, but realising his potential, I wanted to keep the ride so I sold a half share to Jane and Michael Kier, eventing enthusiasts from the Isle of Wight and good friends of Justin Llewelyn, my original agent in the Hackett sponsorship deal.

The talking point of the summer was the new event at Barbury Castle, a lavish, high-profile international with a £5,000 first prize, a bonanza in a sport where the rewards for one-days are often derisory. As expected, a strong field arrived at Nigel and Penny Bunter's estate near Marlborough, and I for one couldn't quite see how I was going to get my hands on the coveted cheque. As Tam was halfway through his preparation for the European Championships at Blenheim in September, he wasn't ready to run cross-country and Max, in his first competition since his heart problem at Badminton, was also on the easy list. So it was up to Bob to carry the day.

Mark Phillips's cross-country was worthy of the status Barbury aspired to, well up to height and quite technical, with some tricky distances. Certainly I wouldn't have wanted my Bramham winners to tackle it at this stage in their careers. As the tally of falls, run-outs and refusals grew on a boiling day, consternation mounted, but Bob galloped cheerfully round, making nothing of it – until he tripped coming out of the sunken road and stopped, so that was that.

Once I got Bob back to the lorry, I had to hurry a bit for Max, scheduled to go third last in the reverse order of merit after a clear show jumping round. My main concern was whether he'd be all right, so I didn't start my watch, merely trucked round at a nice speed. He felt good and I jumped off him at the end thinking, 'Thank God for that.' During my celebratory hugs with Judy and her husband, Jeremy, the announcer said, 'William Fox-Pitt and Ballincoola go into the lead.' 'Result,' I thought. 'He's got ten time faults, but his heart's fine and I'll be third at worst.' As I walked him back, the announcer had more good news. 'So our winner is Ballincoola, ridden by William Fox-Pitt.' Of the two lying ahead of me, Bettina had a fall and Andrew Nicholson a stop. With Diamond Manati picking up £500 for the top score in the show jumping class, it was a very good day at the office.

At Gatcombe, Bad Bob reverted to Good Bob, even Amazing Bob, when he won the British Open Championship for the second time. Just as he hated Barbury, he loved Gatcombe and he made it clear, to Jackie at least, even before we arrived. 'He's in a very good mood,' she said, earning a doubtful look from me, but she's very instinctive and she kept repeating it throughout the morning. I remained sceptical but, mysteriously, Bob is unaffected by the hills at Gatcombe and, with two wins, a second and a third in six years, his record is second to none. This time, he did a great test, he's never show jumped better and he flew round inside the time, only the fourth horse ever to do so – one of the other three is Stunning.

With Dumble and Barney first and third in one advanced, Frog placed in another and Mac sixth in the novice championships, I felt I was on a roll as I arrived in Sweden to ride Max in the third World Cup final. Masterminded by Jack Le Goff, an American based in France, this competition is rather ambitiously presented as the ultimate one-day individual championship. Each country has an allocation and certain events are designated as qualifiers, with the winners flying in from around the world for the grand finale. The timing is difficult and, at the moment, prize money insignificant, so it doesn't attract all the top names, but I'd qualified as a rider at Chatsworth and Thirlestane and Max had been off for much of the spring, so I decided to take him.

The first two finals were held in Pau, but now it was Malmo's turn. Funds were limited and the setting bizarre, a park between the sea and the city. The stables were in a hanger off a street ten minutes away and there was another urban walk to the dressage arena. The course was rather rustic and very impermanent, a twisty track that suffered from a lack of space. This was the first of two successive Malmo finals, but the public park element meant that every cross-country jump had to be taken down after the competition and then reassembled for 2006.

Maybe this is the shape of things to come, a city-centre venue that brings eventing to a wider audience. Certainly the people of Malmo turned out in large numbers to watch us. Or were they there for the rabbit show jumping, a contest the locals rate very highly. The rabbits are on leads, but they have to take their own path down a straight line of jumps, parallels, uprights and combinations, all about eighteen inches high. The handlers can't direct their charges, but they can tickle them from behind to get them going again if they refuse. On the whole, the performances were disappointing, with the rabbits more interested in bonking their rivals than clearing the jumps, but make no mistake, these were Grand Prix bunnies, with pedigrees and performance blurb printed in the programme, much as you'd find at a dog show. No way were they natural performers, but they certainly made us laugh. Only us, mind you: the Swedes watched them with the reverence usually reserved for Wimbledon finalists. Next to the rabbit ring there was a greyhound coursing competition, so you couldn't help feeling the dogs would have much more fun if the two were combined.

With the birth of our baby imminent, I'd agreed with Judy that I would leave immediately if Alice went into labour, hardly the best mindset for a major competition. Max performed a tense test and finished on his dressage score behind two Australians, Clayton Fredericks and Andrew Hoy, with Piia Pantsu, from Finland, third. The Swedes put on a great show, but the event never quite matched up to its World Cup billing. Even with a decent cross-country track and sizeable show jumping, it was basically a dressage competition and, as often happened, we Brits fell a little short of our rivals in this respect, so I finished where I'd started, in fourth place. If it is to take off, it needs a decent prize and a quality venue in England, perhaps Barbury Castle or Gatcombe. In Malmo, the winner got €18,000 (£13,000) and the fourth €6,000 (£4,000), which just about paid for the expense of going there.

Max's 2005 game plan hadn't originally included Burghley, but it all changed when he couldn't go cross-country at Badminton. As this was the last-ever long-format three-day event, I wanted to be there, but then again, I wondered if I could justify risking him on a steeplechase when he'd never need to do one again. I decided I could, but only if I was in contention after dressage, something that seemed extremely unlikely in the run-up to the event. He had made significant progress at Badminton and Barbury, but now, for some reason, he regressed, becoming fractious and resistant. Lizzie Murray tried to rescue the situation, improving him a bit, but I wasn't convinced he'd be good enough.

With the Europeans just one week away, I felt I should make the 400-mile round trip to Dorset to school Tam in the dark on Thursday and canter him in the dark on Friday morning in preparation. While I dashed back to Burghley, Alex was busy hacking and lunging Max ready for our test that afternoon. The moment I got on him, I felt he was going to go well. The edginess of the previous days had gone and he led the dressage ahead of Kim and Winsome Adante, no mean feat for any horse, let alone Max.

Mark Phillips's cross-country was tougher, quite hilly and more physically demanding than the year before. It was also tight for time, a bit of a worry, though it eventually played into my hands, because Max was one of only four or five without penalties. I used up a life at the Dairy Mound, a big parallel landing on sloping ground, followed by a sharp right turn around a tree to a narrow branch with a drop off higher ground. It rode well on three strides, but that meant coming in at an acute angle off a blind bend. Max argues when you turn him and, if he has his head in the air, he wouldn't see the second element, inviting a run-out, so I convinced myself he'd find it easier on four strides. A bad decision, as it turned out, because he landed a bit crooked off the first part, turned sooner than I wanted and got to the branch on three and a half strides, nearly shooting me out the side as he twisted in the air. I thought, 'I've blown it again,' but he managed to right himself and carry on quite unperturbed to finish in the lead ahead of Philip Dutton.

Max is an excellent jumper, with a much better record than the horses behind him, so I felt fairly confident when I walked the show jumping on Sunday. Although it wasn't big or impressive, it caused a lot of trouble and I had a two-fence cushion by the time I went in. Even on a bad day, that should be enough I thought, but after he hit two early on, I realised it could be an exceptionally bad day. Eighty per cent of the horses took out the last, a flimsy upright of planks, so I feared the worst, though I kept telling myself it was a fence like any other, a fence a careful horse like Max would clear with ease. And he did, making the day a fantastic one.

It was a moving moment for me. I'd never seen Max, with his average trot, tense outlook and lack of quality, as a winner at that level, but he would have taken the Burghley title the year before if I hadn't stopped him in the water, so this performance confirmed what a decent horse he is. One thing that has been consistent throughout his career is his amazing jump and I was proud I'd done right by him and Judy, who stood up in front of the crowd and said she'd been waiting for twelve years to win a four-star event. Initially the ugly duckling she couldn't bear to look at, Max had now joined the eventing elite. Winning Burghley has taken the pressure off him. Even if he never wins another event, he owes us nothing and the positive vibes have done his confidence no end of good. It was an emotional day for all the right reasons.

CHAPTER TWENTY-NINE

... And in With the New

S hort format arrived in Britain the next weekend when the European Championships were held at Blenheim. The home fixture meant that Britain could field a team of four, plus eight individuals, giving up-and-coming young riders valuable international experience. As usual, the spring events and summer build-up sorted out the selection process. Initially the regulars, Tam, Primmore's Pride, Shear l'Eau and Over to You would have been the obvious team, but Primmore's Pride suffered a minor injury. Pippa's second horse, Ensign, was at the same stage as Dumble and Frog, competitive but without the top-level mileage required for the team, so she was replaced by Zara Phillips. At twenty-three, Zara was relatively inexperienced, but she is certainly bred for the job, her father a four-times Badminton winner and her mother a European champion at Burghley in 1971. She has deep confidence in Toytown, backed by solid self-belief and an excellent temperament, and she earned her selection for Blenheim with a top four-star performance at Luhmühlen, where she finished second behind Bettina, proving her second at Burghley had been no fluke.

In the run-up to the competition, the press played down our chances; a positive because we didn't have to handle the pressure that goes with being favourites. Team GB had won five European team golds in a row, starting in 1995, but the journalists were convinced we were very unlikely to make it six. The French were strong and the Germans aggressive, fuelled by a desire for revenge for Athens. The German riders are very easy-going individuals, but they turned up at Blenheim as a team on the attack. Of course, you need to be positive to win a three-day event, but you also need to be controlled and relaxed. The Germans and French each had three individuals who were capable of winning, but our morale was high and the vibes were good.

With Pippa sidelined from the team, the running order was up for grabs. She's such a prolific winner that she's earned the right to run in her preferred third slot, with the rest of us falling into place around her. This time we decided Tam should go second so he could do his dressage on Thursday, when there'd be smaller crowds and fewer distractions. His fans are always there to cheer and clap, but we hoped to mislead all but the most dedicated with this change of direction. We also hoped to surprise the other teams in the draw, but the Germans may have learned about our revised order in time to switch Bettina to second in their own line-up, not a natural place for her as she usually starts first or last. As she was sure to get a good mark, it was to my advantage to avoid unwelcome comparisons by going as far away from her as possible, but now there was just one horse between us. This was a double backlash because, as happened with Pippa at Badminton earlier in the year, her excellent score was wildly applauded as Tam went into the ring.

In one sense our strategy worked, because I felt he did the best test of his career, but unfortunately he didn't score well. You always take a punt going on the first day because the scores are lower overall, but I felt the risk was worth it, because if Tam performed, I hoped they'd give him the marks he deserved. As it turned out, he behaved impeccably, but the judges seemed to find the new, non-cheeky Tam boring.

At the end of dressage, Leslie and I shared a beer to drown our sorrows at being out of the top ten. He tried to cheer me up by saying, 'You never know, I was twelfth after the cross-country in Athens,' to which I replied, 'Fair enough, but at least then you had two show jumping rounds to make up some ground.' With the sun shining down on Mike Etherington-Smith's relatively straightforward cross-country course, we waved goodbye to individual medals as we drained our glasses. In the run-up, we'd heard that Mike was turning the familiar three-star track into a true championship challenge, but in fact he only changed a couple of fences. With trees and markers set out as turning points to make it easier still, we thought we'd need a miracle to catch the Germans or French this time.

Astonishingly we got one: a deluge that started in the evening and lasted through the night, turning perfect ground into testing conditions, but would it be enough? It was hardly encouraging to watch Dag Albert, the Swedish number one, blazing round half a minute within the time as if he was riding in a gymkhana. Jeanette set the ball rolling for us in similar style and then it was Tam's turn. Going second, he had much better ground than he'd have had later in the day but, as usual, he was unaffected by the conditions, turning in his customary ebullient performance well within the time. Poor Leslie had a round to forget on Shear l'Eau, who looked wrong from the start. He got him home somehow, though he nearly came a cropper, hitting his chest on a big oxer and having to be withdrawn before the show jumping. Zara went in the very worst of the weather, but she seemed oblivious to the horizontal rain and poor visibility, putting up the performance of the day.

As the day progressed, it became increasingly clear that some of our rivals lacked the fitness required to combat high humidity and wet conditions. Luckily the German team didn't include Ingrid Klimke on Sleep Late, another horse who made nothing of the course, so when Bettina had a stop on Ringwood Cockatoo and two of her colleagues finished with time penalties, Team GB managed to creep ahead. Even losing Leslie and counting Jeanette's dressage score, we had three fences in hand over the Germans and the French at the start of the show jumping. Zara had taken the lead individually, with Pippa, whose stickability had been tested to the limits, in second, ahead of Belgium's Karin Donckers. I was surprised to move up to fourth, and was excited to find myself within grasping distance of the podium. If Tam jumped clear he could well win a medal and avoid the pain of finishing fourth, the worst possible 'nearly but not quite' position.

Tam was in top form, sailing through the vets' inspection with his trademark leap and buck. Experience has taught me that it's wise to jump him in the morning to take the buzz out of him, then put him away before the competition proper in the afternoon, but second-guessing Tam is always Russian roulette. At Blenheim, he was angelic over the practice fence, jumping like a dobbin, so relaxed and easy that I didn't know how to ride him. That wasn't normal and I didn't like it at all. My suspicions were confirmed when he darted into the arena, tail whirling, but should I be glad to have the real Tam back or anxious about the fences he might be about to flatten? It did not bode well when he shot away from a man lowering his arm for manual, back-up timing as we went through the start, destroying my stride into the first fence, and threatening a demolition job. Agile as ever, Tam fiddled it and landed clear, then bounded forward as if he hadn't jumped for a year, fooling about all the way round, but mercifully without faults.

When neither Pippa nor Karin went clear, I moved up to second, but Zara needed to take out two to give me gold. Of course I didn't want her to jump badly, but I can't deny two down would have been nice and it wouldn't have jeopardised our chances of winning team gold. As it was, she jumped a clear and won in style, a much more satisfactory result for both of us than a single error would have been. It was incredible riding for the team in front of the massive home crowd who came to cheer, party and carry us forward on a wave of emotional support.

We had celebrations in the lorry park after the prize-giving. Zara's first senior championship was incredible and she took her victory with her usual grace and natural style. This was a huge personal achievement for her, especially as she had to handle all the extra media pressure she gets because of who she is. She is a rider with great natural talent and she put up a performance way beyond her years.

By the time we got home after several hectic weeks on all fronts, Team Fox-Pitt felt as if it had been flattened by an elephant, but we still had some way to go before we could sit back and relax. While Max and Tam had been going strong, the others were preparing for their next engagements, with the exception of Frog, who was taking an early holiday before going to Lizzie Murray for a winter's intensive dressage training. My first fixture was Gatcombe, a much-needed outing for Dumble, Mac and Barney, but first I had to ride First Mate in the novice class. At that point, I'd had two falls in 2005, both from him when he'd used his lethal buck to good advantage to get me off in the school, so I was on a hat-trick. In the lead after dressage and show jumping on an experienced novice, I hoped the cross-country would be a formality.

Halfway round, I jumped a simple fence and thought, 'Yep, that's another one done.' The next thing I remember is looking up at a ring of very anxious faces. I was trained from an early age to get straight back on, but that was out of the question this time. I learned later to say nothing after a fall, because if you speak gobbledegook you get stood down. When people started to ask me questions, I refused even to give my name, unaware that I'd been babbling away for five minutes while I was unconscious. Going quiet triggered a mass panic and I found myself being strapped onto a board. 'You're going to hospital in a helicopter,' the paramedic told me. 'Isn't that fun?' I said it wasn't necessary, shaking my head violently to show them I hadn't broken my neck, as they'd feared at first. At that point, three men jumped on me and bound my head to the board as well, trussing me up for the journey to Frenchay Hospital outside Bristol.

As I lay there, I read a message above me that said, 'Do not panic. You are in a helicopter,' presumably to reassure those who come round during the journey thinking they're in hell. I was very relaxed during my airlift, drifting in and out of sleep with no fear that I'd suffered any permanent damage. When we arrived, the doctor checked me out to see if I could walk and dismissed me immediately, asking if I wanted him to call me a cab. Extraordinary since, twenty minutes before, I was deemed so bad as to need air transport! However, it is very reassuring to know that every precaution was taken. The rogue fence, a simple rail over a wall out of darkness into light, had been there for several years, but this time it caused an inexplicable number of falls. Maybe the trees had grown up, reducing the light, or the horses had the sun in their eyes at that time of day. I remember thinking here's the fence, here's the stride, now he'll take off, but he didn't, chesting the rail and turning over. My theory is that my head must have hit his neck before I fell, so I was unconscious and relaxed as I went down. Fortunately we landed separately and, although he rolled on me as he got up, my only injury was a tiny bruise on my sternum.

The disadvantage of an airlift is that it doesn't get you home. When Alice, who was having lunch with friends at Shepton Mallet, came out to find twenty-one missed calls, she panicked, so she was relieved to get to the ones from me asking her to pick me up. I was fine the next morning, no stiffness but a bit distracted and unfocused. I was hopeless when Becky tried to get me to concentrate on business matters. For the first few days, I had no wish to ride. Not that I could – in public anyway. Because I'd been stood down for three weeks, Kreuth was taken out of my programme and it was touch and go for Boekelo. The ban started the day I was knocked out and reducing it depended on how long I'd been unconscious. There were conflicting reports on that front, with assessments ranging from two to ten minutes, with some people claiming I'd been talking gibberish and others that I'd been fine.

According to our team doctor, Peter Whitehead, my only chance of getting to Boekelo, which started just before the ban ended, was to take a psychometric test in London. Originally devised for jockeys, it starts with an interview and a balance test. The results are very black and white: you have to stand for thirty seconds on one leg with your eyes closed; if you only make it to twenty-nine, you're toast. You have to recite phone numbers backwards, count down from one hundred in sevens and play a form of Pelmanism on a computer, all of it on the clock. The downside is that once you've chosen to go down the psychometric route, you have to pass it before you can ride again, no matter how long it takes. When Gemma Burton, who I'd known in Atlanta when she was Gary Parsonage's girlfriend, rang me to ask me to ride one of her horses, she told me it had taken her a year to get it. As I felt I could fail it even if I hadn't had a fall, I wondered whether the risk was worth it, but Dumble was in fine form and I wanted to take him to Boekelo, so I bit the bullet and headed for London. The whole thing was a nightmare, because I only had time for one shot before Boekelo and, as the results had to be assessed in Australia, I had three white-knuckle days to wait for the outcome. It was a massive relief when Peter Whitehead rang to say I'd passed.

As I wasn't ready for Kreuth, I asked Mary King to ride Barney, a decision endorsed by his owners. He's not a horse who goes in a conventional way and he has to be ridden tactfully, but he obviously enjoyed his time with Mary because he finished second, ahead of her own horse. He was mid-field after dressage, but moved up steadily as the cross-country took its toll on his rivals. She adapted to him quickly and gave him every chance in the jumping phases, riding him to perfection. He's not very supple, but he's tough and determined. In the early days, his show jumping was weak, but Pete Charles has taught me to cope with his extraordinary technique so he's exceeded my expectations on all fronts. I was sad not to be on him, but very pleased that his owners Michael and Jane got some compensation for Bramham, where he was unlucky not to be third behind Dumble and Frog.

Dumble hadn't run since Gatcombe two months earlier, so despite feeling great he was rather under-prepared to take on the quality opposition at Boekelo. As Blenheim's three-star had had to give way to the European Championships, there were 110 starters, a top-class field that included twenty-five Brits and some of the best continentals. If you think eventing weather in England is dodgy, you should try Holland in October but, for the first time in living memory, the sun shone throughout the competition and the ground, which is usually wet and has sometimes been frozen solid, was surprisingly good. Dumble did an excellent test and he ended up third, behind Ruth Friend (now Edge). Having recovered from his foot problems in the nick of time, Coastal Ties also did the dressage, only to develop colic before the cross-country. For his long-suffering owner, Lady Kelvedon, and me, it was the final nail in the coffin and it was the moment when we decided to cut our losses and give him to Lara Ross, an ex-pupil of mine, to see if she could break his jinx at a less demanding level.

The cross-country course was straightforward at the outset, but the last part was very twisty, making the time difficult to get. That suited Dumble, who is nippy but not a galloping machine and he gave me a good feeling as he powered round inside the time. As the two ahead of me had penalties we edged into the lead, but with half a dozen rivals jammed up behind us. When my three nearest challengers went clear in the show jumping, I knew I'd drop to fifth or sixth if I had a fence down. Yogi was there to help with the warm-up, always tricky with Dumble because the less he jumps the better he goes. Going in with no room for error, I couldn't help thinking he might easily knock a couple, especially as the crowds and the tents were very close to the arena. However, he really tried, pulling out all the stops and giving me one of my most satisfying wins by a tiny 1.2 margin over Andreas Dibowski on his Olympic horse, Little Lemon. It was Pete Charles who gave me the confidence in Dumble to jump that clear round, so he was the crucial factor in our victory. As I rode out in triumph, my accident was well and truly consigned to the history books and my morale was high as I headed home for some quality time with my family.

CHAPTER THIRTY

Father's Day

In 2005, I was runner-up to Pippa at Badminton, Zara at Blenheim and Philip Dutton in the world rankings, but even if I'd won them all, the satisfaction would have paled into insignificance beside the birth of my son. Oliver was born on 19 August and I was there to see him come into the world. When Alice first told me she was pregnant, I'd been excited and scared in equal measure, worried that our comfortable life was about to be thrown into disarray. We first saw our child, a strange, squirming thing, on a monitor at the three-month scan. 'My God,' I said. 'It looks like a naked baby gerbil.' Alice asked the nurse if she could tell how big it would be, to which she replied, 'Very average,' adding 'but I don't imagine it will be for long,' when I stood up to leave. Our fellow parents-to-be had come out looking very serious, but we were in hysterics as we joked about 'The Gerbil'. The name stuck, especially when John McCririck warned Alice on television that it would give our baby a lifelong complex. My mother took up the theme, saying that it would be known as the 'Ginger Gerbil' if it was born with red hair, which was a possibility.

Alice didn't relish the prospect of being huge, but she had an active pregnancy, working until mid-June. We took our mid-season break on Pabbay on our own, a last chance to enjoy the island together as a couple rather than as a family. As we couldn't go lobster potting or take huge walks, we had the perfect excuse to read and sleep, to talk about the future and how our baby would fit into our lives. Alice was quite large by this time, so the invisible third person was always with us and our last moments of freedom passed all too quickly.

On 17 July, we had our first open day at the new yard, a charity event for the Katie and Eloise Memorial Trust. We'd had one the year before at Fontmell Parva in the run-up to the Olympics, but this was a proper affair, a showcase for the stables and a push to make decent money for the Trust. The rain was tipping down when we woke up, but several hundred people braved it and the sun came out by 11 a.m making for a very enjoyable day. Alice introduced a programme of demonstrations, which included Ibby and I on two of the young horses, dressage with Lizzie Murray and jumping on Stunning. The crowds then watched as we resumed our normal activities, lunging, working in the arenas and on the gallops. The local burger van came to sell food, donating a percentage of its profits to the Trust. We were amazed by the turnout, but people rarely get to see behind the scenes in eventing, so maybe it's something we in the sport should do more of.

Gatcombe, Malmo, Thirlestane, Blair, Burghley, Blenheim? As these events were coming up over successive weekends, one of them would coincide with the birth, but which would it be? Our baby was due on Friday, 19 August, but Alice's waters broke on Thursday morning. As I hadn't left for Thirlestane, it was perfect timing and we set off for the hospital thinking that he or she would start to pop out any minute. The nurse said everything was fine and to come back when Alice was having contractions every five minutes. When we asked when that would be, she replied, 'Who knows? If nothing's happened by Monday, we'll have to induce.' We were horrified at the prospect of waiting for four days but that's how it is, so Alice kept her appointment at the hairdresser in Dorchester and I worked the horses under Lizzie Murray's eagle eye.

In the evening, Alice felt tired, but good. As I started cooking supper, she said, 'I think I had a contraction.' 'What do you mean, you think?' I asked, cooking a bit more. It wasn't long before things were definitely happening, so we left our supper on the table and dashed to the hospital. I didn't know what to expect. We arrived at 11 p.m. and Oli joined us seven hours later... I've seen a lot of puppies, foals, lambs, calves and guinea pigs come into the world so I'm not squeamish, but it was the most amazing relief when the head appeared, followed by the rest of our baby boy.

The birth happily went according to plan and the hospital in Dorchester looked after us very well. All four grandparents made a huge effort to get there the same day, my mother from Kent, my father from London and the Plunketts from Oxfordshire. We didn't have to use much imagination deciding on a name, as both our fathers are called Oliver. I remember driving home next day, taking great care and suddenly feeling a lot more responsible. We were so excited we stopped off en route to show him to Charlie and Sarah Church, good friends we've made since we have come to live in Dorset. They cracked open the champagne and laughed at us – the new proud parents.

The first month with Oli was made so much easier by the wonderful Lucy Ross, who came to help us get on track. As Alice wanted to go back to work after three months, we planned to get full-time help, but when we were discussing the candidates, Lucy chipped in with an offer of a more long-term arrangement. She has been with us ever since and without her our lives would be impossible.

Until you have a child, you don't know what you're missing, but I feel very lucky and privileged to be a father. Parenthood has always been something I've hoped for, but Oli has put our busy, selfish lives into perspective, something it's easy to lose when you're as involved in horses as I am. I remember changing my sisters' nappies and I love looking after Oli whenever I can. As soon as he slept through the night, I was occasionally left in sole charge when Alice had to stay away for work. It's extraordinary how such a tiny person with so little to offer held us all enthralled from the start. He always brought a smile to my face and it is the best thing when you get one in return.

Oli's christening in the church in Hinton St Mary in December was unforgettable. Anthony and Val gave us a delicious lunch and our families turned out in force, four grandparents, four godparents, my brother and sisters, lots of cousins and our closest friends, about thirty in all. We'd registered Oli's birth, but this was our first public responsibility to our child. I was totally caught by surprise in the church by how emotional I felt; as I looked around, I couldn't believe how lucky we were to have such a perfect baby and wonderful support. Poor Oli was decked out in traditional Fox-Pitt christening clothes with the Plunkett robe over the top. The christening was part of the regular morning service which lasts for over an hour, way too long in Oli's opinion.

Jackie, who hasn't been confirmed, hit a lighter note when she followed everyone up to the altar for communion. She thought it was for a blessing but, as her hands were in front of her, the vicar put the bread into them. Jackie looked at it blankly until he came back with the wine. 'Just eat it,' he hissed as she tried to stuff it in her pocket. She crammed it in her mouth and gulped some wine, convinced she'd been confirmed at last, while Lucy and her husband Clive creased up beside her.

Of course Oli won't remember his first Christmas, but Alice and I had a great time with the Plunketts at Cradle Farm. They prefer to do the traditional things, church, horses and drinks parties during the day, leaving the evening free for a relaxed celebration. As Jackie also likes to go away for Christmas, we left Alex in charge of the yard. In the past, a lot of horses used to go home for the holidays, but now their owners prefer them to stay at the yard. They reverse the role at New Year when Jackie takes charge and Alex enjoys some socialising.

Christmas Day is a non-riding day, but Alice and I went hunting on Christmas Eve and Boxing Day. Our first family trip got off to a rocky start when the small lorry, with a baby, two horses, two dogs and armloads of presents on board, ground to a halt on the A303 ten miles from home. As it couldn't be repaired at the roadside, Alex rescued us in the big lorry and we switched everything over before speeding off to get to the meet on time.

Hunting isn't as relaxed as it was before the ban came into force in 2005, but it's still an enjoyable day out for both horses and riders. As I don't have the time to get out as much as I'd like to, I particularly enjoyed hunting with Alice and her mother over Christmas. The pressure of operating within the law falls more heavily on the huntsman and the master than the field. Like most other hunts, the Heythrop lays a man-made trail for the hounds to follow. Anthony hosted the last traditional meet of our local hunt, the Blackmore Vale, at Hinton St Mary, an emotional occasion, though slightly less so than their first day under the new system a few days later. I went out with Bob, one of hundreds of people who were there to show their support.

I see the hunting legislation as one more step towards removing freedom of choice. Steeplechasing and shooting are also at risk in an increasingly regimented and restricted climate, as is eventing. Even if the Conservatives get in at the next election, it is unlikely that the hunting law will ever be reversed, but there is the hope that the ridiculous and unenforceable legislation will be relaxed. Of course, that won't help the hunts that have already gone out of business. Whether a hunt thrives under the new regulations is largely a matter of location and luck. The Blackmore and Sparkford Vale, which has had very little trouble with saboteurs, is doing well, whereas the Cattistock, its nearest neighbour, is in trouble, due to a virulent anti who camps at the gates of the kennels, causing stress all round. On a positive note, the ban has shown just how much grass-roots support there is for hunting; in many cases, the number of hunt subscribers has risen.

When the phone rang one morning in November and an American voice on the other end said, 'Hi, I'm Siobhan, Madonna's personal assistant. We've Googled you and she'd like you to be her riding coach,' I was convinced someone was winding me up, but I was wrong. Apparently Hunter, who sponsor the Fox-Pitt Eventing Club, donated seven pairs of wellies to her Live Aid Concert. Now it was payback time. Madonna had had a much-publicised fall earlier in the year, but she was ready to start riding again. Hunter felt that an article linking the two of us with their product would be a significant boost to their sales. She wouldn't agree to any kind of stunt, but she did want to hire me to get her riding confidently again. It took some time for Siobhan to persuade me this was for real, but eventually I agreed in principle.

For three months, it looked as if that was as far as it would go, but in December I got another call from Siobhan to say that Madonna was in residence. She and her husband, Guy Ritchie, spend part of the year on their estate less than ten miles from Hinton. She didn't want formal lessons in an indoor school, but would it be possible for me to bring a horse over and ride out with her on her land? On the appointed day, Bob and I set out for Ashmore, arriving in a small yard with five stables, a barn and a cramped indoor school three miles from the main house. Annette, her groom, introduced me to Tom, Madonna's Welsh cob, Sting's coloured cob and the pony she keeps for her nine-year-old daughter, Lourdes (Lola), but the rock star was nowhere to be seen.

When she arrived, she was very relaxed, with a red furry hat and no make-up. She asked me to ride Tom in the arena first so I could assess him, then she rode him so I could assess her. On the one hand, it felt very normal, but on the other I had to pinch myself as I gave her a few pointers. 'Do you like him, do you like him?' she asked eagerly, clearly keen that I should. In fact, he's very suitable because he's teaching her to ride. She was brought up in the city and she'd never sat on a horse until three years ago. Thanks to her work and her intensive regime, she's very fit, with excellent posture and good balance, so the basics were in place before she started. When we set out for our ride, it became clear that although neither Tom nor Madonna wanted to waste time walking, there was some cause for conflict because Tom favours a spanking trot and Madonna a canter.

It's a beautiful estate, hilly with a lot of wildlife and deer everywhere, distractions for any horse with a tendency to shy, so I concentrated on keeping Bob between Tom and the pheasants that might fly out and spook him. Madonna was chatty and amusing, telling me how her managers and staff are terrified she'll fall off again and put them out of business. She's determined to go on with her riding, because she finds it more exhilarating than anything else she does. She doesn't like being out of control, but she loves galloping, breathing in rhythm with her horse and not quite knowing what's going to happen next. For her, riding is the ultimate escape from the pressures of her life.

She fell in love with Bob, saying he was the most beautiful horse she'd ever seen. She wanted to have a sit on him, but I wasn't prepared to risk the repercussions if she fell off, so I said she'd have to wait until we'd done a bit more. Two and a half hours of trotting and cantering left Tom at the point of exhaustion while Bob, who was fit from hunting, was dripping with sweat. He'd probably have been happy to hear Siobhan tell me that Madonna only wanted a couple of sessions. If so, he was about to be disappointed.

When we went home after Christmas, winter struck with a vengeance, making it impossible for me to ride out with Madonna on the frozen ground. Instead she got her chance on Bob, our quietest horse, in our indoor school. They struck up a great partnership once she found the right buttons and she braved our all-weather gallop in bitter cold and fluttering snow. I rode behind her on Dylan, who was bucking and generally creating mayhem. I was afraid his antics would excite Bob, who luckily behaved immaculately, because Madonna kept glancing over her shoulder and asking if everything was all right. Later, when she saw the true picture on Guy's video, she said she was glad she hadn't known how badly Dylan was behaving. Afterwards she took the time to chat to everyone. It's not every day that Madonna walks on to your yard; how mad it was to have the world's greatest diva hanging out drinking tea in our tack room.

We had an even more surreal New Year's Day with her and Guy, a relaxed family lunch that lasted until 8 p.m. After seeing the New Year in with Paddy and Iona Hoare, we arrived feeling a little the worse for wear and with no idea what to expect. Guy met us and introduced us to the other guests, Gwyneth Paltrow, Chris Martin and their daughter, Apple. I managed to recognise Gwyneth, but although I'm a fan of Coldplay, I had difficulty placing Chris. Alice was trying to signal me to tell me who he was, but she needn't have worried because he broke the ice by saying we looked terrible after what must have been a hard night and we shouldn't feel we had to make polite conversation.

Oli was invited and, with Gwyneth heavily pregnant with Moses, there was a lot of baby talk over a very normal lunch of roast lamb.

My first time at Badminton, with Steadfast in 1989.

On the winners' podium for winning the show jumping section at the University World Championships in Rotterdam, 1990.

Chaka at Badminton in 1993 – our first three-day event together, where we finished seventh. (Dick Cassan)

Loch Alan, never a keen ditch jumper, but here he is jumping the biggest ditch of all – the Cottesmore Leap at Burghley, 1996. (Equestrian Services Thorney)

At the Open European Championships at Burghley 1997. I won the individual European Silver and Open European Bronze and Team Gold, riding Cosmopolitan.
(Barbara Thomson Photography NZ)

Ballincoola showing his excellent show jumping technique in Kentucky, 2004.
(Kit Houghton)

Stunning clearing the water on our way to an individual fourth and team gold at the European Championships in Pau 2001, and (inset) testing the water at Pau with individual gold medallist Pippa Funnell.
(Les Garennes/Julia Rau)

Moon Man performing the best test of his career at Kentucky in 2003. He finished third – his best four-star result. (Shannon K. Brinkman)

Moon Man speeds his way round one of his favourite courses – Gatcombe in 2000.

Tamarillo in full flight at the Athens Olympics, 2004, before disaster struck. (REUTERS/Eric Gaillard)

Lifting the Mitsubishi Trophy at Badminton in 2004 – my lifetime achievement. The happy owner Mary Guinness looks on.

Celebrations at the yard following our Olympic success in 2008 – from l to r: Sylvia Harley, Lindy Best, Lynn Earle, Richard Earle, Belinda Blanshard, Jane Kier and Cathy Butler.

Parkmore Ed powers his way to an impressive win at Burghley 2007.
(© David Miller/Horse & Hound/IPC+ Syndication)

There was a funny moment when Chris started talking to me about his work and Madonna piped up, 'You'll have to tell him what you do because he doesn't even have a clue what I do.' When we went for separate walks, girls and children in one direction, boys in the other, the conversation turned to horses. All in all, it was a real laugh, full of genial banter, and we were made to feel very welcome and very relaxed.

Bob and I went riding with Madonna fairly regularly until March, when she left for Los Angeles to prepare for her world tour and I tackled the new eventing season. She told me that the safety-obsessed Californians wouldn't let her ride interesting horses for fear of reprisals if she had an accident. I suggested she take Tom with her and she did, though different management and the lack of turnout made him much feistier than usual and he returned to Dorset when her schedule got too hectic.

After seeing our facilities, Madonna asked Paddy to build her a larger indoor school so she could ride when she was free in the evenings and in the winter. He's already got planning permission and his target is to have it up at the end of the summer so that it's ready when she returns from America. She loves the idea of learning more about eventing, but this year she's been too busy to come and check it out. However, she sponsored a fence at Portman Horse Trials and made a lot of progress with her riding, and her love affair with Bob remains on track.

After the big freeze, it was wonderful to spend four days in Dubai at the Show Jumping World Cup. The event was the brainchild of Princess Haya, the wife of Sheikh Mohammed Al Maktoum, and implemented by Simon Brooks-Ward through his company, Horse Power International. Her plan was to present all the FEI disciplines to the people of Dubai, so she organised demonstrations of dressage, eventing, carriage driving, vaulting and endurance as back-up for the main show jumping competitions. Toddy and I, eventing's two tall men, were invited to do some fairly basic demos, but our schedule was relatively relaxed so we had plenty of time by the pool at the Jumeira Beach Hotel. Alice was involved as well, putting the finishing touches to the *Horse Tails* series she had been working on for the last few months for Animal Planet.

With so much sunshine to enjoy, we never got to Dubai's celebrated ski slope, reputedly the most challenging indoor black run in the world. The idea of hiring skis and kit to hit the snow in Dubai wasn't tempting, even less so as we were heading out to Sainte-Foy soon after we got home. Venture Ski had offered a chalet holiday as a prize for winning the 2005 British Open Championship. Ever the Gatcombe specialist, Bob had secured it for us, so we toasted him enthusiastically throughout the trip. Paddy and Iona travelled with us and Tintin and Tess, his Swedish girlfriend, drove through the night from Belgium to join us.

We divided into two compatible ski groups, with the experts, Paddy, Tintin and Tess, heading off into the powder snow, while Alice, Iona and I took a more cautious approach on the piste. I love skiing, but I have no desire to become more adventurous. I still have plates in my leg as a result of my riding accident in 1997 and they act as a restriction, similar to driving a lorry with a governor set at 80kph. I'm always aware of it and I know that improving would mean going for it and possibly getting injured. I take a bit of a chance doing it at all, but I'm prepared to accept the risks involved in cruising along in my comfort zone.

Sainte-Foy is expanding rapidly, but it's also brilliantly placed for day trips to Val d'Isère, Tignes and Les Arcs, so we had plenty of slopes to choose from. Venture Ski's chalet was very luxurious and the food was delicious, so we were very well looked after. They were talking about offering the prize again this year, an effective promotion from their point of view because so many eventers are enthusiastic skiers. Given the meagre prize money in the sport, I'm surprised that more events don't take the initiative by asking companies to give back-up prizes to owners and riders. Meanwhile, I'm very grateful to Venture Ski and, of course, to Bob, who is hopefully on top of the job of guaranteeing our return to Sainte-Foy in future years.

CHAPTER THIRTY-ONE

All My Ducks in a Row

With luck, I will be able to compete in at least two more Olympic Games, Beijing in 2008 and London in 2012. Tam has always been my likely first choice for Beijing, partly because he is my top horse and partly because he would be the best at coping with the heat and humidity in Hong Kong, where the equestrian competitions will be staged. Although I hope he might go on a lot longer, I've always planned it as his swansong. Realistically, you have to accept that the horse you take to Hong Kong might not bounce back, so it makes sense to take an old campaigner rather than a younger prospect who has it all to come. Whether we like it or not, Beijing will be another Athens, so the competition itself won't ask a lot of the horses, but the climate, the journey and the quarantine certainly will.

At this stage, my back-ups for Beijing are hopefully Max (Ballincoola) and Frog (Idalgo). Max is the most exposed, a tough, sound, determined contender who is building steadily on the confidence he got from his Burghley victory in 2005. His show jumping would be a big plus in an Olympic competition and, by then, his dressage should have become even more consistent.

Frog is an amazing animal, a bit like Tam in that he'll be truly astonishing if he comes good. It'll take time to prepare him successfully, for mental as well as physical reasons, as he needs to take everything on board slowly. At eleven, he's already capable of better dressage than Tam and his thoroughbred blood makes it easy for him to do the time cross-country. After a fiery start, he's finally beginning to settle, so we could have it all to play for in Beijing or London or both.

It may seem premature to lay the foundations for 2012, but it can take six years or more to produce a top competition horse, so I spent much of the winter looking at eighty or ninety potential contenders. I hope this will be the last big push of my career, the basis for a string that will be successful over the next decade. One of my problems is knowing exactly what I should be looking for at the start of the short-format era. As the cross-country is of decreasing significance, the theory is we'll need horses with more scope for dressage and show jumping. If so, the emphasis would switch to warm bloods, yet the early stars of 2006 were quality horses who can gallop and jump, led by Andrew Hoy's Badminton winner, Moonfleet, which was bred to win the Gold Cup. Maybe we need different types of horses for different events and conditions. Then again, we'd need a crystal ball to select our best options when the entries go in, given there's no way of predicting the weather or the course builder's whims.

As a result of my owners' shopping expeditions, I have half a dozen promising young horses, of which I'd expect half to make the grade for next season. They come from Ireland, New Zealand, Australia, France and Britain, a diverse collection of bloodlines hopefully resulting in a range of options. The most precocious is Chuckleberry (Chuck), a handsome, eight-year-old grey that Catherine Joice bought to replace Arctic Knight, who was sold in 2005. Part warm blood and well produced by event rider Jo Geddes, he won two novices and came fifth in his first intermediate. Navigator (Bart), owned by a consortium called Bart's Ladies, is the same age, a chestnut thoroughbred who came from Sharon Ridgeway in Australia, and he too has shown some good form at novice level.

I have two promising seven-year-olds, All That Jazz, who spent much of the spring on stallion duties, and Cool Mountain, who was sent to me by Theresa Stopford-Sackville, when her older horse, Silver Dollar, developed wind problems. After winning his last two events, he has upgraded to intermediate and he really does seem to have it all.

I also found Walk the Line, a large grey with the jump to come second in the Australian six-year-old National Championship, through Sharon Ridgeway's yard for Judy Skinner.

So which are the geese and which the swans? At this stage of my career, my aim is to find horses with the ability to be top class if things go their way, rather than good all-rounders like Bob. The law of averages dictates that some of the novices won't make it, so I try to cover all the bases. If I'm honest, I can never turn down an opportunity, so I take on a lot, maybe more than I should, and ride them round a few events to see how they shape up. The year 2006 saw Andrew Hoy win Kentucky on Master Monarch, not a horse you'd buy for his movement, and Badminton on Moonfleet, initially an inconsistent jumper. It just shows you never know.

In February 2006, we held the inaugural open day for the Fox-Pitt Eventing Club, which we hope will be the first organisation of its kind to succeed in our sport. Racing has some fantastic success stories, notably the Elite Racing Club, who own the prolific winner, Soviet Song, and the Royal Ascot Racing Club, who hit the jackpot with the 2005 Derby winner, Motivator. Eventing has dabbled with the idea, but never with much conviction. I'm hoping we can get people involved who could never afford a horse outright, but would like to share in the action. The plan for the open day was to meet the members and show them Dylan and Imran, the two six-year-olds who would be running in the club colours when the season got under way. Imran is generous and industrious, as talented as Bob ever was and the kind of horse who might well take a young rider to the top or even go well for an amateur. Dylan is probably the better horse, but being big and weak he still needs a lot of time.

Fortunately it was a brilliant blue-sky day, ideal for me to work the two horses in the outdoor school while Alice pointed out their finer points over the public address. We had 170 people, members, who came for free, and their guests, who paid a small fee. We gave them breakfast in the office when they arrived – coffee, croissants and bacon rolls served by Alice and Lucy – showed them round the yard and finished with a general meeting to discuss our aims and approach to the season. Club members were allowed to take photos of themselves with their favourite horses, mainly Tam and Bob, the latter's army of fans boosted by his much-publicised success with Madonna.

The club campaign got off to a flying start, with Imran winning a novice class at Portman Horse Trials and Dylan coming second at the South of England. Event organisers have welcomed us and the turnout was good for my course walk at Badminton. Our club manager, Tom Gittins, who also runs the Countryside Alliance Racing Club and other syndicates, has done a great job and somehow persuaded events to make room for the members' tent we usually put up whenever one of the horses runs.

Alice and I own the club horses and we guarantee that at least one will be running throughout the season, so if both are off the road, we have to provide a substitute. Several members have approached us to say they'd like to be more involved, so we're thinking of running a syndicate in tandem with the club next year. Members could follow the club horse, as they do now, or pay more for fractional ownership of the club syndicate horse. If it was a winner, they'd be eligible for their share of the prize money and the proceeds of any sale.

As Max had won Burghley, I was in a position to try for the Rolex Grand Slam, a $250,000 prize for winning Burghley, Kentucky and Badminton consecutively. My plan was to take Coup de Coeur, a ride I'd taken over from Leslie, and Dumble to America, keeping Tam and Max for what I hoped would be the grand finale at Badminton a week later. After a couple of minor setbacks in the winter, Fred went very well at Belton and Dumble had won his last two three-day events so things were looking good.

The journey to America went smoothly and we arrived to find good conditions, with the ground drying fast after rain. The draw wasn't in my favour. I would have liked to have started on Dumble, but it was Fred who came out of the hat first. In such a new partnership, it's not surprising he wasn't settled for the dressage. Although he put in some great trot work, his canter work showed some tension. The four-star atmosphere is so much bigger than that of a three-star and Dumble spooked a bit and didn't perform as well as he could have done either. They ended the phase twelfth and eighteenth, disappointing for what are potentially my best dressage scorers and even more so with the Grand Slam on my mind.

Fred set off enthusiastically on the cross-country, but lost a shoe on take-off at one of the corners, as I realised when it flew over my shoulder. He was slipping a bit on ground that was now quite firm, but I thought he'd be okay. As we came into the Head of the Lake water complex, I wasn't aware the other front shoe had gone as well. If I'd known, I'd have pulled up. As it was, he reached the point of take-off and I thought he was going to stop. What happened next passed in moments, but it felt like ages. With minimal grip, he slid into the base of the fence and never came up, rotating straight over the rail into the water.

We fell over the big drop as if in slow motion and I have haunting memories of lying there waiting for him to land on me. I was trying desperately to get out of his way, but my foot was momentarily stuck in the stirrup. As it came free, he came down next to me and lay there, much as Briarlands Pippin had done at Badminton in 1992. I jumped up before he did and it was such a huge relief when he got up and we walked away together. My blood ran cold when I saw he'd lost both shoes because he never had a chance. He'd cut his shoulder and neck and was quite sore, but remarkably we were able to walk away pretty much unscathed.

My focus switched to Dumble. He had come out with a big hock for his dressage, the result of a bang in the stable. We X-rayed it after his test and he was deemed okay to start. Doing his first four-star on a tough, hilly course was a big ask and he was never firing on all cylinders, never relishing the challenge. As he was jumping to the left and failing to make the distances in the combinations, I took the long way out of the coffin. The time wasn't looking good as I approached the Head of the Lake and I asked myself what I was trying to achieve on a young horse with his future before him. It's very hard to pull up with the adrenaline flowing and the owners waiting eagerly for good news, but it was the obvious thing to do. At that point, he'd had a good experience. Much better he should finish safe and sound so he could go on to fight another day. Talk about disappointment, but at least we enjoyed staying with my best man, Julian Dollar, then managing Dr Ryan's stud in Kentucky, with his wife, Georgia and my god-daughter Daisy.

On their return from Kentucky, Dumble's owners decided once again to put him on the market and Judy Skinner and Margie Hall were very excited when they received an offer they couldn't refuse. No one deserves a big sale more, but I was sad to see him go, because I haven't had many horses as consistent as he is. After turning down a six-figure sum for Wallow, only to have him go chronically lame shortly afterwards, I'd be more likely to accept a big offer, even if meant losing an Olympic dream, and I'd always encourage my owners to do the same. Wallow spent his enforced early retirement with us, dogged by injuries and arthritis that eventually resulted in partial paralysis behind. After discussions with his co-owners, we put him down in 2005. It was a sad end for a horse who had promised so much for so long.

Back at home, Badminton was coming up fast. Tam and Max were on great form. Unlike Burghley, where he felt on edge during his preparation, Max had been very relaxed all spring, carrying his condition well and working through in a settled rhythm. Again the draw wasn't ideal: Tam, who is usually among the last to do dressage, had to go on Thursday morning, with Max taking his usual spot on Friday afternoon. Ironically, Max peaked on Thursday. When I worked him with Lizzie, he was on the button, cooperative, soft, the best I've ever known him at an event but, on Friday, he wasn't there. Maybe he would have settled if I'd warmed him up for another hour, but he'd definitely got out of bed on a different side and I never really had him. We would never have rivalled the leaders, Andrew Hoy and Moonfleet, but we could have been much closer. Producing your horse at his best on the day is one of the challenges of eventing, but there was some consolation in the fact that he'd felt great on Thursday as he usually produces his best work at home.

Tam too felt very good on Thursday and I was confident he was about to produce an exceptional test. He did some of his best-ever trot work, but was unsettled in the canter and scored 49.8. He was never going to win from that mark, so I withdrew him before the cross-country, quite unaware of the furore that would cause.

Back in the winter, Yogi told me Tam was excused Badminton in advance of the World Championships in Aachen in August. Toytown and Call Again Cavalier were in the same privileged position, but Zara, Mary and I were still free to take our horses to Badminton if we wanted to. They chose not to but, with the Grand Slam in the offing at that stage, I entered Tam with every intention of running him. By the time the competition came up, my prospects for Aachen were looking more fragile. Fred and Dumble were out of contention after Kentucky, so Tam might be my only option. If he'd done an amazing dressage and won a second Badminton, I could have lived with not going to the World Championships should I have injured him. As he hadn't, I wasn't prepared to risk him.

M W Guinness always has Tam's best interests at heart, so she was happy with my decision. Not so Tam, who was all dressed up with nowhere to go. He'd have loved to do the cross-country as much as I'd have loved riding him round it, but you have to look at the bigger picture. I also had to take my responsibility to the World Class Performance group into consideration. Funded by the Lottery, it was set up after the fiasco at the Atlanta Olympics to produce winners at championship level. As far as it's concerned, victory at Badminton counts for nothing compared to a completion in the World Championships.

No doubt Hugh Thomas, who runs Badminton, would disagree with that assessment, but I was surprised by his outrage at my withdrawal. He seemed to take it personally, saying that entering meant running and that I was treating Badminton as a tin pot event. I now see that I'd have done better if I'd explained myself before the word went out but, as far as I was concerned, withdrawing was a private decision that I was perfectly entitled to make, just as entitled as the other five competitors who did the same thing. We pay to be at Badminton, £380 per horse for the entry, stabling and meal vouchers, and no one receives appearance money, so what exactly was the problem?

Hugh's argument was that you shouldn't enter a top event without the intention to run, but I would have run if the circumstances had been different. He claimed that I was depriving other riders of the chance to compete and disappointing the public by not starting one of the sport's most popular horses. Once I'd announced my decision, Brian Giles of the *Daily Mail* wrote the article that fuelled the flames and Simon Barnes followed up in *The Times*, but the fact that they wrote about Tam at all was great for the sport's profile. Mark Phillips said that I should either keep my mouth shut or make up a good story about what went wrong. Maybe he's got a point.

Clearly Hugh was disappointed to be left with just sixty-nine starters, but I'm not responsible for the numbers game. He accepts one hundred entries and assumes about eighty will turn up. They used to have a waiting list, but it was scrapped, rightly, because it's difficult to prepare a horse for Badminton if you don't know whether you're going or not. Maybe Hugh should accept 110 entries, but that's up to him. I do feel very strongly that the entry fees should be scrapped at Badminton, if nowhere else. The event makes a significant profit, so everyone who qualifies and wants to go should at least not have to pay. The £50,000 first prize is considered acceptable because it's the highest in the sport, but I would love to think that £100,000 is an affordable target in the near future and more representative of what competitors have to do.

With Tam safely wrapped in cotton wool, it was time to get going on Max. I was impressed with the big, bold fences when I walked the course. Although the run for home was very straightforward, the first half asked a lot of serious questions and it seemed more challenging than it had in recent years. It's only human to feel a frisson of fear and the bounce into the lake looked particularly imposing though, as it turned out, you could climb through it and take the long route out without wasting any time.

I thought the course would have a significant influence on the outcome but, as the early horses romped round, it became clear that the fences were much too forgiving and the time much too easy to get. Why risk all the direct routes when you can take two long ones and cruise round in second gear within the time, as Moonfleet did? He was one of nineteen horses to finish without time penalties; far too many to make a good all-round competition. A solution I often promote is to wheel the course tightly and leniently to produce two optimum times, one for good conditions and one for bad, with the ground jury deciding which to use on Friday evening. That aside, it really shouldn't be possible to take long routes at top level and complete without time penalties.

Call me old-fashioned, but I felt the first short-format Badminton was lacking something. Despite the school of thought that says horses hit a wall in short format and get more tired than you'd expect, my own impression is that they finish better overall than they did before. Setting out on phase A in long-format events always made me feel sick, but I enjoyed the anticipation and doing the roads and tracks and the steeplechase certainly helped put you in a pattern. Inevitably there has been a lot of discussion about how we should warm up for short-format cross-country, but most people worked out what would be best for them. I hacked Max out in the morning, then got on him forty-five minutes before our start time, giving him a few jumps and a canter to loosen him up and open up his lungs. With fifteen minutes to go, I dismounted and let him relax, allowing his respiration and temperature to return to normal.

As befits the true pro he's become, Max cruised around within the time, an effort that did little to advance his cause because most of his rivals did the same. As he's one of the best jumpers in the business, I hoped he'd go clear over Sunday's unusually testing show jumping track, but he had one fence down, again like most of his immediate rivals. He'd have been third if he'd gone clear, as would several of the others, but a single error at an upright into a double put him down to ninth. Although that was disappointing for a Burghley winner, it was really another plus in a remarkably consistent record; first, fourth, ninth and eleventh in four out of five four-stars is good solid form – and he's still only thirteen.

After two highly embarrassing falls, I'd love to draw a veil over Chatsworth a week later. The first was on Macciato, who was trying to get his CIC qualification for Bramham. As he jumped out of the water over the Normandy Bank, I leaned back and slipped my reins, only to find I'd fallen out the back. Then it was Bob's turn. He'd already won a World Cup qualifier at Burnham Market in April and he was very handily placed after dressage this time. He'd jumped the course four times in previous years, so I set out with justifiable confidence. That lasted until he banked the second fence, slipping as he touched down on the woodchips in the flower bed on the top and losing a foreleg as it slid down the front sleepers. The result was a head plant for both of us. I was both winded and in shock, because he'd never fallen before.

Having missed out on Badminton, which he probably wasn't ready for aged ten, Frog was on course for Punchestown. After winning the three-star CIC at Burnham Market, he was improving fast and I thought Tommy Brennan and Hugh Lochore's course, a big, bold track with plenty of technical questions, would be an appropriate preparation for his first four-star at Burghley in the autumn. From the moment we arrived, it rained as if there was no tomorrow, creating rivers in the stables and turning the going into a bog. The organisers were commendably proactive rather than reactive, determined to run the competition and equally determined to run it safely. If they hadn't had all-weather surfaces for the dressage and show jumping, it could never have gone ahead, but it did and Frog produced a stunning test, maybe the best I've ever done on any horse. He got thirty-three penalties, with Pippa second on forty-two, so for once the tables were turned!

The course caused more trouble than I'd expected and no one got round within the time. Frog went clear with fourteen time penalties, the fastest of the day, and he had seven fences in hand for the show jumping on Sunday. Sadly it was not to be. He tends to assess fences very quickly, deciding whether to treat them with respect or contempt.

He didn't rate a small, dilapidated stone wall, 3ft 6in at most, so he whacked it with his knees, then did the same at the gate a few fences later. He had a nick on his knee when he pulled up but soon bruising appeared very quickly on the tendon just above it. Although he could bend his leg, it hurt him to lift it up. I was very relieved there was no serious damage, but I had no option but to withdraw him. If I'd been able to jump, I'd have had nine fences in hand by the time I went in, a position I doubt I will ever be in again, but that's eventing for you and we took consolation from what was so nearly an outstanding performance.

Now we're a family, we've discovered a system for major three-day competitions, with Alice and I sleeping in the horsebox and Lucy and Oli in the camper van. It worked well when we tested it at Badminton in 2006, with everything running smoothly in beautiful weather. Could we accommodate two babies next year? It was an alarming thought, but we'd have to try. When I was competing at Belton with Bob in April, Alice rang to say she was expecting our second child in late November. Win or lose at Aachen, 2006 would be another landmark year.

CHAPTER THIRTY-TWO

Déjà Vu

As soon as we were back from our holiday, the spotlight moved onto the World Equestrian Games (WEG) in Aachen. All being well, the team, announced back in the spring, would be three of the Blenheim gold medallists, Zara, Mary and me, with Pippa making a welcome return on Primmore's Pride. The individuals were Daisy Dick with Spring Along and Oliver Townend, who earned his place with his third at Badminton on Flint Curtis. Jeanette, the fourth member of the Blenheim squad, was very disappointed to miss out with Over To You, especially after he proved his form by finishing fourth on his dressage score at Badminton. At the age of eighteen, it made no sense to run him as an individual, but we were all surprised the selectors put him way down on the third reserve list because he'd be an invaluable replacement if anyone dropped out of the team.

It wasn't long before someone did. We weren't worried when we started training at Waresley Park without Pippa because we were expecting her to arrive late, but soon the terrible news came through: Primmore's Pride had had a recurrence of the injury that had kept him out of Blenheim. My first thought was, 'That's our team gold gone.' The Germans, French and Australians looked strong on paper and we needed our best riders to have a chance of matching them. Pippa, Jeanette and I had been together since 2001 and I'd been on several teams with Mary. Zara had made the best possible start at Blenheim, but we'd lost Jeanette, who is an outstanding rider, and now we'd be without Pippa, our banker and our backbone. Daisy

Dick was a very experienced and talented replacement, but you never know how a rider making their team debut will react to the pressure of world championship competition. Her promotion opened the door for Sharon Hunt and Tankers Town to compete as individuals.

Fortunately Yogi is always very upbeat, able to see the positive side of any situation, no matter how negative it appears, and I felt a lot better after I'd discussed it with him. Even so, it was worrying to start using reserves in June. Poor Pippa had a disappointing season, with Ensign, her second string, not coming up to expectations. Primmore's Pride is still young enough to make a comeback but seeing a top horse go wrong made us all realise how vulnerable we were and dented our confidence at a time we needed it most. Toytown, Spring Along and Tam have all had time off for injuries during their careers and Call Again Cavalier and Toytown hadn't had preliminary runs in the spring of 2006 so we were on tenterhooks over the eight weeks before the Games started.

Although team training stalled a bit when the news came through, Yogi worked hard to get us focused and thinking forwards again. We might have used up our share of bad luck with Pippa but nothing was guaranteed for our rivals so we should get stuck in and see how things turned out. As the competition drew nearer, the press focused on the fact that Britain's eventers hadn't won a world championship team gold medal since 1994 or an individual one since Ginny Leng in 1986.

Mary and I travelled over to Aachen in a day with Tam and Call Again Cavalier. Max had been on standby all summer but, with Burghley a couple of weeks away, Judy and I decided not to risk taking him to Germany. We expected it to be boiling hot, but we arrived in torrential rain, similar conditions to the ones that had suited us so well at Blenheim. The venue was impressive. The long-established international show jumping venue is set in a relatively cramped site for Games that include vaulting, endurance, reining and driving in addition to the Olympic equestrian disciplines, but the Germans created the best possible stage for all the competitions.

At some events, Tam and I are on the same wavelength from the start; at others, we're slightly at odds. In Aachen, the omens were good, although arriving on Sunday afternoon left rather too much time to fill before the dressage on Friday. Five days would have given Max the time he needs to settle, but Tam has to be kept busy. There was nowhere to hack and the more he goes round and round the same arena, the more he develops his homing instinct, looking for his friends and food from the moment you get on. At least he was coping better than I was. Normally the first two days of a big event are fun because you have only one horse to ride and lots of time to look around the area, but on Monday and Tuesday, I was lying in a heap in the lorry, unable to ride because I'd been struck down by food poisoning. By Wednesday, I was back to normal and, as Jackie pointed out, better me than Tam.

After Tam's dressage at Badminton, I'd taken a new approach in an attempt to make him accept more discipline. I've never sent him to Lizzie, partly because I don't want him to leave my yard and partly because he might not appreciate such intensive dressage. The problem with Tam is not merely that he's naughty when he's fresh, but he is also lazy and determined to do things his own way. After discussing methods of working him with Lizzie, I'd suggested she come over and ride him at home. The theory was that she'd be asking him to knuckle down and I could then be more relaxed with him.

After several visits, Tam felt more cooperative. I did dressage and show jumping at a lot of events in the hope of keeping his brain active. It's always a fine balance with him; over-compete him and you risk injury; do nothing and he gets bored. By the time he got to Aachen he was going consistently better, so much so that I dared to feel a bit more optimistic. Usually I hope he'll go well, but realise he might not. Now I felt he should go well, a confidence that was dented when out of the blue he tried to turn round in the first halt as I saluted.

Usually the dressage scoreboard displays each judge's marks for each movement, but Aachen's revolutionary system announced the overall percentage for the movement and the placing compared to all the other competitors. Fortunately I had no time to look at it, but my mother was distraught to see that I was in 68th place following the botched halt. After that Tam buckled down, not going as well as he could, but a lot better than he had for a long time. Even so, it took the whole test for him to rise up the order to eighth, where he finally finished.

Our score of 45 helped the team, as it needed to do because Mary and Daisy, going on Thursday, had not performed as well as we'd hoped. Mary finished the dressage in the low fifties, less well than expected because one of the judges marked her exceptionally harshly. After the worst test Spring Along has ever done, Daisy was ten marks further adrift, disappointing because although he's not a dressage horse, he normally performs well. On Friday morning, Zara pulled us up the order with an excellent test and a mark of 38 and my result put us in second place, surprisingly good considering how far back we'd been the day before. With some of the French and the Australians falling short as well, it was a tight contest for the minor placings. We all knew we'd be pushed to beat the Germans at dressage but as they were the only team to deliver across the board, they were much further ahead that any of us had expected.

Our first impressions of the cross-country course were very positive. As we walked the course, it didn't look terribly difficult, but it appeared to be a proper championship track with some serious fences. Designed by Rudiger Schwarz, it was the best short-format championship course so far, more interesting than Athens or Blenheim. On a busy course that needed thinking through, you wanted a horse that would could check and turn on the twisty sections and cover the ground on the galloping stretches. The terrain was naturally wet, but the organisers had spent a million euros digging out the track, then filling it with stone topped with sand and turf to create excellent going. The time would certainly have been too easy to get if conditions hadn't been a bit soft but, given that they were, it was difficult to take long options and finish within it. Bettina was in the lead after dressage, but not by her customary huge margin. A danger was that she might have been able to take two or three long routes, get ten time penalties and still end up ahead. In the event, she took the long routes and got the time penalties, but they cost her the lead and ultimately an individual medal.

Our greatest worries were the two water complexes, the first an out over a boat and the second over two angled houses off a slope on the approach. Coming four from the end when horses might be tiring, this one asked a lot of questions because the slope was not only steep, but heavily cambered. Would it be best to take on the houses or eliminate risk by circling and jumping them separately, a loop that would add an extra fifteen seconds. We discussed it as a team, but ultimately the decision was left to the individuals. Mary, as our pathfinder, thought she would play it safe, but Call Again Cavalier was going so well that she decided to risk it. I stood on her line to watch her and she was spot on, but the horse ducked out at the last moment.

This was a terrible start because even if the rest of the team went clear, we'd have to use Daisy's dressage score so we were already playing catch-up. Poor Mary was devastated, furious that she hadn't resisted the temptation to take the fence on. However, Daisy flew round clear, giving us a tremendous boost. She was always planning to the take the houses straight, but now she changed her mind for the benefit of the team. Even so, she finished well within the time. She's a very positive rider and she made it look easy, so although we were nowhere to be seen on the scoreboard, Zara and I had something to play for.

Zara definitely had a lot more fun riding the course than her team-mates did watching her. She really went for it and took all the direct routes but in doing so used a couple of lives especially when Toytown climbed over the boat at the first water. There were moments when our hearts were in our mouths, but everyone needs a few things to go their way if they're to win gold and Zara's determination and skill were rewarded with a faultless round. Then it was my turn. Tam set off feeling very chirpy. My first cause for concern was the fourth, a double of hedges set at an angle over a road that we'd crossed all week on our way to the stables. Would he think it was time for a quick break? Not at all. He jumped it beautifully, although my anxiety was well founded because several of the other horses did run out.

We'd gone slowly at his warm-up runs at Salperton Park and Aston-le-Walls so he was fresh and cheeky, really up for the big one. As he hit the minute markers, I knew the time was well within his reach. He went through the first water effortlessly, but disaster struck at the Normandy Bank, a log up to a bank followed by four downhill strides on the turn into a narrow triple brush. Tam has always taken me through the flags on the narrowest of fences with never a thought of running out, but on this occasion, he was going too fast when he jumped the log. As a result, he came into the brushes on three and a half strides and ducked out. Even though he'd got away from me, he could have jumped it, but he didn't.

Once I'd seen our chances evaporate, all I wanted was to be swallowed up. I knew I should crack on and get as few time faults as possible for the team, but what was the value in that if we were going to come fifth rather than sixth? Then again, with the Lottery funding in mind, we needed the best possible result. The bottom line was I'd been saving Tam all year for this and now I had to get on with it. He responded enthusiastically, eating up the ground and taking the direct route at the second water without a hint of hesitation.

After I went through the finish, Yogi was quick to offer consoling words. I'd done my best and no one could do more than that. I said my run-out was unforgivable but of course Yogi wasn't having any of that. Being the optimist that he is he ran through a scenario designed to give us hope. If the last German, Swedish, Australian, American and French riders did X, Y and Z, the team would end the day in third place. And the major boost was that Zara was still in the lead, though Ingrid Klimke and her Badminton runner-up, Sleep Late, could still beat her at this stage.

I looked at Yogi with complete disbelief, wondering where on earth he'd clutched these straws from. But even as he talked us through it, it was beginning to come true. Ingrid had a terrible day, leaving Zara in gold medal position. And one by one, our main rivals made mistakes. Andrew Hoy and Jean Teulere, the reigning world champion, came to grief where I did, Linda Algotsson had a run-out at the angled hedges and Andrew Nicholson and Kim Severson also had refusals. When the numbers were crunched, Team GB was in second place.

Secretly, I thanked God I hadn't let Tam cruise to the finish, clocking up the time faults that would have left us lower down the order. Silver was not what we'd come for, but there was still hope. The Germans had put in fantastic performances, riding their luck and ending up with a lot of fences in hand for the show jumping the next day. However, their horses still had to pass the vet, by no means a certainty, as I knew as well as anyone. We felt jubilation for Zara and some consolation in the fact that the team position wasn't as bad as we'd thought it might be. It wasn't over yet.

Jumping in the main Aachen arena in front of a massive crowd would be a huge honour, but I knew it would be an ordeal for Tam. He hadn't got to the final day in Athens and even though he was fourteen, his exposure to this sort of atmosphere was limited. Mary went first for Britain, putting in a fantastic clear. Then it was Tam's turn. His behaviour was entirely predictable, eyes out on stalks, lurching around all over the place, but he too jumped immaculately to keep us in the hunt. We still had two fences in hand over the best of the rest, a huge relief as it gave Daisy and Zara a little bit of a cushion as the climax approached. Daisy also went clear, finishing on her dressage score in twelfth place, and then it was up to Zara.

Going last, she had one fence in hand for individual gold and two fences for team silver, but what happened next is the stuff of nightmares. When I was watching with her parents during the early stages of the jumping, the Princess Royal warned me that some of the riders weren't hearing the starting bell. Once it rang, you had forty-five seconds to go through the start, but if you missed it, you could be stranded at the other end of the vast arena with too little time to get back. Presumably this message had been relayed to Zara, but the huge burst of applause for the previous rider who'd secured team gold for Germany gave her little chance of hearing the bell. While waiting for it to ring, she did one circle, then another and turned away from the start. Watching helplessly, you could only wonder if this was pay-back time for Bettina's experience in Athens.

As the crowd realised what was happening, they started whistling and suddenly Zara clicked. Her look of furious desperation as she turned and galloped to the start told the whole story. She crossed the line five seconds late so she already had time to make up before she reached the first fence. Given that Toytown is not the most reliable of show jumpers, she could easily have become flustered and racked up a lot of faults, but Zara stayed calm. Cool to the end, she hit the second last to finish with four faults and one time penalty, good enough to take gold ahead of Australia's Clayton Fredericks and America's Amy Tryon. By finishing fourth, fifth and sixth, the Germans displayed the consistency required to win team gold by an impressive twenty-four points, with Australia and the United States behind Britain in third and fourth.

There was plenty of joy and jubilation in the British stables as we celebrated with the owners, supporters and grooms. Zara was overwhelmed by her back-to-back championship victories, but as always she was very humble. Finishing ninth and eleventh, Sharon and Oli took a lot away from their first Games but I was left with a haunting feeling of déjà vu. As it had been in Jerez, so it was in Aachen, even down to my final placing: fifteenth on both occasions.

Two years down the line from Athens, the Germans were gracious winners, with none of the desire for revenge they seemed to feel at Blenheim in 2005. Eventing is still very much a minority sport in Germany, far behind show jumping and dressage, but this was a good competition. The organisers didn't have a lot of ground to work with so they needed to plan well and they did. Their efforts were rewarded with a three-day event in June 2007 held at the same time as the celebrated Aachen show, excellent news for all of us.

In Dorset, it was business as usual, with Blenheim the next weekend and Burghley the one after. Barney and Mac were doing their first three-stars at Blenheim and I also had Parkmore Ed, sent back to me by his owner-rider Philip Adkins because he was about to lose his three-star qualification. I hadn't ridden Ed since Boekelo eighteen months earlier, but as soon as I got on, it was as if he'd never been away. He fitted back into his slot as only a really good horse can. His dressage and show jumping were in great shape and he went well cross-country in the Open Intermediate at Iping, but he surprised me with a stop at a straightforward table at Gatcombe so I knew we weren't quite there yet. After I'd schooled him a few times, I felt I had him spot-on for Blenheim and that he could win. Mac had missed Bramham after our fall at Chatsworth so Blenheim was new territory for him and Barney can be a bit of a wild card in the show jumping so I was delighted to have Ed in my corner.

I rode Mac first and he went as well as I could have hoped. He doesn't find dressage easy but he's improved enormously. He's fine when he's in his comfort zone, but he loses confidence very quickly when you ask a bit more. At Blenheim, he was marked in the mid-fifties, a lot better than Highland Lad or Max on their first outings in a big arena. When I walked the course, I was surprised to see how little it had been modified since the European Championships.

It posed a lot of questions for an inexperienced eight-year-old like Mac. If he answered them well, I'd know I had a good horse, and he did, going smoothly through all the direct routes. As his dressage score wasn't competitive, I let him to gallop round within himself, so we had ten time faults. Although he's a thoroughbred, he got a bit tired and it showed on the Sunday when he had four fences down, disappointing for a reliable show jumper. Even so, he finished twenty-first, a promising result for a tough, sound horse who should have it all to come.

Barney delivered the test of his life, but had a run-out cross-country which is very unlike him. The mistake occurred at an angled combination in the main area. He jumped the first hedge very big, then threw his head in the air and slipped behind when I asked him to turn, so I had to circle. He does have a tendency to be argumentative and we usually get away with it, but not this time. I never like parting with a horse, but his owner, Jane Walter, and I decided he should go to Harry Meade for the 2007 season.

Ed did a very good test, but forty-six penalties put us behind Pippa and Daisy and that's where we stayed. The schooling paid off in the cross-country when he came into a double of houses at the top of a hill on the wrong stride. He could easily have stopped but he bailed me out and although he tired towards the end, he completed with a couple of time penalties and jumped an easy clear on Sunday. It was a fantastic performance, one that could have resulted in a win on another occasion, but Pippa and Daisy were better on the day. When Pippa had a show jump down, Daisy moved ahead of her, but third was the best I could do. Philip was delighted but it was mission accomplished and I was soon waving Ed goodbye.

Next stop Burghley with my two redheads. Max was defending his title, while Frog tackled his first four-star. He'd showed me at Punchestown that he was ready and I was looking forward to seeing how he'd perform. Unlike Badminton, which had failed to ignite, Burghley was a great competition, with a real buzz to it. Max did his test on Thursday morning, a tricky draw as it doesn't give him quite enough time to settle in. He'd had a quiet summer, missing a run due to a minor training setback and hanging around in case I needed him for Aachen. In 2005, he won Burghley off the back of a busy summer which suits him better. This time he was fragile and fractious in the dressage and his score of 47 could easily have been 57. He was certainly generously marked, but then so was everyone else so it didn't help him much and I knew he hadn't performed as well as he had in the two previous years.

On Saturday morning, I was a passenger on the cross-country. He's not a naturally relaxed horse, but he's developed into a true professional and it was a luxury to ride him. He finished the day in fourth place, but knocked two fences to finish sixth. Considering he's technically one of the best eventing show jumpers, his three-day record is frustrating. Out of four attempts at Burghley, he's had two down on three occasions, only going clear the year he had a run-out on the cross-country. Just as at Badminton, his Burghley errors were expensive.

Because of his injury, Frog left Punchestown on a cross-country high instead of submitting to the discipline of the show jumping. He had a couple of runs in the summer, but at Burghley he was on his toes and boisterous. After a lot of work, I got him where I wanted but by the time he went into the arena, he'd lost his flair. His test was way below what he's capable of, but at least he behaved and hopefully it will stand him in good stead for the future. He can easily react to the pressure of a big occasion, but this time he just made a few silly mistakes which proved critical. As is often the case, this cloud had a silver lining. Fifty penalties meant I could ride the cross-country for the future, taking the direct routes but not trying to make the time, whereas if he'd had forty, I'd have had to have gone for it. As it was, he learned a lot and excelled over a tough show jumping track on Sunday, one of only five clears in the whole competition.

He finished nineteenth, a performance that underlined the fact that he is a seriously impressive horse whose day will come. When I tried him in France, I got off thinking he was amazing, but that I'd have to learn to ride him because he's a very complex character. He is volatile mentally, usually forward going, but sometimes backward and cold. His stride is inconsistent, varying very quickly between one and seven metres. At times, he shortens before I'm ready and turns on a dime, at others I couldn't turn him round a harbour, but hopefully he'll become more predictable. Sometimes he's so gung-ho he jumps himself into trouble and he doesn't come back very easily which makes it difficult to capitalise on his natural speed. He's potentially a winner, with outstanding looks that impress the dressage judges, and the quality and athleticism to succeed at the highest level. After four years, I know the struggle is worth it, but I still have to find the key.

On Sunday at Burghley, excitement mounted as Andrew Hoy made his final assault on the $250,000 Rolex Grand Slam. Moonfleet was in first place, the dressage leader and clear within the time across country, but he didn't look quite the horse he was when he won Badminton in the spring. There he cruised to a victory that looked as effortless as a walk in the park, but he had to be pushed along at

Burghley and his jumping lacked its earlier elan. Did the other riders want Andrew to win the Rolex? Yes and no. On the personal front, he's very popular and everyone wished him well, but we all know how difficult it is to win one four-star event. Now he was threatening to repeat Pippa's feat of winning three back to back. If that could happen twice in three years, what on earth were the rest of us doing.

For Andrew, the pressure was immeasurable as he went into the arena with one fence in hand over his compatriot Lucinda Fredericks. For the spectators, it was inconceivable he could be beaten on a horse who'd put in such a magnificent clear at Badminton, but that was to overlook Moonfleet's inconsistent record. As the drama unfolded and the poles fell, it became clear that this wasn't one of his better days. He was so far ahead at Badminton that he could have won with three fences down. Now three errors cost him a quarter of a million bucks in addition to the Burghley winner's cheque. As serious prize money is scarce in eventing, no one would have grudged Andrew his pay day but it is still out there for the taking

My three-day season continued with the two-star at Weston Park, a chance for Trinity Hill and Irish Moon to stand up and be counted. I'd bought Trinity Hill, for Lindy Best, Sylvia Harley and Jeremy Hackett, sight unseen from New Zealand the previous autumn, but he arrived in Britain very late. He looked terrible. At the South of England, one of his first events with me, he stumbled in the water and cut his knee to the bone. When he recovered after several months, it seemed more sensible to backtrack to Weston rather than push for a three-star.

As Irish Moon led the dressage with Trinity Hill in fourth, I was in a strong position going into cross-country and an even stronger one coming out as Trinity Hill moved up to third. Surely this time I could win the three-day event that had been eluding me all year. No way, as it turned out, because both horses knocked two fences, ending up third and fourth. As she's been on the show jumping circuit, I didn't expect Irish Moon to make one mistake, let alone two, but she didn't bother over the smaller fences. Sadly her owner wants to keep her at home so she has a local rider for 2007.

Trinity Hill gave his owners a bit of consolation for their slow start to the season and something to hope for in the future. At least my loss was Piggy French's gain because it gave her the two-star North of England grand slam, awarded to the winner of consecutive Weston Park events with Sansaw in between. There were a lot of jokes about Piggy paying me off and I'd like to say I had the fences down on purpose, but it wouldn't be true. Even so, a two-star victory wasn't anything like as important to me as the £25,000 prize was to her, so it was the best possible result.

When Becky texted me at the end of the season to say I'd come first in the British rankings for the sixth successive year, with 1333 points to Andrew Hoy's 1306, I was amazed because I didn't feel I'd had the best of seasons. Andrew topped the world rankings, decided on international results, but again I could hardly believe it when I learned that I was second. I had a great team of horses and they were going well with very few injuries, but all the way through, I felt we were just missing the mark. With no three-day victories, my success was thanks to strength in depth, with a lot of the younger horses playing their parts.

My two seven-year-olds, Chuckelberry and Navigator, put down serious markers for the future in the Novice Championships at Gatcombe. This competition is often a tough one to win so I was delighted when Chuck and Bart were first and second after dressage and show jumping. I set off on the cross-country on Bart thinking there was a lot to jump for a relatively green horse. But jump he did, going into the lead with half a dozen time faults. With the competition already won, I was in a difficult situation with Chuck. Although I had no preference as to which should win, I'd obviously be taking an unnecessary risk asking him to race round to beat Bart's time. In the end, I went as fast as seemed right for him and he too was foot perfect. As Bart's a thoroughbred and Chuck has an element of warm blood, he was eighteen seconds slower which put him in second place.

Bart was the more backward of the two and he'd done a lot of work since he'd flown in from Australia back in the winter, so he took an early holiday while Chuck tried to qualify for the seven-year-old championship three-day event at Le Lion d'Angers. Basically he had to complete a CIC two-star, normally pretty routine, but not if you have two run-outs, as he did at Longleat, and a fall in the water, as he did at the second Gatcombe in September. He'd done a great test, but failed to put down his landing gear and crashed heavily, cutting his knee quite badly. It came up like a football and I thought there was no way he'd be ready for one last attempt at qualifying the next weekend. Even if he was, he might have lost some confidence with water.

Back at home, Alex did an incredible job on his knee with physio and spa treatment and he seemed unbelievably unaffected by the fall when I schooled him through water. Although he wasn't lame, his knee was not a pretty sight. Then again, a horse only gets one shot at the seven-year-old world championship and, qualification apart, he was ready for Le Lion d'Angers. Catherine, his owner, said I should do whatever I thought best so I took him to the South of England and he did the business with a good dressage and a double clear. He came good in the dressage at Le Lion as well, finishing second behind one of the last horses to go, and went on to confirm both his placing and his promise across country. After all my near misses, I should have expected my final three-day of the season to end badly – and it did. Chuck tore a muscle in his hindquarters, a relativly minor injury but one that kept him out of the show jumping. If he'd jumped clear, he'd have won so it was disappointing, but I was pleased about the bigger picture because he was everything I hoped he'd be.

The other novices also played their part in my top British ranking. Bee Animas won six pre-novice and novice classes, and Imran, competing for the Fox-Pitt Eventing Club, won four. Despite doing stallion duties through the spring, All that Jazz came out on top on three occasions, as did Cool Mountain, while Dylan, also in the club colours, and Walk the Line made promising starts to their careers. Dylan could easily make a good amateur ride so we sold him at the end of the season and we kept All That Jazz at novice level so he could get more experience in the spring of 2007, but the others performed well in their first intermediate classes and they should be ready to do their first two-star three-day events next season. With the two French horses I bought in the autumn of 2006, I should have a very competitive team for the future.

I will eventually find out more about which ones have top-class potential.

At the end of the first year, I felt we'd laid solid foundations for the future success of the Fox-Pitt Eventing Club. Imran and Dylan gave the members a lot of fun and eighty-five came to the end of season party in Anthony's tithe barn. It was weird doing pre-novice dressage at the start of the season in front of a crowd of enthusiastic supporters instead of the usual one man and his dog in an empty field. Ten members wanted a bit more involvement so they've invested in our first syndicate to buy a really nice horse and run it for a year. As they'll be part owners with a cut in the proceeds of any sale, it's an affordable and potentially rewarding way of taking their interest a stage further.

And what of Bob, now my designated one-day specialist? After starting well at Belton, he won the World Cup qualifier at Burnham Market before turning upside down at Chatsworth. He won again at Aston-le-Walls, a speciality track for him, then went to the championships at Gatcombe. That's supposed to be another of his favourites but this definitely wasn't a performing day and I withdrew him after he knocked four show jumps. The next weekend, I took him to Hartpury CIC*** on a mission to win a Mitsubishi Warrior. Show jumpers often compete for cars, but in eventing such a rare occurrence attracted a field of over a hundred. And guess what, the winner was Bob. He did his best test of the year, show jumped clear and flew round the cross-country to beat Moonfleet very comfortably. As I was sponsored by VW Touareg at the time, I couldn't accept the car, a disappointment for Mitsubishi who would have got much more publicity out of a different winner, but the money I received for selling it was my highest prize of the season.

As I detected a bit of a breathing noise towards the end of the cross-country, Bob had a wind operation on his return. I never noticed it before and he's always been very clean-winded so it was never clinically diagnosed, but it could explain his puzzling stops near the end of three-day event cross-country tracks. The operation was successful, but to his distress as much as mine, his convalescence kept us off the hunting field until February. Will he emerge as a rejuvenated sixteen-year-old Ferrari in 2007 and beyond? With Amazing Bob, you never know.

CHAPTER THIRTY-THREE

Family Values

F rom the outset, Thomas Fox-Pitt was ahead of the clock, coming into the world eight days early on 22 November 2006. Alice was still working when she was eight and a half months pregnant so Thomas featured regularly on Channel 4's racing programmes before he was born. We both thought we'd have another boy but there was no particular reason why. Having two boys so close together will hopefully work out well and it won't be long before they will have a lot of fun, but if they are anything like Andrew and I were, there will be plenty of fighting too.

While Alice was willing Tom out as soon as possible, I was making the most of the quiet before the storm and rushed about looking at prospective horses. I was in Ireland when she called me to tell me to keep my phone on through the night. I thought that was a sure sign but luckily I never received the call and I cancelled my trip to France the next day when I got home. That night alarm bells started ringing and the déjà vu from 15 months earlier began. Only this time everything happened at double speed. We were in Dorchester Hospital at 11p.m. and Tom was born by 2a.m. With Alice and Thomas both safe and well, I went home for a short sleep and returned in the morning to bring them home for lunch. However, this was not before I was woken up at 6.45a.m. by a UK Sport Doping Control Officer. As part of the deal of being a lottery funded athlete, all the elite riders are subject to random doping tests. I was not happy to be woken up by this poor man, and it took me a while to forgive him his appalling timing even though it was not his fault. Babies were arriving at a rate of knots so the maternity unit was keen to free up beds as soon as possible. In August when Oli was born, Alice quite enjoyed the luxury of a couple of days' rest but this time all the celebrations happened at home.

There was no pressure from the horses, November being the perfect time of year for an eventer to have a child, so we really enjoyed the first few days together as a family of four. Naming him was quite straightforward. Our list ran to Thomas and George, with Ben as an outsider, but as Oli's monkey is called George, a potential source of confusion that might have scarred Thomas for life, the decision was made for us. Oli was very excited by the new addition, but a bit disappointed by the lack of action. As each day passes their age gap becomes less significant and it won't be long before they are well matched.

By chance, Oli had a hilarious first birthday party last August just before I left for Aachen. It was a Saturday, one of the very few during the season I was not competing, and as it was a perfect day we had the party in the garden. We had no idea how many friends would brave the occasion so it was a nice surprise that several did. However, it was my Aunt Sarah and her trio of Touareg musicians who stole the show. She had met the band at a music festival in Timbuktu while travelling in the Niger region and she had offered to look after them during their trip to Europe. When she had replied to her invitation she mentioned that the three men would have to come too, but I'd forgotten to pass the message on to Alice. Our conversation came back to me as the six-foot tribesmen, resplendent in blue robes, hats and jewellery, emerged from Sarah's car, and Alice's jaw dropped.

Once everyone had got over the shock and been introduced to our French-speaking guests, we persuaded them to play some music. Hinton St Mary vibrated to the African beat as the older children looked on in amazement, but they were not half as surprised as the village was when we joined them outside the pub to wish the Hinton float good luck in the Sturminster Newton carnival. Sadly Oli won't remember his first birthday, but there are plenty of pictures to show him one day.

He took his first steps in October while I was competing at Weston Park. He was staying with Lucy at the time and she rang in a state of high excitement to say he'd walked across her kitchen. Alice had seen him take a couple of steps and then grab something, but this was real walking and typically neither of us was there to witness it. We had to wait until we were in Kent for my parents' fortieth wedding anniversary celebrations to see him in action. His shrieks of delight were more than matched by ours.

Since becoming a father, I have been overwhelmed by the emotional impact parenthood has had. Babies are so fragile and their well being is so dependent on the right environment, but we are really enjoying the responsibility. Everyone who told us that they would get more and more rewarding was absolutely right . . . so far. It is as if they move in, take over and train you in your new role in the process.

Of course I was impressed that Oli's first recognisable word was dada, although that is very normal and he was not very selective as to what he applied it to. In 2006, my equestrian achievements came a distant second to his rapid progression and while I felt as hungry and keen as ever, I realised my main priority had changed for ever.

My parents' fortieth anniversary celebration was a very special night. They had invited a small gathering of friends to enjoy an evening of drinks, classical music, dinner and dancing. The only bone of contention concerned the speeches: my mother hates them and my father enjoys making them. The compromise was that Laurella and I would say a few words at the dinner. No matter how successful the marriage, forty years is a long haul and it seemed appropriate to pay tribute to our parents in front of their contemporaries.

Sadly although I failed to emulate them in my first marriage, their marriage is a strong role model for me and one that I'm determined to live up to with Alice. Being a father has definitely changed the way I see my parents, as I am sure it does with many new fathers and mothers. You are suddenly more appreciative of their achievement and massively more aware of the importance of your relationship with them. After the freedom years, having your own children brings you back into the loop of your parents' lives and Oli and Tom are incredibly lucky to have four wonderful grandparents. As a child and an adolescent, you have no idea what your parents are going through because you do not appreciate how important you are to them. All parents are annoying but only because they want the best for their children, and the love they give is second to nothing. I see that now but it will be a long time before Oli and Thomas understand what I am saying.

I love every moment I spend with them, which is sadly not enough because of eventing's antisocial nature. On the other hand I am lucky as I see them during the week, something many fathers with hectic jobs can never do. In the quiet season, I try to be back for Oli's bath at 6p.m., a pretty reasonable target until I actually try to meet it. I am looking forward to the time when they are old enough to come to more events and spend time at the yard.

By the dawn of the New Year, I was working on my campaign for the European Championships at Pratoni in 2007 and the Beijing Olympics a year later. Tam hadn't struck gold in Aachen, but he was in great shape when he came back into work.

While he enjoyed his annual holiday, I struggled with the ongoing problem of finding the key to his enigmatic personality. Lizzie and I had made progress with his dressage; perhaps it was time to review my overall strategy.

He won Badminton off one run and went well in Athens and Blenheim after very few outings, but I've come to believe I'll have to risk him more often. He's a very lazy horse, but he does get over-excited at competitions which means that he can get over-zealous when I actually do push him on. His mistake in an otherwise foot-perfect round at Aachen came when he got the bit between his teeth and refused to listen to me. With Tam, tactics can work because they're new rather than intrinsically better, so breaking the pattern of taking him quietly, then going for broke at the big events could yield dividends, at least in the short term.

The plan for him is to run several times before Badminton, then miss Pratoni in the interests of Beijing. Yogi wants all the potential team members to get their Olympic qualification as early as possible in 2007 to avoid the kind of last-minute cliffhanger I had in 2004. With Athens just three months away, I had to qualify Tam round Badminton in the mud, luckily as it turned out because we won, but hardly the most risk-free preparation for the Games.

All being well, Frog will join Tam at Badminton and Max will stand in as reserve. His owners decided they did not want him to go to Kentucky again but he could easily end up at Badminton. If Frog is to be competitive he will need to knock a good ten marks off his Burghley dressage score and I would be happy if his jumping stays at the level he reached at the end of 2006. He is an obvious Badminton type of horse and I am really looking forward to riding him there. If he goes well he could be ready for Pratoni, leaving Max free to have a go at adding to his impressive Burghley record.

On the team front, we will be defending the European gold medal we won at Blenheim, a stern challenge in the light of German excellence at Aachen. With her individual gold at stake as well, Zara will be under ever greater pressure, especially as Toytown is still her only horse capable of competing at this level. Given reasonable luck with finding more horses of Toytown's calibre, she will surely play a major part in the London Olympics in 2012. In December, Yogi, Pippa, Mary, Daisy and I joined her for the final of the BBC Sports Personality of the Year. We were delighted when she was nominated, because she thoroughly deserved it after winning the European and World titles back to back and because eventing, like all minority sports, needs all the publicity it can get.

On the big night at the National Exhibition Centre in Birmingham, we were part of an audience of 5,000, the first time members of the public have been invited to buy tickets for the show. In the run-up, the commentators underplayed Zara's achievements to the point we felt she had no chance of beating Darren Clarke, the favourite after his brave showing in the Ryder Cup shortly after the death of his wife, Heather.

Luckily we were wrong and we watched with amazement and disbelief as Zara, looking slightly bemused, went up to receive her trophy.

In response to negative vibes both within the sport and in the press over the choice of Greenwich Park as the venue for the equestrian events of the London Olympics, the British Equestrian Federation (BEF) organised a site visit for potential owners and riders last December. Usually the dressage, show jumping and eventing venues find themselves out on a limb, staged far away from the main stadium and the city centre, but for the first time they will be fully integrated into the Games.

Objections focused on traffic problems, which will inevitably be an issue, and the size of the park, at least as big as Aachen at 170 acres. The main arenas and grandstands will be constructed on the main front lawn between the Queen's House and the main road. Never before will equestrian arenas have such impressive surroundings but it will be a tight fit. Sue Benson, the first woman to design an Olympic cross-country course, will have plenty of interesting terrain to work with, including potential leaf pits, a quarry area and a massive pond. Her appointment was greeted with hostility in eventing circles, mainly because her Bramham track for 2006 was too twisty and horses finished exhausted, but I have usually enjoyed riding her courses, admiring her flair and imagination. Greenwich may not be rolling parkland, but there is plenty of scope for galloping stretches among the loops. As a bold cross-country rider herself, Sue knows how important it is to create a true competition by testing competitors' bravery, technical ability and judgement of speed without pushing horses too much.

Many of the 250 people who attended the BEF presentation in the National Maritime Museum were sceptical initially, but the mood shifted after Andrew Findings's speech and most came away agreeing with Lord Coe that the site at Greenwich Park was one of the jewels in the crown of the London Olympics. Having climbed up to the Observatory, I can confirm that this is a spectacular venue, its sense of history enhanced by the view over the Thames and half of London stretching away beyond it. My only concern remains the space for the grandstands which does not look large enough on paper to accommodate the crowds.

Because of the timing of the Olympics, in August, the equestrian competitions have in recent years been held in inappropriate climates on the outskirts of cities. However, with optimum conditions in London, particularly for equestrian sports, and the accessibility from Europe, I imagine we will never have seen crowds like it. Furthermore if our team is in with a chance there will be no limit to the number of enthusiastic supporters who will abandon their TVs and head for Greenwich Park for the greatest showcase our sport has ever known. In my dreams it will be an ideal swansong for my eventing career. Then again, eventing is addictive. Look at Ian Stark, Ginny Elliot and Lucinda Green who all tried to give up unsuccessfully on several occasions. Would I really quit if I was lucky enough to be ahead?

Update for the
2009 Edition

CHAPTER THIRTY-FOUR

The Road to Beijing

———⚬⚬⚬———

We started 2007 in high spirits, with three top horses in Frog, Tam and Max potentially aiming for Badminton. However, the spring season turned into a depressing game of skittles. Tam had been competing well and was feeling at the top of his game, but suddenly a replay of 2004 was underway. As a result of running more times in the build-up to Badminton, he picked up another minor injury that put him out for the season. There was no point worrying about it; we had managed it before so I was hopeful that the road to Beijing would work in the same way. With Tam out of the equation three weeks before Badminton, I concentrated on Max and Frog, only for Frog to develop some heat in a leg on his last gallop. A minor tendon injury was diagnosed, which was very depressing news as I had been very excited about the prospect of his becoming a true Badminton horse. Frog also needed to have the rest of the season off to rehabilitate, so all our hopes were pinned on Max – could this be the year when Max could represent Great Britain at the European Championships?

Off we set to Badminton with our one survivor, only to be met with the very concerning news that the general opinion of the going on the cross-country course was that it was unacceptably hard. As I was relying on Max to fly the flag for me that season, I immediately felt worried about taking a risk if the ground was unsuitable. Sadly, all concerns were well justified. I only needed to walk as far as the third fence to decide that I could not possibly take the risk of running him. The previous weeks had been dry and no rain was forecast. The park was as dry as a bone and even preparing for the dressage was going to do the horses no good. I spoke to Judy Skinner and Yogi and we decided there was no point in even presenting at the first trot up. My notion that I could then slip away unnoticed, without making a big deal out of the situation, completely backfired. The press took it as a huge statement and made a real thing out of the conditions. The fact remained that the course was in a wholly unsuitable condition and, whilst everyone was made aware of how much effort would be made to improve the conditions, my opinion was that without watering the entire course no temporary measure would improve the going sufficiently.

Inevitably there were significant withdrawals and a very downtrodden Badminton 2007 it turned out to be. The highlight was a brilliant win for Headley Britannia who, after her Burghley victory, annihilated the field and coped easily with the hard ground.

The ramifications of this year were huge, and gave Badminton the boost it needed to move on in the future. The endless discussions which followed were to move Badminton forward to its most significant development since I started competing there in the '80s.

Luckily for me, several of the potential team horses ended up withdrawing from Badminton, so the selectors decided to delay making a choice for Beijing until later in the spring. At this stage I hoped I had a good chance. However, as luck would have it, or not, Max shrivelled like an ant under the magnifying glass once the focus was upon him. Yogi came to watch him at his first OI run of the summer at Salperton, only for him to be so tense in the dressage that he nearly left the arena. Then, when he could have made amends for that, he put in another lacklustre performance, again mainly in the dressage, to finish a rather mediocre twenty-first at Barbury. A phone call that evening from Yogi to congratulate me on being selected as second reserve for the Europeans left me feeling rather empty and the phone call I then had to make to Judy Skinner was a sad one that I will never forget.

We had thought that if Max was to go to a championship his place would have been in a team. As second reserve, the best he could have moved to was an individual slot. Tam, whose shadow Max had always been in, had at last left the door open, and it was typical that Max's form should take such an uncharacteristic and untimely dive. Needless to say, as soon as the pressure was off, Max stood two inches taller and put in a brilliant Burghley performance, finishing fifth.

Whilst team dreams had gone belly-up, the rest of the string could not have been going better. I was particularly excited by the return of Parkmore Ed. That spring, he had gone particularly badly for his owner, Philip Adkins, and only marginally better for Tristram Owers, who he had substituted initially. Philip knew that I would be keen to have Ed back and I was very excited as he joined my string for our first run together since Blenheim 2006 at Brigstock. However, Ed's confidence had been dented slightly more than I had anticipated, and two refusals at the Normandy Bank forced me to retire and have a big rethink. Plan A had been to have a go at Burghley but we were already in May and I found myself gloomily looking plan C or D in the face.

Having grown up hugely from his three-star debut at Blenheim, Macchiato (Mac) won Bramham with an excellent jumping display. His dressage left him well placed and, after a mature cross-country round, it was his clear show jumping that moved him from fourth to first. This was a real thrill for all of us and his owners whose first horse he is. It is always very satisfying to achieve a result like this on a horse that you, as the rider, have produced from the beginning.

At two-star level my horses were flying, with Navigator winning at Houghton and Trinity Hill winning at Tattersalls in Ireland. Navigator had won the Novice Championships the previous season and at this stage was turning out to be a seriously exciting prospect. Trinity Hill had just missed out on qualifying for Bramham so I had hoped that Tattersalls would be well within his ability. He put in a really professional performance in all the phases but despite this I had a niggling concern that he was slightly too small for me. At one-star level I had a first and second at Houghton, and a second and third at Tattersalls, so things were looking pretty rosy for the future.

Over the next few weeks I gradually felt the real Ed coming back but he still kept me on my toes with the odd blip here and there. After several schooling sessions and a good OI run I decided that if he had any chance of going to Burghley he would have to run at Barbury. In my heart I felt this was crazy, but I had ridden him round three three-stars and he was fourteen years old, so it was something that I convinced myself I had to go for. He was well up there after the show jumping so I set off on the cross-country in very positive frame of mind. The first half of the course went well but he put in a naughty stop at the ski jump into the quarry and came home a little too gingerly for my liking. However, it transpired that he had lost a shoe and I hoped that perhaps his confidence had been a little weakened by that only. It still was not ideal – if he was going to go well at Burghley, he would need to jump a clear round at Barbury, even with no shoes on! Luckily, he then ran very confidently round two more advanced events, so I decided Burghley it was. I had him entered at Blenheim the following week just in case. I explained my plan to Philip and that I thought Burghley was still going to be a tall order. Philip's confidence in Ed, however, never waived and he would probably say to this day how he knew all along that Ed was going to win.

As usual the August focus was Gatcombe and Moon Man excelled as he often did there, finishing second just behind Mary King with Call Again Cavalier. Bob rounded off a very busy weekend which included Cool Mountain winning the Novice Championship, taking over Navigator's crown.

The week before Burghley was Blair and I decided that it was a good target for Mac, having already done Blenheim and not being quite ready for a four-star. If nothing else Mac proved his Bramham win was no fluke with a very confident display, leading from the start. I do have to admit to one very lucky moment in the cross-country when Mac banked a table and landed on his stomach. He picked himself up and carried on unperturbed but of course this did not go unnoticed and caused some consternation amongst the stewards – was it a horse fall or not? They decided not, as his shoulder had not hit the ground, but this was something that Andrew Nicholson was not going to ignore. However, his objection at Blair was rejected. Bee Animas won the two-star at Blair, making for a very happy journey back home, through the night, en route to Highclere with my three horses on board.

So far that season, I had won six three-day events. I hoped that Max could make amends for his disappointing start to the season with another good Burghley performance. Ed was drawn first of my two rides which I was relieved about because I thought Max would benefit from the better draw. Ed lay third at the end of dressage and though Max was a little disappointing, he was potentially close enough. On walking the course I realised that it was a big question for Ed, and I had a very clear plan in my mind as to where I could pull him up if he was still to go to Blenheim. This may sound a bit negative, but I was determined not to raise my hopes, the media's, or anyone else's. Even for Max I felt the course was a serious question and the biggest Burghley he would ever have seen. I set off on Ed very much thinking, 'Here we go, lets see what happens,' and after a little hesitant beginning he gave me the best ride I could have hoped for, coming home just outside the time. He was tired, understandably, having only been prepared for three months, but he had given his all and surprised us. Clayton Fredericks collected some time faults which left only Nicholson ahead of him going into the show jumping. Max gave me an excellent ride, finishing on exactly the same time as Ed, and for that rose considerably up the order. This is where the press got very excited about the Fox-Pitt/Nicholson duel, egged on by Clare Balding and Clayton Fredericks who had sat in the press conference and announced, 'Well, the referee is here – where are the boxers?' Excellent!

Show jumping day came and when both horses trotted up the thought crossed my mind that I could actually win it. Andrew's horse, Lord Killinghurst, was not a very reliable show jumper. Philip arrived for the first time that week to support and he was clearly dressed for the prize-giving. As far as he was concerned, Ed was going to win. The show jumping course was causing considerable trouble, particularly the planks at the last, with hardly anyone clearing them. Max jumped well but had the planks down, as did Ed, so the order remained very much unchanged. When Andrew had a fence down early on in the course everyone held their breath as he came to the last, only for it to fall, handing me one of my most satisfying four-star wins. Ed was a horse I was very fond of and for him to have come through his ups and downs in such style was incredible. Highland Lad's victory had been equally surprising in 2002 but in Ed I felt I was riding a truly great horse who had more to offer.

The press conference that followed was very entertaining, with Philip's confidence remaining the prevailing factor, but the Beijing Olympics were approaching fast and Ed had thrust himself into contention.

The rest of the season was slightly disintegrated after Burghley; however, morale was high with the seven three-day wins providing me with one of my best ever seasons, and Tam, Max and Ed hopefully looking to be exciting Olympic prospects.

Alice and I managed to have a very enjoyable winter break joining Lesley and Leslie Law in Florida to celebrate their marriage, followed by a fantastic trip to Costa Rica.

We headed home and Olympic mania was in full swing, with various meetings and training sessions planned. I discussed my plans with Yogi, which involved Tam and Max heading to Badminton and Ed taking the CIC one-day preparation route. With Beijing taking five weeks out of the season there would be an inevitable strain on the team at home to fit in each individual horse's programme. I was dreading the logistics.

Unlike 2007, 2008 began very smoothly, with the horses running well. Instead of the challenge of taking horses to Kentucky the week before Badminton, I decided it was a good idea to take some of the younger ones to the international one-day at Ballygraffan in Northern Ireland. We had a very successful trip; it was a high-class event that gave me a healthy distraction. Had I been at home, I may have been tempted to overwork the Badminton horses.

Tam and Max were on top form so I was very excited about their chances at Badminton. As it turned out, Max put in one of his best performances – his dressage could not have been any better, his cross-country was foot perfect and he jumped a brilliant round in the show jumping, despite a fence down. Going into the show jumping in fourth place I was very aware I needed to jump a clear round if I was to put the pressure on the leaders. None of the horses ahead of me were considered good jumpers but once I had had a pole down I knew I had given my leaders a cushion. They duly used their fences to get the upper hand over me, and victory was frustratingly no more. I was thrilled with how Max had performed but in my heart I felt it was one of those missed opportunities when victory was uncomfortably close.

Tam's Badminton did not go to plan. His dressage was pretty good and had him right up amongst the leaders, but disaster struck four from the end of the cross-country, when we ran out at the Little Badminton Houses – this should never have happened; it was a fence that I never gave a second thought to. Looking back, Tam was definitely beginning to tire. Unlike 2007, there had been a lot of rain over the previous days, and the going was soft. The optimum time was proving very difficult to get and I set off knowing that if I was close to it I would take the lead. Tam is usually very nimble and adjustable but on this occasion I let him get long and I had no stride to the first half. This resulted in a terrible jump; my turn to the B-element ended up being in the lap of the gods and to my utter disbelief we found ourselves running out. The sinking feeling was indescribable, but all was not in vain – there was still Olympic qualification to be gained. Tam happily pulled up sound and, with two down in the show jumping, our ultimate goal had been achieved. Despite Max's achievement I left Badminton with a very empty feeling; for what so nearly could have ended up being a first and second to have ended up the way it did was disappointing. However, there was still a lot that was good over the weekend and I had two sound horses.

Badminton had had a serious revamp over the twelve months following 2007's hard ground, and provided a fantastic competition with improved benefits for owners and riders. I thought Hugh Thomas's course was his best yet and certainly the ground preparation had never been so extensive. Ironically, there was plenty of rain so the work had not been essential, but for the future it was very promising.

The following weekend was a big one for Parkmore Ed in the World Cup qualifier at Chatsworth. What I thought was going to be an enjoyable weekend with five good advanced horses turned out to be quite a drama.

There was a fair amount riding on the weekend as a whole, with Seacookie competing in his first advanced competition with me. He had been bought for me by Catherine Witt from Ingrid Klimke, and I was very excited to have him in my team. He'd shown a lot of promise with Ingrid in Germany and I was very much looking forward to the future with him. Nevertheless, expectations were high and, having given him a gentle spring, this was his first test.

Kaleidoscope, another new ride, needed to get his qualifications finalised for Bramham. He was also a lovely horse owned by Jess Thomas, who had produced him herself.

All five horses performed pretty much as well as I could have hoped, but Ed got a little bit tense in the main arena during the dressage. He was lying well but, with the Olympics in mind, his performance had been a little bit disappointing. Philip Adkins had made it quite clear that he was unhappy about Ed being listed along with Max and Tam for the Olympics, rather than ahead of them, and here he used Ed's below-par dressage as a vehicle to voice his concerns. Unknown to me, he had organised for Ed to be collected after his show jumping round, during which he clinched third place, and taken back to Philip's stables. Looking back, I wish I had let him take him, but at the time I felt Ed had a vital role to play as my Olympic horse, or at least as a backup. However, Philip was determined to force the selectors and Yogi to list Ed as my number one choice. After the show jumping, high drama unfolded. Lisa Maynard arrived in her lorry to pick up Ed, but I felt that at the very least Phillip should talk to me directly, explain his thoughts and listen to what I had to say about Ed's performance. I finally reached Philip on the phone and persuaded him that if Ed had any hope of going to the Olympics he did not need to have his routine disrupted by changing yards.

This was the beginning of the end of my relationship with Philip. The previous year had been a real success, with Ed's win at Burghley being a dream come true, but the whole 'Olympic thing' caused a real difficulty between us. Yogi became the vital mediator, an unenviable role for which I shall always be grateful. For the first time ever, and the last, my only means of communication with one of my owners was through Yogi, and it worked. Relations improved and Ed felt great as he moved into the final two months of his Olympic preparation.

June was a busy month, with four three-day events over four weeks. The end of May had been manic, preparing the ten horses involved. The younger horses went well at two-star level in both Ireland and the UK, and then we headed north to Bramham with Navigator and Kaleidoscope. As is often the case with Bramham, this was a mission into unknown territory, with neither horse having competed at this level before. However, I was full of optimism.

Kaleidoscope had not been with me very long, so I was worried about his fitness and with good reason, as he did get a bit tired towards the end of the course. He had felt more than ready in his work at home but a competition at this level can catch you out if a good depth of fitness is not established. He was lying fourth after the cross-country but had three rails down in the show jumping, which was definitely due to his feeling a little worse for wear. Navigator surprisingly got a very disappointing dressage score, which left him right down the order in twelfth, but he was fantastic around Bramham's taxing course. He did the time easily, but as we went into the show jumping in fifth place it never entered my head that he could win. He did, however, jump one of the very few clear rounds which amazingly shot him into the lead, giving me my fifth Bramham win. It was a brilliant moment for his owners, Barts Ladies, who had seen him develop from his early days.

The following week I took Macchiato to the four-star at Luhmühlen in Germany. As the least experienced of my three horses, he had been my backup for Badminton. As it turned out, the cross-country track in Germany was very different and was a very good step up from Blair. I had gone hoping for a good all-round performance so to win far exceeded mine and his owners, the Kiers, expectations. His dressage was as good as he could have possibly done and left him just in the top ten. He is not very flashy in this phase but is unbelievably trainable and improving all the time. He was a little bit green in parts on the cross-country but kept on trying and coped far better than some of the more experienced horses, moving up to third. With Moonfleet, winner of both Badminton and Burghley, in the lead going in to the show jumping with several fences in hand, I never dreamt that the order would change. But, as my father would say, it is never over until the fat lady sings, and, to my amazement, Mac's clear round clinched a victory when Moonfleet and the French horse had several fences down. Jane and Michael Kier could not contain their emotion and shed more than a tear or two. To win three out of three events is an unbelievable record for any horse and particularly for Mac who is not an obvious superstar. It just shows how far a good brain and a good heart can get you.

Being listed for the Olympics with a choice of three horses was a fantastic position to be in but it did not come without its complications. Even though each horse was very different I would have been happy to have ridden any of them. The problem was that each horse had different owners. Mary King – who was the other team member listed with two horses – was in the fortunate position of having her horses share the same owners. There was always a chance that my horses would select themselves either through injury or by one performing significantly better than the others, but this was not to be. All three were going brilliantly and I felt it was going to be a very tough call choosing between them. Any which way, there were going to be two disappointed owners and a feeling of dread lingered through June and into July. Sentimentally, I was hoping to ride Tam, who had lost his chance of individual honours in the Athens Olympics with a fractured stifle, but he was sixteen and I knew the run-out at Badminton would stand against him. Ballincoola had also been a long and trusty servant. Was this his chance? He had never felt better and I knew the jumping and twisty cross-country would suit him. Ed was generally felt to be the best overall on his day, but his patchy record was perhaps a concern. My loyalty lay with Skinners and Guinness's who had been supportive owners for years. Having said that, the choice was always going to be made on which horse was likely to be the best performer on the day.

Barbury Castle was to be the final run for all British Olympic horses and I thought that the decision would surely be made clear for the selectors, who would be letting me know the following week. As it turned out, Ed, Max and Tam finished second, fourth and fifth – all performing right up to scratch.

The following day Yogi rang to let me know Ed was the one they wanted, and it was a huge relief to finally know who would be going. M W and Judy took the news well and I hoped that Philip would now relax. There was still a month to go, so the plan was to get Tam and Max fit as backups. As we were preparing for the extreme temperatures of Hong Kong, it was going to be a pretty tough few weeks for all of them. The thought of taking horses to Hong Kong had initially been met with dread, but time was flying by and the excitement was setting in. Media interest was gaining momentum and this was highlighted by the huge turnout at the team press day during final team training session. At this stage, Zara Phillips and Toytown were still in the team and the draw of a 'princess' competing in the Olympics was enormous. Devastatingly, within the next few days, Toytown suffered an injury and Zara had to drop out of the team – this was not only a huge blow to Zara but also to all of us, her teammates, who knew the chance of a team gold had drastically diminished with her withdrawal. Despite her huge disappointment Zara managed to remain upbeat and generous in her support, acknowledging that as a previous European and current world champion, she was probably due some bad luck. Shortly afterwards there was another casualty in Lucy Wiegersma whose horse, Shabrak, had not been quite sound. This did not bode well, but Yogi was typically upbeat, emphasising how a tricky preparation can often result in a good performance. We were also very lucky to have two such good reserves in the wings; in Tina Cook and Daisy Dick there were no two better riders to stand in. Daisy had already been in the British squad three times and Tina would have been in the team in the first place had Miners Frolic been a little more experienced. Having said that, the remaining five of us now needed to stay in one piece if we were going to give Germany, France and Australia a run for their money.

I had been dreading quarantine. The thought of having three horses in Stow-on-the-Wold whilst trying to give the horses at home a chance to keep up their work for ten days was giving me a fair amount of worry. We were very lucky to have the horses at the Unicorn Centre but, although the facilities were excellent, we were all unsure as to how the horses would react to being so restricted in space. Tam would certainly find ten days quite boring. As it turned out, everything went very smoothly, the horses were very happy and we all got some good work into them during their final preparation.

We knew the work space in Hong Kong was going to fairly limiting so the horses had to leave the UK in top form and fully fit. The excitement had really begun to set in and the team camaraderie could not have been better. The final weekend before we were due to fly I had ten horses entered at Wilton which, if nothing else, would be a very good distraction. My horses at Stow could enjoy a relaxing weekend with Jackie while I was away but, in the end, Yogi and I decided that the risk of riding so close to the Olympics at an event was not worth taking. All the horses therefore did the dressage and jumping which still proved a very useful exercise. They were about to have a long break, so going to Wilton shortened the gap between their competitions as much as was possible and would hopefully mean that they were a little less fresh on my return.

I was also aware the next few weeks were going to be quite a trying time for my owners who were keeping horses with me in work but without the opportunity of competition. Fortunately they were all supportive and understanding and had busy schedules for their horses to look forward to. I was also in the lucky position of having Jackie to go with Ed to the Olympics and Alex to keep the yard going at home. Alex's was going to be a huge job as, on my return, I had eight horses preparing for three-day events in the following four weeks.

Finally the day came when the horses were due to fly and it was a huge relief to get Ed to the airport in as good condition as I could have hoped for. It was also a good feeling to see the five horses take off with no further setbacks or changes to the squad. Jackie was one of the designated grooms to be on the horse flight, which was certainly an added bonus and gave me great piece of mind. I then took Tam and Max back to Wood Lane for a couple of easy weeks before they would start their final build-up to Burghley. The riders flew out the next day comforted in the knowledge the horses had all travelled well and were safely in their stables at Sha Tin. With us on the flight were Yogi, Kenneth and Tracie. Dressed in our Olympic travel wear we stuck out like beacons and, as there were still two weeks until the opening ceremony, there were no other athletes to blend in with. We travelled in luxury in club class, as did all the athletes, and enjoyed our last few hours of calm before the Olympic tension set in. I wondered what it was really going to be like – was it just going to be too hot and humid? Getting off the plane I was dying to know how the weather would feel. Tina and I dived outside and said simultaneously, 'It's OK!'. However, if it stayed like that, it was pretty hot and very humid compared to anything our horses had experienced. I had Atlanta to compare it to and it was definitely hotter in Hong Kong, but this time we were well prepared. The horses had been galloping in fleece rugs and making the most of any hot weather that had appeared to help them acclimatise. They had coped well in training and, although the heat worked their respiration and muscles hard, their recovery was good and morale remained high.

CHAPTER THIRTY-FIVE

. . . And Beyond

⎯⎯◆⎯⎯

The first few days were spent finding our bearings and getting ourselves into a routine. I was very fortunate not to suffer from jet lag but some of the others took a few days to adjust. Due to the climate the competition timetable was going to be something that none of us had experienced before. The plan was for the dressage to be done in two sessions on each day – one from 0700–1100 and the other from 1900–2300. In this way we would miss the heat of the day, but the mornings were still incredibly humid, though less hot. The horses needed to get used to being ridden at these bizarre times. Being near the equator, it did not get light until quite late, so some people would be warming up for their early dressage test in the dark. However, they would not be competing under floodlights like those in the evening session would be. We all needed to get used to very early starts and then have time for a siesta in the middle of the day to cope with usually quite late nights. Not being the best morning person, our dark early starts felt more like the middle of the night for me.

Initially the horses were being exercised gently and seemed to feel very bright and happy. With only one horse to ride each there was a temptation to do too much. However, Jackie was not totally happy with Ed. She felt that he was not adjusting in the same way as the other horses were; his drinking was sporadic and he was less interested in his food. Basically he was struggling to get his feet 'on the ground'. I felt that this was probably not very surprising given the fact that he is a very sensitive horse and that he had not flown before. I remained conservative with his work plan and watched slightly enviously as the others began to build theirs up. Around day four I got the phone call I had been dreading. Jackie was unhappy with him and was pretty sure he was showing early signs of colic. If caught early, colic can be easily cured, but we were getting close to the start of the competition and any medication that he needed would have to be declared to the ground jury and it would be at their discretion as to whether or not I would be able to compete. Our team vet Jenny Hall treated him and felt it was caused due to the early onset of dehydration. Given the humid weather and how much he was sweating it had been very concerning that his water consumption was less than it had been in the UK. Jenny had been less concerned about this than us but now she felt it was time to give him some fluids to help him rehydrate. The horses were all monitored daily; urine and blood samples were taken as well as their temperature and respiration to help detect any early signs of change. Though Ed's readings were erratic, he was feeling better and I needed to step up his work schedule. Our next setback happened when a blood test following a jumping session showed some signs of muscle damage. This was far more concerning and we were very limited as to what treatment could be carried out to help this. However, the damage was very mild and everyone kept convincing themselves that it would amount to nothing. As a result, Ed had a couple more easy days with plenty of walk but very little else in preparation for the evening when all teams were allowed to have a practise jump in the main arena and experience the atmosphere and floodlights. Instinct told me not to jump him but I was torn – I knew how important it was for him to jump, being a spooky horse and quite a worrier. We jumped in torrential rain and Ed felt OK, though was perhaps not his usual exuberant self. Walking him down having jumped I felt straight away that something was not quite right. He was happy to walk but he felt tight and short in his stride. Basically, his muscles were cramping. Jenny came to have a look and the next treatment phase was soon underway: more fluids, more walking and very little else. We were now two days before the vet inspection and

I could not believe that I would be starting the competition. Jackie and I had done more walking than we had ever done in our lives. A pedometer would have helped alleviate the boredom. Poor Ed became more depressed by the day and, as we walked, all I managed was a lot of watching and wishing I had a healthy horse to ride. In fact, any horse would have done. How I wished I had been able to have had Tam or Max out there as a backup. If I'd have had a reserve, Ed would most certainly have been withdrawn. If this had been a normal competition in the UK I would not have even put him on the lorry. But this was the Olympics and the only option was to get him right and hope that he did in time.

As everyone focused on Ed's blood tests and hydration levels a new problem bizarrely appeared. He developed a haematoma in his girth area. It looked as though it must have been caused by an over-tightened girth, but as he had not had a saddle on for the past two days and had hardly worn one for the ten days prior to that, it was very hard to understand. The main reason we thought it was there was because his system was now full of fluids and they were pooling in that particular area, as it was the lowest. Initially, no one was concerned as there were more important things to focus on, but on the day of the trot up these two swellings had grown into 'elephant's boobs' and you could not miss them. In another wave of panic, icing was added to his already busy routine in an attempt to reduce the swelling. This was all in the end too little too late and the ground jury decided to put Ed in the holding box for further re-examination. Jackie, Jenny and I all knew the reason why and that Ed was perfectly sound, but no one else did. There was a deathly hush followed by a lot of whispering as the vets conferred prior to Ed being represented. I could not believe that here we were at the Olympics and that I had been held because of a girth gall. It even made me smile to think how ridiculous the situation was. As it was not Ed's soundness that was a concern I was not needed to re-present him at trot. Having stood there for what felt like an eternity, I walked away quite relaxed that they could not spin me, but nobody else knew that and I will never forget the look on my teammates faces of complete disbelief. Starting with a team of four instead of five would be a serious disadvantage. After a long conflab the commentator announced, 'Passed'. The gasp from the public and the intense relief was palpable. At least now everyone thought that the reason I had been walking Ed in hand for three days and not riding him was because of his girth gall. The ground jury and vets had decided that he was fit to compete but he would undergo further monitoring prior to being allowed to start the cross-country. At this stage this did not worry me as I was convinced it was very unlikely that he would even be doing the dressage.

With that hurdle out of the way the dressage was my next concern. Yogi had decided to change the team order. I had initially being going fourth but he decided to move me to second to give Ed a day to recover between the dressage and the cross-country. I had no idea how much work to give Ed for the dressage. His blood tests were back to normal but we were terrified if we overworked him that the problem would reappear. Although he was quiet in himself, he was bored and I knew that when he went into the arena he would light up. I was advised to do very little warm up, but there was no point going into the arena and producing a test that would be no use to anyone in our bid for gold. I decided to do ten minutes' gentle warm-up in the air-conditioned indoor school, and then ten minutes' in the heat in the final practise arena. Ed worked well and felt quite relaxed but as he went into the main arena he went solid with tension. He would not have gone in at all had it not been for Tracie holding on to his head. He wiggled like a worm underneath me as we trotted around the arena hanging for the exit and rooted to the spot as I tried to pass the imitation Olympic torch and camera positioned between the judges' box. The bell to start went all too soon and I knew I was in for a tricky four minutes. Inevitably his test was disappointing, littered with small blips through lack of concentration, and he suffered badly from not having been able to participate in the arena familiarisation the evening before. Ed had a tendency to get very insecure in that sort of environment and unfortunately he gave the judges the very clear message that he did not want to be there. At the end of my test, I hardly dared look up at the scoreboard, but I was very relieved to see his score was 50.2. It could have been an awfully lot worse. However, no one outside had any idea what a miracle it was that he got through his dressage so to them Ed's test had been a disaster.

After the trot up Ed's close shave had been big news back in the UK and now his dressage was more big news on the bad start for the GB three-day event team. Daisy had done a good job with Springalong but her mark was also in the 50s, meaning that we were well out of contention after the first two team members of each country had gone. The second day of dressage raised British hopes with excellent performances from Tina, Sharon and Mary, but it was another day off for Ed prior to the big move of all the horses up to the cross-country venue at Bees River.

The logistics of moving seventy horses for forty minutes in air-conditioned lorries were complicated, as any time spent waiting in the heat could be potentially detrimental. As was typical of the whole organisation, the move was carried out to precision and the horses were very comfortably stabled in their big air-conditioned boxes by teatime. From the moment Ed arrived, Jackie reported that he was on much better form. I will remember that bit of good news as being the only bit of good news I got from Jackie that week. Over the previous days we journeyed out to Bees River to walk the course. It had been designed by the English course designer Mike Etherington-Smith and was beautifully presented. With seven jumping efforts in the first minute it was clear, over the undulating and twisty track, that the optimum time would be unachievable. The course had been shortened right down to eight minutes – two minutes shorter than we had been told earlier in the year – but the number of jumping efforts was at a maximum. The questions were evenly spread over the course and provoked considerable debate, but the second last fence was where I felt the competition would be won and lost. This consisted of a double of hedges to be taken either on an acute line or via the slow option of circling between them, which was the safer alternative.

Cross-country day came and, as luck would have it, the weather was significantly cooler with rain forecast. Daisy gave the team a great start with a clear but got several time faults. After the first few had been, it was looking as if the time would definitely be impossible to get, but the good news was that the competition was working and that the horses were finishing well, albeit quite hot.

Once more there had been much discussion about my warm-up with Ed and, in the end, we all agreed that less was best. My warm-up normally works to a very set pattern with the horses having 30–40 minutes of exercise including a gallop to open the lungs, and a small period of jumping five or six fences. This time there was no gallop and I allowed myself and Ed one fence. I found it hard to believe that this could work, but it was time to go for it. This is what we were here for; Ed's dressage had put him out of individual contention and if our score was going to be any use to the team result I had to get him round as close as possible to that optimum time. He felt pretty good in the warm-up and showed no signs of tying up, which gave me a very welcome feeling of optimism. We had come this far, and I was sure that if the first minute of the cross-country went to plan, Ed would give the rest his best shot. I set off in a determined frame of mind, jumping the first few fences a good notch quicker than I would ever have done before, and quicker too than I would have liked, but from watching the first few it was very clear that if you were slow in the first minute it was pretty much impossible to make up that time later on. Ed gave me a dream ride and galloped right to the end. The last fence was our only breath-holding moment, where we ended up taking off a little bit too early. Ed's length of stride had become quite unalterable and I made the split-second decision to leave him alone rather than interfere and get an extra stride in. I think many people watching missed a heartbeat, but I watched it a few months afterwards and thought it looked much less dramatic. Ed's lack of TB blood had been a concern, particularly given the conditions, so to have him finish the cross-country in the second fastest time of the day was particularly rewarding, not only for myself but for the team at home, who had put so much into producing him. Tina and Mary both had good jumping rounds but sadly Sharon had an annoying run-out at the second last. The top three scores from each team are what count towards the final result and, incredibly, at this stage Ed was in the equation. He'd finished the cross-country well but, just as we had become accustomed to this, there was further drama to follow when Jackie noticed a small cut on the front of his hock. It looked like nothing but rapidly became very painful, suggesting either severe bruising or the early stages of infection. By the evening, Ed was lame. I thought it had all been too good to be true; the next twelve hours were going to be as stressful as ever. We just had to hope that antibiotics would curb any brewing infection and that icing would alleviate any bruising. The encouraging part was that he always improved for walking. Jackie and Jenny did all they could for him overnight and all I could do was to wait for that phone call in the morning. Miraculously he did improve and, with the trot up not being until late afternoon, we had time on our side. He sailed through the trot up with Team GB once again breathing a sigh of relief. His score could have been critical in the final results depending on the show jumping.

It was a testament to the Hong Kong team and the years of preparation that had gone into the competition that the horses had come through the toughest part of the competition so well. However, we still had the show jumping to come and for the top twenty in the standings there would be another round to do which would surely test fitness even further. Lying in twelfth place, Ed had a rail down in the first round, but he jumped well, leaving him on a counting score for GB's team bronze. He remained in the top twenty but without any chance of an individual medal. This was a bitter pill for Philip to swallow. He had been convinced that Ed would win gold much as he had been convinced Ed would win Burghley.

Mary did not have luck on her side and had some uncharacteristic poles down, dashing her hopes of an individual medal. She had come into the competition on top form, brimming with confidence, and I thought she looked like she would be hard to beat. Tina, on the other hand, got a fantastic tune out of Miners Frolic to jump two clear rounds and clinch individual bronze. This was a truly deserved result; Miners Frolic is a class horse and Tina had suffered several years out of the limelight having been the unlucky travelling reserve for the Sydney Olympics. Although team bronze would appear a little disappointing, given how strong we could have been, I felt that we had fought for every little bit of it. We went into the Games probably as one of the top four nations i.e. with a chance of a gold or a fourth so, given how the competition panned out, we should be pretty happy with our bronze. It was certainly my best Olympic performance so far. After my Athens disappointment, completing in twelfth place individually can only be a highlight.

At the end of the competition we all stayed on in Hong Kong for a couple of days to unwind. It was great opportunity to be able to spend a bit of time with our families, who we had seen very little of during the competition. Alice had come out without the boys, both my parents and parents-in-law were there as were my brother, his wife and two sisters. How lucky I was to have had such a support team. We all took a boat together for a very enjoyable day, giving everyone the chance to relax and actually appreciate what had been achieved. So often in eventing you have to rush from one competition to the next and it is very easy to never stop, think or even enjoy.

Back in the UK, Alex was very happy with how the horses were coming on. One of the challenges with having a string of event horses is how best to manage and prepare them at home when I am away at competitions. It is always my aim to produce my horses so that they get to their three-day events in the best possible condition and with the best possible chance of doing well. Each horse can have an entirely individual programme and having a backup team able to carry this out is something that I am incredibly fortunate to have. When I am away the team know exactly what work each horse should be doing, and while I was in Hong Kong I had two working students – Leohna Rowland and Sinead Halpin – putting a lot of work into the horses. Though I never necessarily expect or aim for a horse to improve whilst

I am away, it is very important that they are kept supple and happy in their work and that they are made to concentrate from time to time. Most of the schooling work would be on the flat but some of the less experienced horses might have the occasional jump down a grid of fences to keep their eye in and their backs down. Alex was more closely involved with the fitness work and knew exactly how often and how much they needed to canter, as we very much stick to a set pattern. We are very lucky to have a five-furlong, all-weather gallop at home, so it is easy to get the right amount of work into each horse, and for a four-star like Badminton or Burghley their last piece of hard work would be five times up. I like to do as much of the canter work as I can myself, as I then get to the three days knowing how fit each horse is, and the horses are used to my weight. With most of the three-day events following each other in a cluster, it can be difficult to do this, but wherever possible I at least canter them myself when they do their last main session.

Alex, Becky and some of the owners had organised a party at the yard so that everyone could watch and cheer on our event team together. This was a fantastic idea and, looking at the photos, Alice and I missed out. There was a plaiting competition judged by Alex where each owner plaited their own horse – just the forelock – and some hilarious unicorn lookalikes were produced. Prizes were awarded, and then everyone had dinner while they watched the TV.

On returning from Hong Kong there was no time to relax and, after a few days, we were off to Blair Castle with two one-star horses and one two-star horse. Cool Mountain, one of my future hopefuls, was second in the two-star behind Sarah Cohen, five months pregnant, on the very talented Irish Jester. Blair is quite a journey, but it has so far always been worth it; it is one of the most enjoyable events in the calendar. As well as having a wonderful Scottish feel and atmosphere the competition provides superb experience for up-and-coming horses.

Highclere was sadly cancelled due to the wet, so we had a bonus day at home to get ready for Burghley. As Jackie had been away in

Hong Kong, Alex would be doing Burghley. Between them another quick turnaround was masterminded before we left for Burghley early on Tuesday. After my win in Luhmühlen there was more hype surrounding the HSBC Classic Series so I had to get to Burghley early for some filming.

The Classics was a brand new series linking the five leading four-stars around the world excluding Adelaide, and points were awarded to the top ten finishers. The final prize money fund is the highest eventing has ever seen and stretched generously to fifth place. If the series continues, its impact on riders will be significant. It will undoubtedly influence how riders target their team of horses and plan their season.

Tam and Max were both on good form and, despite having not competed since Barbury in July, they were both reckoned to be amongst the favourites. Philip Dutton was also in the reckoning for the HSBC series and he certainly was thought to have a good chance. While I was gunning for a top placing I am sure there were many in the other camp hoping that if I did not do well the HSBC competition would stay alive. If I was to win Burghley I would win the series, and those involved with HSBC could not be blamed for thinking but that would lessen the excitement of Pau as the last leg.

Max was drawn first of my two rides yet again and produced a reasonable test. As torrential rain set in on Friday I wondered if he had not got the better deal. The going in the dressage arena deteriorated to such an extent that by the time it came to Tam's test it was hard to anticipate what would happen. Tam, uncannily, decided that he had to concentrate, and produced one of his best ever four-star dressage performances. It poured with rain throughout his test in exactly the same way it had at Badminton 2004. Overnight, he lay in third place with one of his best scores in the 30s and, whilst he was not in the lead, I felt he was close enough, particularly given the conditions. The rain had really set in and the cross-country course would undoubtedly see some alterations overnight. On the Friday evening it was hard to believe that it would not be cancelled. It rained solidly, but the Burghley team never gave up. They put in tracks for emergency vehicles, and a lot of the ground work around the fences was re-enforced. When they announced on Saturday morning that the competition was still on, I could not have been happier. Several fences had been taken out, but none of them significant. I knew it was going to be a serious test but I also knew that I was on two of the best cross-country horses in the world. Max flew round the cross-country with a few time faults to take an early lead. The course was causing trouble and even Max, who had gone brilliantly, had had to work hard and finished a bit tired. Philip Dutton, as predicted, went well and overtook Max, but Tam made nothing of the track or the going to finish easily inside the time, and went into the lead with two fences in hand. Both Mary King's horses put in classy performances to lie in the top five. Sadly, Philip dropped out of the competition on Sunday as his horse was unsound. However, this left me in the comfy position of lying first and second with Tam having four fences in hand over Max. Max, jumping out of order, had one down and left the door open for Mary to put some pressure on. She too had a fence down on each of her horses which meant that I knew I had won my fifth Burghley title before I jumped Tam. Tam used up two of his four fences in hand and became one of the few horses ever to win Badminton and Burghley. I could not have been happier for him and the Guinness's, who had been so disappointed at missing out on the Olympics. However, Tam had not show jumped brilliantly and two down at the Olympics would have been expensive and could well have been the reason why he was not meant to be there.

Determined to enjoy the moment, Alice and I stayed at Burghley on the Sunday night and celebrated with my owners. It was a moment to be savoured, particularly as Ballincoola was to be taken on by Fergus Payne to campaign on the Young Rider circuit for the remainder of his career. Judy, Michael Payne and I had decided at the beginning of the season that Fergus should take on Max before he got too old and, as he had given us all so much, we were keen to 'retire' him at the top. Max had never felt better, so I will always remember him at the top of his game. I will certainly miss him and his incredible talent for cross-country. Of all the horses I have ridden, he would probably have to go down as one of the most consistent and genuine.

Tam, at sixteen, was also nearing the end of his career. Knowing him, I would not dare predict his future, but I and all his connections were very aware that we could have enjoyed his last big win. The added excitement was to know that I had secured victory in the HSBC Classic which, financially, was a huge boost.

My focus now turned to Idalgo who, having had a year off, desperately needed to retain his four-star qualification. One of my big gripes in our sport is the unnecessary wear and tear that riders are forced to put on their horses in order to keep qualified. This is particularly an issue at four-star level, when horses have proved themselves time and again, yet have to requalify if they suffer an injury and subsequently have time off. Idalgo was in danger of falling over the two-year period, so I was aiming him at the four-star at Pau in the hope that he would safely get into Badminton 2009. The event calendar had suffered all year due to the weather and each time Idalgo had been due to run it had either been too wet or too hard, so his first run ended up being at Gatcombe at the end of August, which was late enough given that Pau was in October. I knew he would be on his toes but the ride he gave me in the cross-country was one I would like to forget; the course there is not the most imposing and he tackled it with complete disrespect. Fortunately, we survived the experience, and his next run, which was advanced, went reassuringly to plan.

From then on, we ran into trouble, with him suffering endless small setbacks resulting in him getting to Pau under-prepared and not as fit as I would have liked him to be. I was so frustrated that had the qualification for Badminton not been essential I would never have taken him. With Tam, Ed and Max off the scene I very much was considering Idalgo as my next team horse and, if he was to be selected for the European Championships, he would have to prove himself at Badminton. Miraculously we got him to Pau, thanks largely due to the Endell Vet Practice in Salisbury who had extracted a splinter from his knee and managed to prevent infection just days before departure. Pau was in its second year of running a four-star and I had heard that the cross-country course was very much up to standard. When I walked the course I could see what everyone meant; there were serious questions all the way round requiring a very brave and accurate horse. Idalgo was predictably a bit lively in the dressage but he very much contained himself and earned a respectable mark of 48. He can be one of the most exhilarating horses to ride cross-country and he gave me a superb ride, far better than I could have hoped given that he had only had two runs in the last two seasons. Unfortunately he did get a bit tired towards the end, which resulted in a frustrating 20 penalties caused by crossing our tracks. However, this was still a qualifying result so provided we completed the following day with no more than four show jumps down, things would be OK. This he did easily, jumping a really pleasing round after annoyingly knocking the first fence down. For his owners George and Jane Apter it was such a relief to see him back to his best, particularly as they had been incredibly patient allowing him the necessary time off. After the season I had been having I could hardly be dissatisfied with his eleventh place, but it was good to know that he would have been right up there in good company without his cross-country blip. Bettina Hoy was the deserved winner on her amazing old horse Ringwood Cockatoo; brilliant for her after her huge disappointment of missing out on the Olympics.

The HSBC prizes were awarded at the end of the competition. Nicolas Touzaint in second and Frank Osholt in third had narrowed my lead, but it was a great feeling to have won. To win again would not be so easy. Two four-star wins, a second and a third in a season doesn't come along very often.

Looking ahead, I have some exciting up-and-coming four-star horses in Navigator and Seacookie. Both these two went really well at Boekelo in Holland, finishing sixth and tenth. This had been Seacookie's first big test with me and he was impressive, which gave me the feeling that the Kentucky four-star would be a realistic target. My plan at this stage was to take Navigator with him and aim the two more experienced horses – Idalgo and Macchiato – at Badminton. It will be very strange taking first-timers there again, having ridden either Max or Tam there every year since 2002.

My younger horses were also performing encouragingly well. Lionheart, a lovely six-year-old owned by Judy and Jeremy Skinner, finished second in the six-year-old National Final, and Oslo won the six-year-old World Championship at Le Lion in France. I had never had such a forward six-year-old and therefore never even competed in the six-year-old final, but Oslo had given me the feeling all year that he had a very real chance. The final turned out to be an incredible week with Oslo performing brilliantly in all three phases; he is owned by the Fox-Pitt Partnership, made up of ten shares, and most of his owners were there enjoying the greatest highlight of his career so far. The Le Lion organisers were bemused by the number of owners one horse could have, particularly as finding a single owner for a horse is hard in France. Oslo's owners were very well looked after and enjoyed the French hospitality fully. As this was their first experience of owning Oslo at a three-day event, it could well be a hard act to follow.

At the end of the season I found myself as the new world number one, a position of great honour and a great way to finish off one of my best years. This year, however, there was the new focus of the Express Eventing Competition in Cardiff's Millennium Stadium, to take place at the end of November. Express Eventing was a new concept, being a compact version of the sport designed potentially for arenas and stadiums around the world. It condenses all the drama and excitement of traditional eventing into a single day, with all the action visible from one seat, and aims to bring the understanding of the sport of eventing to a wider audience. With £100,000 on offer to the winner, the twenty invited riders from around the world embarked on a frenzied November of preparation.

The competition started with a freestyle dressage programme, set to music, where horse and rider were judged not only on the degree of difficulty, but on their artistic interpretation. Having never ridden a dressage test to music before, it was a serious challenge to find a suitable test matched to the right music for Ballincoola. Lizzie Murray was a huge help. She organised for someone to choreograph the music we had chosen, and helped me tackle some of the more difficult movements. The level of dressage was intended to be higher than the four-star level we are used to. For example, we had to include half pirouettes in canter and three flying changes every four strides. This was a quite a question for Max, who did not enjoy dressage at the best of times. For the first few weeks he embraced the challenge but, as Cardiff grew close, he threw in the towel and I had to hope that we had done enough.

As far as the show jumping training was concerned I took Max to Peter Charles, a former European Champion show jumper. Peter has helped me a lot over the last few years with my show jumping; he has got a great way with horses and very clear methods of putting his point across. All in all it was an action-packed November, far removed from a normal November when things have wound down and we get a good time for a break.

I got to Cardiff the day before thanks to a very generous invitation from HSBC to watch the Wales vs. Australia rugby match; it was a great game but I could not imagine how the pitch was going to be turned overnight into a site for an equestrian extravaganza. That evening we had a rider briefing, which included the running order draw, and you could sense the feeling of anticipation. Everybody in the room had a good chance of winning and everyone was hungry for the high prize fund. Riders and owners were generously invited to a reception dinner, which was an enjoyable evening, but in a way surreal. Everyone was there to have a good time but by 10 p.m. it was very clear that riders were getting edgy and wanted to get to bed. However, Mark Todd reminded me that it was mine and Alice's wedding anniversary. He knew that because it was his and Carolyn's too, so we had a quiet drink back at the hotel. Luckily, Alice had forgotten too!

The logistics of the competition could not have been more complicated. To produce a show jumping course and a cross-country course overnight from a bare rugby pitch was going to require military organisation and an expert team to carry it out. This they had but the time schedule was impossibly tight. Everyone worked throughout the night to produce what was undoubtedly an impressive course. The presentation was such that it could have been at a championship.

The day of competition started very early and in darkness for all the riders, as there was a particularly busy schedule. We could walk the course first thing but it was still not quite finished, there was then the trot up followed by press breakfast, dressage warm-up and then dressage. This was all meant to be finished by 12 noon, giving us some time to walk the finished course. However, by the time the course was ready the celebrity riders were in action, leaving only fifteen minutes to walk the course and fifteen minutes for the first riders to then warm up. The celebrity riders were Jodie Kidd and Tara Palmer-Tomkinson and, although they were brave to tackle a minute show jumping course in freezing conditions, on slippery ground and with no studs in their borrowed horses' shoes, they added little to the excitement. However, the one thing they did do was show us how important it was to have some decent studs in our horses.

The show jumping and cross-country was due to start shortly after their display but time was running out, and riders had to choose whether they had a last look at either the show jumping or the cross-country, adding to the pressure. The show jumping course was made up of nine fences of 1.30m; there was then a compulsory and timed pit stop, followed by thirty cross-country fences to jump. With this many fences condensed on to the pitch, the course was cramped and complicated, and, with such tight time constraints, riders had difficulty learning the course let alone focussing on how it should be ridden. Given the prize fund, Stuart Buntine had hired Pierre Michelet, a top French course designer, to build a serious track, but it turned out to be too testing.

The dressage warm-up was quite novel. There was a shortage of space and the last ten minute area was an underground space of about fifteen metres with a concrete pillar in the middle. The main arena was very spooky with lots of marks in the grass covering rugby pitch lines, but Max coped really well. My first worry was that the right music would come on at the right moment and happily it did. My test to the music from *The Lion King* went pretty much to plan, although I did get a bit ahead of myself. Andrew Lloyd Webber and Arlene Philips were the celebrity music judges and it was an excellent idea having them briefly interviewed in between each test. Sadly, they were not blown away by my performance. Max was a bit off the pace after the dressage but by no means out of contention and actually in the end the result would have been no different if there had been no dressage.

The jumping and cross-country ran in reverse order and it was quite apparent after the first few riders had gone that we had not been given nearly enough time to learn the course. Riders were going the wrong way and horses were clearly having difficulty reading some of the questions.

After eight starters and one clear round I entered the ring with one thing in my mind; I had to go the right way. I had tested myself endlessly and I hoped that I would not go blank. Max show jumped really well but had one down, and our pit stop was not a success as I had trouble doing up my chin strap. This was infuriating and it ultimately cost me second place and £30,000, as Max jumped a fast clear. Even Max, with all his experience, found the course confusing, particularly the first water which he all but stopped at. He can be quite spooky and suspicious and our round was far from foot perfect, surviving a couple of hairy moments. I was so lucky to be riding him and not a less experienced horse, as he needed to draw on all his experience and genuineness to cope with the intensity of the course. My feeling on finishing although I had gone into the lead was of utter relief. Fortunately, as the afternoon progressed, riders did make fewer errors and some of the horses appeared to cope very well. Shabraak and Lucy Wiegersma, who finished second, made it look easy and Oli Townend, the eventual winner, put in a fantastic performance.

Sadly, the whole afternoon was ruined by Mary King's horse Call Again Cavalier breaking a hind leg. The horrific situation was made far worse by being in a stadium where everyone could see exactly what was going on. The Cardiff team and vets were very professional, taking him swiftly off the course. He was an incredible horse, probably the most talented horse that Mary had ever had, and I feel privileged to have been in a team with him.

Reviews were mixed but there was a lot to come out of it that was positive. It was an exciting competition and at a time of year when the event season is usually dormant. However, there was criticism about the organisation and the fact that too much had been taken on in too tight a timeframe. My main concern was that some of the best riders in the world were made to look under too much pressure, and some of the horses did not look to be enjoying themselves. I feel that if there is another time, the cross-country course needs to be more friendly without being too easy and it needs to be ready the day before. There was something awe-inspiring about competing in the Millennium Stadium but a less prestigious venue would hopefully be more flexible, giving everyone more time to get organised. I dread to think how long it took everyone who had worked overnight to put the course together and overnight again to dismantle it to recover. Hats off to Stuart and John Peace, the financial guarantors of the project, for everything they did.

Through the 2008 season I had been carrying an injury to my shoulder and with Cardiff out of the way it was time to get it sorted out. I had been recommended the top surgeon Geoff Graham by Andrew Thornton, a leading NH jockey. His operation had been very successful, so I was grateful for the introduction. It was a good time for me to get it sorted out as it would take three months to recover and my horses would only be coming back into hard work by then.

During December we were devastated by the loss of Moon Man who died from a bout of colic after a days' hunting with Alice. Poor Alice and the Hook Norton Vet team stayed up with him all night but on operation found he had a growth in this small intestine which had compromised the blood supply to thirty-four feet of his gut. He had been part of the family for thirteen years, and was just one of those rare horses that you were lucky enough to have in a lifetime. He would turn his hand to anything and, having competed at top level for seven years, was a brilliant hunter, hack, schoolmaster and a horse that even our two small boys enjoyed riding. Every animal on the place is now called Bob!

Looking ahead to the 2009 season, there is a lot to be excited about. I have got some very talented horses, a great team at home and loyal supportive owners. Who knows what the next four years will bring? Hopefully we will see a superstar for the London Olympics and many future successes, both for me personally and for Team GB.

My Top Ten Horses

Tully, 14.2hh, grey gelding, Connemara

If little Minnie Monster was kick and go, Tully was kick, kick, kick and go, my first grown-up pony who gave me the confidence to compete in Pony Club teams. He was a brilliant jumper who never refused, but he was quite lazy, so he taught me to ride forwards. As he was stocky and lacking self-propulsion, I felt totally safe and I was happy to tackle fences I'd never have expected to jump. So long as I pointed and kicked, he did the rest. I took him to my lessons with Wil Lewicki, so he was the first pony I essentially learned to get on the bit. Although he was wonderfully reliable, he wasn't a winner, but he did come first in the Pony Club midnight steeplechase, largely because he was the only one to jump the first fence at the first attempt.

Solitaire (Runt) 15.1hh, chestnut mare, homebred TB Connemara cross, by Suvarov, out of Hirola (out of Go Try)

I remember loading Runt into the Land Rover to go back to the stables after watching her being born in the field. She was a quarter Connemara, too small to be of interest to my mother, so I took her on when she was four and I was thirteen. She was a feisty, opinionated, chestnut mare who'd jump anything, but she was impossible on the flat. My mother didn't take her seriously, so she let me make my own mistakes on her, and in doing so she taught me an awful lot. I'd build pretty nasty cross-country fences out of boxes and bales in Leicestershire and she'd fly over them. I hunted and evented her and she was the first horse I took through to advanced. Dressage was a bone of contention, hardly surprising as it wasn't in her genes and she was being ridden by someone who didn't have a clue. I grew to 6ft 5in during our time together, so we made an increasingly odd couple. Progress was slow, but

I learned a lot from her. When she retired, she joined my mother's breeding programme, but she didn't turn out to be the easiest brood mare.

Steadfast (Steady), 17hh, bay Irish gelding, by Ascertain

Although it was anything but love at first sight, it's entirely thanks to Steady that I'm where I am today. Never was a horse more appropriately named, because he was incredibly consistent through the seven years we spent together. He was a novice when my mother bought him in 1984 and we progressed through my first international competitions in junior and young rider European Championships. Our individual silver medal at the Junior Europeans in Pratoni in 1987 was a highlight. It kick-started our campaign at this level and we went on to take team gold in the young rider European Championships at Zonhoven and Rotherfield. He took me round my first Badminton in 1989 and got into the prize money two years later. In 1991, we were first reserves for the Senior European Championships at Punchestown. He completed twelve three-day events with me and two more with my sister Laurella. Steady gave me the eventing bug and, for that, I am forever indebted to him.

Loch Alan, 16.hh, grey gelding, homebred TB cross, by Alan Rod, out of Islay

My twenty-first birthday present wasn't a superstar, but he was a real clown, with more character than most human beings. He was one of a tribe of four young horses, all rogues, who became quite feral while they were growing up. He was the wise one, stirring the others up, then standing aside to watch the mayhem that followed. If you tried to lead him, he'd tow you along until you let go and then run off, delivering a little kick to prompt you if you didn't release him quickly enough. He found eventing hard work and I was too big for him, which didn't make it any easier, but he had a very short, strong back, which he put to good use to buck me off whenever he needed to. He was capable of good flat work, and he was a good-looking horse. He produced his best dressage test at Burghley to lie in fourth place, I fell off at the Dairy Mound, remounting to finish, but with our chance of victory gone. Technically, he should never have completed a four-star, but he was a trier. He'd sigh, almost talk, let himself out of his stable, roll with his saddle on and take his rugs and boots off, but you couldn't help laughing.

My mother still keeps him as a companion for her youngsters. No doubt he's teaching them all his old tricks.

Chaka, 16.3hh, brown Irish gelding, by Spectrach

Chaka was truly regal, the first amazing horse I rode. Thanks to his early training with Judy Herbert (now Hancock), he introduced me to serious flat work and the feeling of movement and power was a revelation. He was quite lazy, but he had a real engine once you found the gears. Everything came easily to him, perhaps too easily, because he'd only deal on his own terms. I had to learn what made him function and then take a very firm line, because he'd never cooperate unless he liked and respected you. Certainly I respected him. He gave me my first four-star win at Burghley in 1994, my first British Open Championship a year later and my first place in the senior team at the European Championships in 1993. He showed me just how good the big time could be, but he also paved the way for eventing's inevitable disappointments by failing the vet when in the lead at Badminton.

Cosmopolitan II (Cosmo), 16.2hh, bay Irish gelding, by Pennistone

I've always believed in eavesdropping since Cosmo came to me out of the blue as a result of a conversation I'd overheard at a cocktail party. He was a stocky sort yet he gave me my most unexpected period of success. He won at Bramham in 1995, my first three-star three-day success, and was part of the gold-medal-winning team at the European Championships later in the year. We also made the team for the 1996 Olympic Games in Atlanta, not a happy experience, but that certainly wasn't Cosmo's fault. In 1997, he was third at Badminton, my first podium place at an event that initially haunted me, then won team gold and individual bonze in the Open European Championships. He had so much more to give when his career was cut short by soundness problems at the age of eleven, but at least he's enjoying a long and happy retirement with Alison Quinlan, his devoted groom from Atlanta.

Moon Man (Bob), 17hh, bay Irish gelding, part TB, by I'm a Star

By the time he was three, Bob was hard at work in a trekking centre in Sligo, carrying heavy weights on day trips into the surrounding countryside.

Vere Phillipps bought him in the hope of selling him as a hunter, but although he's brilliant at it now, he was having none of it then. From the moment I saw him, he reminded me of Steady, which is why I bought him, much to Vere's surprise, because he didn't see him as having the movement to be an eventer. Like Steady, he's given far, far more than I ever expected, representing his adopted country – he stood in for Tamarillo on the gold-medal-winning team for the Punchestown European Championships in 2003 – and winning many glittering prizes, especially twice at the British Open Championships at Gatcombe. He has a warm and generous personality, very shy but very kind. He gave Oli, my two-year-old son, his first ride, the only horse I'd trust with such an honour. Despite the quirks that have resulted in some serious disappointments, he's my favourite horse of all time, a view now endorsed by Madonna, who enjoyed riding him.

Stunning, 16.3hh, chestnut gelding, New Zealand TB, by Ring the Bell

Mark Todd was convinced Stunning would be a world-beater when he brought him over from New Zealand, but their good results had been marred by some not so good ones by the time I took over. At least Stunning was accustomed to a tall rider, but it's never easy to follow someone of Mark's calibre and it took a while to strike up a workable partnership. When I did, he turned out to be a wonderful servant, enduringly sound and one of the fastest horses I've ever ridden. He was thirteen and didn't have a natural talent for eventing – he didn't have the calmest temperament or an amazing jump – yet he won more for me than any other horse, including Blenheim in 2000, team gold in the European Championships in 2001 and one British and Scottish Open Championships. He was still going strong when we retired him at eighteen and he's with us today, on permanent loan to Jackie, his biggest fan.

Ballincoola (Max), 16.3hh, chestnut gelding, part Irish TB, by Highland King

Max came to me as a goose, as his owner would agree but, at thirteen, he's become a swan. I bought him because he's one of the most careful jumpers I've ever known, but for a long time that seemed to be his only asset. He's a tense, quirky horse, very unfriendly, and his conformation didn't suggest he'd be a world-beater on the flat. Not that he had any wish to be, putting up fierce resistance to all my attempts to improve him. Thanks to Lizzie Murray, he's turned the corner and developed into a real pro. You've got to be in it to win it: for the past three years, Max was my only Burghley runner, with all my other entries falling by the wayside. And win it he did, leading the dressage to my astonishment and giving me my third victory in 2005. In 2006 he confirmed his four-star status by coming ninth at Badminton. He's incredibly tough, brave and consistent, digging deep to deliver the goods, no matter how testing the conditions. He may be a hard horse to love, but I wouldn't be without him now.

Tamarillo (Tam), 16.2hh, bay gelding, 36.5 per cent Arab, by Tarnik, out of an Arab TB mare, Mellita

What can I say about Tam, my iconic Arab prince who thinks he rules the world? He's the most extraordinary horse I've ever ridden or could ever hope to ride. Like Cosmo, he arrived with baggage, his nerve was fragile, and it took patience to build the relationship we have today. That probably stood me in good stead, because patience is a quality he tests to the limit on a daily basis. He's the ultimate chameleon, lazy, excitable, spooky and perverse. On some days he's a dobbin, on others you can't catch him in the stable, let alone the field and, at the age of fifteen, he's well up for pretending he's never worn a saddle in his life. He's the ultimate cross-country machine, feline in his ability to react and adjust at lightning speed, and he's usually a careful show jumper, but if it takes a buck to spoil a winner's test, he'll usually put one in. He fulfilled my dream with his Badminton victory in 2004, finishing with frustrating seconds both there and in the European Championships at Blenheim a year later. As the world knows, since I withdrew him from the Athens Olympics, he's alarmingly accident-prone, so nowadays I play it Tam's way, only competing when the stakes are high and the odds are good. Win or lose, he's my horse of a lifetime, a charismatic star with an army of fans. I keep telling him he should never be beaten, something he's well aware of, but only time will tell if he has any plans to prove it.

Index